Victorian Women

Other books by the author

It's Never Too Late
Women and Marriage in Nineteenth-Century England

Victorian Women

JOAN PERKIN

NEW YORK UNIVERSITY PRESS
Washington Square, New York

For my grandchildren
Nathaniel James Perkin Smithies
and
Hannah Lily Perkin Smithies
*In the hope that they will always believe
that men and women are of equal worth*

© Joan Perkin 1993

First published in 1993 by John Murray (Publishers) Ltd., UK

First published in the U.S.A. in 1995 by
New York University Press,
Washington Square, N.Y. 10003

Library of Congress Cataloging-in-Publication Data
Perkin, Joan.
 Victorian women / Joan Perkin.
  p.   cm.
 "First published in 1993 by J. Murray... London" – T.p. verso.
 Includes bibliographical references (p.   ) and index.
 ISBN 0–8147–6624–2 (cloth) – ISBN 0–8147–6625–0 (pbk.)
 1. Women – England – History – 18th century. 2. Women – England – Social
conditions. I. Title.
HQ1599.E5P47   1995
305.42′0942 – dc20   94–42382
                                                                  CIP

Printed and bound in Great Britain at
the University Press, Cambridge

CONTENTS

ILLUSTRATIONS

(between pages 120 and 121)

1. Yorkshire village tombstone
2. *The Fashionable Mama or The Convenience of Modern Dress* by James Gillray, 1796
3. A lesson in housewifery, board school, 1893
4. Girton College students, 1875
5. Almack's Club, by R. Cruikshank, in *Tom and Jerry*, 1821
6. *The Ladies' Accelerator*, by R. Cruikshank, 1819
7. Women archers, from the *Graphic*, 1892
8. *The Sensation Novel*, by John Leech, in *Punch*, 1864
9. A registry office (Mrs Hunt's, Duke Street), in Sims' *Living London*, 1902
10. Telephonists, in the *Graphic*, 1883
11. Woman mine worker, *Parliamentary Papers*, 1842, vol. XV
12. Pit brow woman, a 'filler' at Rosebridge Pits, Lancashire, 1866
13. Lancashire cotton mill, *Illustrated London News*, 1851
14. The Westminster Union poorhouse, by Hubert Herkomer in the *Graphic*, 1877
15. *The Haunted Lady*, in *Punch*, 1863
16. *The Foundling Restored to Its Mother*, by Emma Brownlow, 1858
17. Sweated trades, at the *Daily News* Sweated Trades Exhibition, 1906
18. 'The Crawlers', photograph by J. Thomson, 1876
19. Annie Besant, with the Strike Committee of the Matchmakers' Union, 1888
20. Differences in social class attitudes, *Punch* cartoon by L. Raven Hill, 1902
21. Prostitution, in *The Day's Doings*, 1871
22. Suffragettes released from Holloway Prison, 1908

The author and publisher would like to thank the following for permission to reproduce illustrations: 2, 3, 5, 6, 7, 8, 9, 10, 11, 13, 14, 15, 17, 18, 20, 21, courtesy of the Stapleton Collection; 4, courtesy of the Mistress and Fellows, Girton College, Cambridge; 12, courtesy of the Master and Fellows, Trinity College, Cambridge; 16, courtesy of the Thomas Coram Foundation for Children; 19, courtesy of the Welfare History Picture Library; 26, courtesy of the Museum of London.

ACKNOWLEDGEMENTS

I would like to thank John Murray Ltd. for having the confidence to propose that I should write this book, and Editorial Director, Grant McIntyre, for his unfailing enthusiasm and support throughout the writing stages. I also want to thank my original editor, Ariane Goodman, for her encouragement when I was drafting the proposal, and Kate Chenevix Trench for her careful editing of the manuscript and help in finding appropriate illustrations.

My good friend, Madeleine Ginsburg, has read the finished manuscript with great care and attention, and saved me from making many errors in her field of expertise. Madeleine is a distinguished authority on historical costume, formerly a member of the Department of Textiles at the Victoria and Albert Museum, and author *inter alia* of *Victorian Dress in Photographs* (1982). I am most grateful for her invaluable help in finding suitable illustrations for this book.

As ever, I am profoundly grateful to my husband, Harold Perkin, for his continued support and encouragement.

INTRODUCTION

For most of recorded time, and in most societies, women have unfairly been regarded as inferior to men. In nineteenth-century England the myth was perpetuated. Male writers pointed to the biological differences between the sexes and said firmly, without feeling that any proof was necessary, that certain consequences followed automatically. Alexander Walker, a noted physiologist, asserted in 1840:

> It is evident that the man, possessing reasoning faculties, muscular power, and courage to employ it, is qualified for being a protector: the woman, being little capable of reasoning, feeble, and timid, requires protection. Under such circumstances, the man naturally governs: the woman as naturally obeys.

Sigmund Freud in the 1880s also assumed that women were biologically inferior to men, and in a lecture on 'The Psychology of Women' claimed that envy of a man's penis caused a woman to 'feel depreciated in her own eyes' and to wish for her husband's penis, a wish that was fulfilled when she gave birth to a son. It did not occur to him that it was men's power, not their appendages, that women envied.

Christian teaching, too, implied that women were inferior in the story of the creation of Eve from the rib of Adam. Divine providence held that women should be subordinate and resignation to her lot, with true Christian humility, was the only proper response of a good woman. To cap it all, some people thought that males and females belonged to two different species, their characters operating on different principles. Surprisingly, there was no shortage of *women* writers who accepted these ideas. For example, the influential educationist Elizabeth Sewell (1815–1906) wrote in 1865:

Boys are to be sent out into the world to buffet with its temptations, to mingle with bad and good, to govern and direct . . . Girls are to dwell in quiet homes, amongst a few friends; to exercise a noiseless influence, to be submissive and retiring.

Few women really believed they were inferior to men, since experience and the evidence of their own eyes disproved it, and there were always 'strong-minded' women who hotly disputed their assigned position. The 'woman question' created lively and constant debate down the century, yet the biological and religious arguments remained very powerful, and were reinforced by the laws concerning women.

This book looks at the lives of English women, from birth to old age, in the 'long nineteenth century' between the French Revolution and the First World War. Chapter 1 assesses how families viewed the birth of a daughter; how a girl was brought up within the home; and how girls came to terms with menstruation and the knowledge of 'where babies come from'. Chapter 2 considers how girls were schooled, both before and after the 1870 Elementary Education Act. Full-time attendance between the ages of five and ten did not become universally compulsory in law until 1880, and in practice even later. Only a tiny minority of girls benefited from the 'new' private schools which provided an academic curriculum and paved the way for women to enter universities in the last quarter of the century, but this was the thin end of the wedge for improving women's education and giving them a chance to enter the male-dominated professions. Consequently, spurious alarms were sounded against women receiving higher education.

Chapter 3 examines the public prudery of Victorian England about sex, and evidence of pre-marital sex, also looking at courtship patterns and wedding customs, family limitation and methods of contraception, including abortion. Chapter 4 looks at relations between husbands and wives, considering law, theory and actual practice. Most women regarded marriage as a fixed fact of nature. English people married comparatively late in life, compared with most non-Western societies where people married as soon as they reached puberty. On average, women of all classes married between the ages of twenty-three and twenty-six; men between twenty-five and thirty. Chapter 5 deals with the lighter side of women's lives – their interests from shopping to fashion, from travel to tennis.

Chapter 6 is concerned with the problems of those who were

unhappily married, a woman's lack of legal power over her children and the difficulty of getting out of 'holy deadlock'. Legal separation and divorce were rare, though desertion, bigamy and sale of wives were less rare than official statistics suggest. Chapter 7 looks at widowhood, which came to most women. Marriage rarely lasted more than fourteen years, before the death of one or other partner.

Chapter 8 examines the lives of unmarried middle-class women, and the difficulties they faced in providing for themselves if they did not marry and had no private income. They had little choice of work up to mid-century, most having to choose between being a governess, paid companion or seamstress, but they benefited from the later growth of commercial and government office work, and the expansion of the retail trade. There were half a million more women than men at mid-century, and a million more at the end. It was just not possible for them all to find husbands (assuming they wished to), despite the opinion of the *Saturday Review* that an unmarried woman had 'failed in her business in life'. So a passion for meaningful paid work became the centre of their lives.

Chapter 9 is concerned with the lives and work of unmarried working-class women, most of whom had to start work at a tender age, for very poor pay. Only in 1876 were children under the age of ten forbidden to work for an employer. There were more women and girls in domestic service than in any other trade, even at the end of the century. It was a life of unremitting toil which most of them hated. Many women preferred factory work, street-selling or manual labour. Most fortunate were the minority of working-class girls who became pupil-teachers in elementary schools from the 1830s up to 1914.

Chapter 10 looks at married women workers. Throughout the century many wives worked in small workshops in their homes, often in appalling conditions that allowed no ease, and some in the 'sweated industries' that were exposed by the Fabian Women's Group in 1905. Other wives worked full or part-time in agriculture or in factories, or did casual work to supplement the family income. Such work was rarely declared to the census takers, but few autobiographies fail to mention that their mothers or they themselves earned money this way. But the Victorian ideal was that a wife should concentrate on her housework and the care of her children, and only late in the century did *feminists* come to believe that a wife had the right to work outside the home if she wished to. By then, almost all the forces of society were opposed to married women

working, and it is certain that many women gladly left work when their
husbands earned enough to keep them.

Chapter 11 considers philanthropic, voluntary and political work,
which provided for so many upper- and middle-class women an opportunity to spread their wings outside the home. Religious belief gave
many the courage to tackle social evils such as poor prison conditions
and slum housing; and women had more time than men to devote to
these causes. Some of the earliest attempts at united political action by
women came not from ladies, however, but from working women. Later
in the century, upper-class women aided them to speak and organize
publicly for change, for example in the Women's Co-operative Guild
and through trade unions for women.

Chapter 12 looks at what the middle class regarded as the greatest
social evil of all – prostitution. The behaviour of women of the *demi-
monde* did not fit the bourgeois ideal of women as sexually passive,
demure and respectable. There was a wide spectrum of women making
their living by selling sex, ranging from the highly paid courtesan to
those who worked with thieves or were also thieves themselves. Most
typical, however, was the underpaid working woman aged about
twenty, who was using part-time prostitution to supplement her low
wages. Most of them later married and gave up 'the game', but Victorian
kept mistresses seem to have been happier than many respectable married women. The organized harassment of prostitutes under the Contagious Diseases Acts of 1864–9, which left undisturbed their male
clients, was bravely opposed by Josephine Butler and others and led
eventually to the repeal of the Acts. Some feminists believed that if
women had been properly paid for respectable work, they would not
have become prostitutes, and this is probably true for large numbers of
them.

A concluding section draws together the main themes of the book,
looking at what specifically changed in women's lives down the century,
and to what extent.

Throughout the book, the term 'upper class' refers to that small but
closely welded community consisting of the gentry and the aristocracy.
Only a fraction of them counted as London 'society', the leisured rich
who took part in fashionable life. The untitled gentry was a group with
ties to the nobility by marriage, though they could rarely afford their
lifestyle. They also had ties of family and interest to farmers and the
middle classes, whom they married when 'landed' partners were not

available. In 1803, Patrick Colquhoun estimated that there were 287 Peers in Britain, 540 Baronets, 350 Knights, 6,000 Esquires and 20,000 Gentlemen. Bessie Rayner Parkes calculated in 1865 that if the population were divided into thirteen units, one would represent the aristocracy, three the middle ranks and the remaining nine the 'masses'. The upper and middle classes ranged in income from over £5,000 a year down to under £100. The manual labour class ranged from £73 a year down to £10.10s a year.

A major theme of the book is how women at different levels of society in nineteenth-century England managed to cope with their unequal situation, which for many was inescapable, but also how some women came more and more to resent their disabilities and to press for change. It was the nineteenth century, infamous in historical legend for the selfish and domineering Victorian father and husband, that was the turning point in the legal and social emancipation of English women. We are still struggling in the late twentieth century to banish the social inequities that constrict women's lives, marriages and careers. But Victorian and Edwardian men, who alone had the legal and political power, were spurred on by their womenfolk to begin the emancipation process and lay the foundation for a better life for their descendants.

This is not a book for scholars, although students of history and of women's studies will find it useful. It is for those ordinary women – and men too – who would like to know how their forebears fared at the hands of inequitable man-made laws and customs. It is based on a wide range of contemporary sources, and those readers who would like to follow up the various leads will find ample references in the Bibliography at the end of the book.

Finally, this book concerns the lives of women throughout the 'long' nineteenth century, from 1800 to 1914, but it centres on the reign of Queen Victoria. It is not too misleading, therefore, to call it *Victorian Women*.

1

What Use Were Girls Anyway?

CLASS AND THE
IMPORTANCE OF GENDER

Had it been a male the matter would be more acceptable.

Karl Marx to Engels,
on the birth of his daughter Eleanor in 1855

We just got instilled in us the feeling of being second best, of not coming up to scratch. We were girls, you see, and what use were girls anyway?

Victoria Wignall, one of six daughters, born 1900

Girls learned early in life that they were less important than boys, and the welcome a girl could expect when she was born depended to some extent on social class. The primary concern of the aristocracy was to beget a son and heir, since only a male could inherit family titles and sit in the House of Lords. To give birth to an heir was the major service a wife could provide for her husband, and everyone was on tenterhooks until a boy was born. Lord Londonderry gave his wife a set of pearls worth £10,000 (a huge fortune) when she presented him with a son in 1821. His wife, Frances, a great heiress in her own right because her parents had not had a surviving son, wrote later, 'Certainly the moment when I found myself the mother of a boy was the happiest I ever experienced before or since.' She was depressed because her next two children were girls. Imagine the feelings of Lady Westminster, who kept on trying to have a son, when she gave birth to her eighth daughter in

1834. She wrote, 'The catastrophe of a daughter was a bore, but what can't be cured must be endured and never mentioned.' A friend of Lady Stanley of Alderley told her in 1859 that her life 'would be a blank' if her pregnancy did not result in the birth of a boy. Male heirs were as important at the end of the century as at the beginning. In 1895, the American heiress Consuelo Vanderbilt married the Duke of Marlborough and was told by her mother-in-law, 'Your first duty is to have a child and it must be a son, because it is intolerable to have that little upstart Winston become Duke.' Consuelo produced two sons during her loveless marriage.

Once the longed-for heir had been born, daughters were welcome in most aristocratic families, if only because they made good companions for their mothers. Lady Sarah Napier said in 1790 that she wanted another daughter 'to comfort me in my old age, when my boys are gone to school.' By the marriages of their daughters aristocrats might also form alliances with other great titles and estates, or bring wealthy, untitled sons-in-law into their own families.

Middle-class parents wanted sons to carry on the family name and business, but there was no sense of calamity when a daughter was born. They did not expect to spend as much money on a girl's education as on a boy's, or to have to set her up in business. They expected daughters to be emotionally closer to their parents than a boy could be, to remain in the family circle up to and beyond marriage, and to be available later to care for ill or aged parents. Mary Howitt, daughter of a land surveyor in Staffordshire, said her Quaker parents had so convinced her they *preferred* daughters that when a stranger asked her in 1808 whether she and her two sisters would like a brother, she replied in all seriousness, 'Oh, no, our parents do not approve of boys.' But when her brother Charles was born that year he became the spoilt darling of the family.

The vast majority of English girls, however, were born to working-class parents, who accepted whatever God sent, but were somewhat disappointed if it was a girl. Any child was an extra mouth for a poor family to feed, but also a potential wage-earner. Flora Thompson, daughter of a farm labourer in Oxfordshire in the 1880s, said that even when girls went away into domestic service, and saved money from their meagre wages to send home, mothers still favoured their sons:

Strange to say, although they were grateful to and fond of their daughters, their boys, who were always at home and whose money barely paid for their keep, seemed always to come first with them. If there was any inconvenience, it must not fall on the boys; if there was a limited quantity of anything, the boys must still have their full share; the boys' best clothes must be brushed and put away for them; their shirts must be specially well-ironed, and tit-bits must always be saved for their luncheon afield.

Victoria Wignall, born in Lancashire in 1900, and one of six daughters of a working-class family, said, 'I was the fourth down, and as we grew older we would hear people saying, "What, all girls!" I couldn't believe it, and they said it in such a way as though, really, poor father, poor mother, to have all girls.' In the early 1900s the birth of a girl was a disappointment, because men were in short supply and it was still a man's world. Possession of those faraway countries of the Empire, coloured pink on the globe, depended on the *men* of the Army and Navy who wore colourful uniforms, marched into battle, served on the great ships, and ruled the natives. A girl could only sing, 'All the nice girls love a sailor' or 'The British Grenadiers' and wear a dress with a sailor collar.

Whatever the sex of a baby, however, parents wondered how long it would live. The chance of survival was better in an affluent family than in a poor one, though in all classes the death of a child was commonplace. In Bath between 1839 and 1843, one child in five from a middle-class home died before the age of five, but one child in two in a working-class home. In Liverpool as late as 1899, the difference between the social classes was just as stark. In upper-class areas of the city, one in seven children died under the age of one. But in the poorer districts it was more than one in four, and in the most wretched streets of all, one in two. The risk was highest in the first weeks of life, when babies are most susceptible to diseases of the chest and stomach. From 1838, when births were first registered, to 1900, one quarter of all recorded as being born in Britain died as babies (this was fewer than in most other European countries). Illegitimate babies died at twice the rate of legitimate ones. Poverty was the major problem. Things began to improve only in the early twentieth century, when living standards rose and there was a government campaign to teach mothers more about hygiene and baby-care.

Despite women being called 'the weaker sex', we now know that they are hardier than men through all stages of life. So it is surprising to find that until mid-century the death rate for young girls and women was higher than that for males, and continued higher for young girls until 1914. A major reason was the high rate of tuberculosis (also called consumption) in areas with large numbers of unskilled workers. It appears that boys were fed better than girls, particularly during the adolescent growth spurt. In poorer homes they tried to keep the male breadwinners well fed, even during hard times. Girls had less access to washing facilities and changes of clothing. They also nursed sick members of the family and so ran a higher risk of infection. Diphtheria and chorea (St Vitus's Dance) were diseases to which girls were more prone.

There were also deaths from accidents. Children were sometimes burnt at work, or even at school as they huddled round open fires, but as coroners' records show, more perished by burns or scalding in their own homes. Little girls were often left at home to look after the house and the babies, when mothers had to go out to work, and accidents happened. There were even some deaths of girls that were deliberately planned. The town clerk at Stockport gave evidence in 1843 to a parliamentary commission on deaths from arsenic poisoning. He quoted the cases of two families of hatters who had poisoned four daughters. The boys were spared, he said, 'because the parents considered them likely to be useful'. An anecdote like this does not prove that such a practice was widespread, but it is a chilling reflection of some attitudes of the time.

Poverty may have blunted some parents' emotions, but most of the poor were as concerned for their children's welfare as the better-off, and grieved as much over their illness or death. When they could not afford a doctor, poor people resorted to a range of home remedies. In 1822 William Varley, a handloom weaver of Burnley, bought some new milk, some ling-liver oil, and a mustard plaster for his daughter who had consumption. But it was no use, and she died. Four years later he said children were dying by two and three a house of smallpox and measles, and commented, 'Well may they die, for there is no aid, no succour to be had for them.' Outpatient departments were more popular than hospitals at mid-century, because the high death rate of inmates roused people's worst fears. From the 1840s, when the Manchester Clinic for Children was opened, it was besieged by nearby families, women sometimes spending the night in the street with their children to get a better chance of early attention.

Death, not only of children but of people of all ages, was the great leveller for all the social classes. The mother of Charlotte, Emily and Anne Brontë died of cancer in 1821, aged thirty-eight, leaving six children. Two of the little girls died of TB a few years later. Mary Howitt lost three children at birth, and in 1828 her two-year-old son died. Dr Tait, who was later Archbishop of Canterbury, lost five of his seven children from scarlet fever within a month in 1856. Illness and death were much more familiar to nineteenth-century children than today. Large numbers lived through much of their childhood having lost at least one parent; most had a brother or sister who died in infancy; and all were aware of the deaths of other relatives and neighbours. Children's religious literature throughout the century seems obsessed with deathbed scenes, and dying children were often alleged to express joy at the prospect of 'passing to a better world'. Beatrice Webb was probably more typical in saying of her childhood in the 1860s: 'Almost continuous illness . . . from inflamed eyes to congested lungs, marred my happiness, and I spent much time building castles in the air in which the picture of a neglected child enjoying her own melodramatically forgiving deathbed was succeeded by a more cheerful vision of courting lovers.'

The rich had very elaborate funerals and lengthy mourning periods. Up to the First World War, the poor kept the corpse at home until the burial, often laid out in the only living-room, in a coffin placed on a door taken off its hinges. Death caused terror in many girls, but Kathleen Betterton, born in 1913 and the daughter of a liftman on the London underground, thought the cemetery was 'the nicest place' and was 'quite overwhelmed by the beauty of the marble angels'. The ceremonies connected with death appealed to a morbid streak in some children, who would play at funerals, make toy coffins and tell jokes about death. Children saw backyard slaughter-houses, the pig-killer and dead horses in the street or on the way to the knacker's yard. Ethel Clark told of dancing with her girl-friends round a dead carthorse, and trying to lift its hoof, but she hated pig-killing and said, 'While the pig hung in the back kitchen I was terrified . . . it really haunted me.' Ruth Howe was fascinated by but afraid of 'a fearful person called Charlie the pig-killer, who was a dwarf and travelled the countryside driving a small, depressed-looking pony and cart, with the knives of his calling hanging from his belt.'

Poorer people prepared for family deaths by taking out insurance policies to cover the cost of the funeral, and by keeping shrouds or 'grave clothes' in a chest of drawers. Some kept memories alive with souvenirs of the dead; in the parlour of a friend's house in Liverpool in the 1890s Daisy Cowper saw framed mourning cards of the children who had died and a photograph of a dead baby in its tiny coffin. Kathleen Hilton-Foord remembered a neighbour's baby dying, when she was a small girl in Dover in 1910: 'All the tenants went in to kiss her and pay their respects. I was very frightened, but made to go.'

Rose Ashton's baby sister was one of the many whose births went unrecorded and whose death was unmarked by a headstone. In 1904 she was called to her mother's bedroom where she saw her newborn sister lying dead on a pillow, 'looking like a little doll, a beautiful thing'. Rose was told to collect a soap box from the grocer, put the baby inside and take it to the gravedigger for burial. Rose tore the lining out of her father's old coat to upholster the tiny box, then set off for the graveyard with her baby sister tucked inside the makeshift coffin. The gravedigger was not at all surprised to see Rose, clutching her small box, and pointed her towards a heap of similar boxes and packets near the church. She was upset, and asked where he was going to bury these tiny babies. He explained that many people could not afford to buy private graves, so when a public grave for paupers was ready for filling he put one baby in at the foot and another at the head, until he got rid of them. Rose said she came home broken-hearted.

Girls of all social classes said they were comforted by religious beliefs when they were coming to terms with death. And religion was the basis for attitudes towards child-rearing. The traditional Christian view, expressed by Hannah More in 1799, was that a child was born with Original Sin:

> It is a fundamental error to consider children as innocent beings, whose little weaknesses may perhaps want some correction, rather than as beings who bring into the world a corrupt nature and evil dispositions, which it should be the great end of education to rectify.

Her view – that a child's will had to be ruthlessly suppressed by parents, schoolteachers and others in authority – prevailed throughout the century, in all classes of society. The reforming Earl of Shaftesbury said he and his sisters had been brought up in the 1810s 'with very great severity, moral and physical . . . the opinion of our parents being that, to render a child obedient, it should be in constant fear of its father and mother.' Kindness, he said, was 'a dish, tho' much relished was rarely ever tasted'. For years his father vented 'malignity and horror' on his eldest daughter Charlotte, only ceasing when his other children grew up and intervened.

Upper-class parents handed over their children from birth to servants, nurses, nannies and private governesses. Most parents were remote or authoritarian rather than as cruel as the sixth Earl of Shaftesbury. Lady Caroline Ponsonby (later Lamb) belonged to one of the greatest Whig families of the early nineteenth century. When she was four years old her mother had a paralytic stroke, and she was sent to Italy to be out of the way, spending five years there in the sole charge of a maid, Fanny. She was then rescued by her grandmother and returned to London to be educated with her cousins at ducal Devonshire House. She said the children were 'neglected by their mothers, served on silver in the morning and carrying their own plates down at night . . . thinking that the world was divided into dukes and beggars.' Her education was at first minimal: 'I wrote not, spelt not, but I made verses which they all thought beautiful. For myself, I preferred washing the dog or polishing a piece of Derbyshire spar.' Later she learned Greek, French and Italian, as well as becoming a good musician.

Life at Devonshire House was not as dismal as at some aristocratic homes, for when Caroline's cousin, Lady Georgiana Cavendish, married Lord Morpeth in 1801 and went to live at his home, Castle Howard in Yorkshire, she found an unfamiliar world of formal patriarchy in which no affection was shown to children. Her sister, Lady Harriet, was also shocked by this, and wrote to her grandmother, 'Lord Carlisle certainly keeps his children in great awe of him. They are in their behaviour to each other more like a Prince and his followers, or a General and his *aide de camp*, than a Father and children.' Lady Morpeth refused to carry on this family tradition and was a loving and devoted mother to her own twelve children. Queen Victoria resented the fact that her mother, the Duchess of Kent, had been so cold and detached from her, saying later, 'To miss a mother's friendship – not to have her to confide in – when a girl most needs it, was fearful. I dare not think of it – it drives me wild now.' The Queen did not care for young children, but was very close to her daughters as they grew up.

Lady Dorothy Nevill said her father, the Earl of Orford, was an autocrat whose rule over his family was unquestioned in the 1830s. She described how, at breakfast 'my mother would on certain days catch my eye and significantly look down at her plate where her knife and fork had been carefully crossed – a sign that its head was in no mood for conversation.' She said, 'Children at that time were kept in great order, and generally forbidden to do anything they particularly liked – more, I think, on general principle than for any sufficient reason.' Yet Lady Dorothy said she did not have an unhappy childhood; she recalled how simple it was and how much pleasure she had in riding with her father in Dorsetshire.

Upper-class children were usually confined to the east wing or nursery floor of a large house, so they did not intrude on adult life. There was no smell of babies in the grown-up quarters, no noise and no evidence of toys. The children ate separately, which saved their parents a lot of indigestion. Their lives were ruled by the nurse, a paid servant who made the laws about nursery life. Some were benevolent and beloved, others cruel. Georgiana Sitwell, member of an aristocratic and eccentric family, was born in 1824 and recalled her nurse Penny, or Pay as she called her, as 'a little, round, black-eyed woman who wore great white caps, sang to the children and played on a paper and comb for their dancing.' But the children had long hours of study beginning at 7 am, with no holiday except Christmas Day. Sundays were Sabbatarian, with only the Bible or tracts to read, and catechism to learn. As a child in the 1820s, the future Queen Victoria had lessons from 9.30 to 11.30 am, then play out of doors, lunch and a walk, lessons again from 3 to 6 pm followed by play, supper and bed. She learned English, French, German, history, geography, writing and arithmetic, as well as needlework. She had a governess she loved, and more toys than most children, but as an only child was often lonely. She said she had been 'extremely crushed and kept under, and hardly dared say a word'. She made up for this later in life.

The author Charlotte Yonge thought in the 1860s that nurseries were becoming more comfortable than her own had been in the 1830s:

I hear now of carpets, curtains, pictures in the existing nurseries. They must be palaces compared with our bare little attic where nothing was allowed that would gather dust. One bit of drugget by the fireplace, where stood a round table, at which the maids talked and darned stockings, was all that hid the bare boards; the walls were plain as those of a workhouse . . . there was a deal table for meals, and very plain meals they were.

This was a gentry household of moderate means. In that of a rich and noble family things were not much different. Lucy, daughter of Lord Lyttelton, described her nursery in the 1840s as being a large, plain room with massive furniture, and books only for consultation by the nurse. The walls contained prints of foreign scenes, a portrait of the Queen, and an old map which Lucy loved. At the age of thirteen, Lucy wrote this heart-rending account of her governess up to the age of seven:

Miss Nicholson managed me ill; over-severe and apt to whip me for obstinacy when I was only dense, and punishing too often . . . At Brighton I used to be taken out walking on the Parade with my hands tied behind me . . . At home my usual punishment was being put for a time into a large, deep, old-fashioned bath that was in one corner of the schoolroom.

This governess was followed by one who was over-indulgent, and then another who exposed Lucy's faults unsparingly. Lady Lyttelton loved her children, but would not listen to their complaints and did not interfere between them and the governess, so the children continued to suffer, as did Lucy's cousin, Mary Gladstone, daughter of the Liberal leader. She was born in 1847 and wrote in old age, 'My governess from ten to seventeen years continued to treat me as half-witted, so I grew up a nonentity. I have never outgrown it.' B.L. Booker recalled her childhood in London in the 1870s: 'We lived upstairs in a different world and were at the mercy of our nurses, one of whom terrorised and starved me when she got me to herself.'

Not all girls were so abused. Jane Ellen Harrison, born in Yorkshire in 1850, and later a lecturer at Newnham College, Cambridge, said the governesses she had up to the age of thirteen were 'all grossly ignorant, but they were good women, steadily kind to me'. They taught her 'how to enter a room, how to get into a carriage, that little girls should be seen and not heard, and that I was in the schoolroom to learn, not to ask questions.' She learned a lot of facts and a quantity of poetry while lying on a backboard, which gave her a well-stocked memory and a perfectly straight back. Dame Ethel Smyth (born 1858) said, 'Our governesses never stayed long and they pass before my mind's eye in dreary procession: some English, some German, some with dyspepsia, others with unfortunate natures . . . nearly always ugly and quite invariably without the faintest notion of making lessons pleasant or profitable.' Beatrice Webb said of her governesses in the 1860s, 'For the most part I liked them and they liked me' and Sybil Cuffe (later Lady Sybil Lubbock, her father having become an Earl) had in the 1890s a governess she loved, an excellent teacher who 'made no attempt to invade our emotional life, and was kind, just and reserved.' Barbara Lister, daughter of Lord Ribblesdale, loved her governess 'Zellie' and learned perfect French and German, but her general ignorance shocked her uncle, Prime Minister Asquith.

From 1851 a magazine called *The Monthly Packet* was produced by Charlotte Yonge, especially for girls in the nursery and schoolroom. It was serious and instructive, and contained stories in which girls predominated. From the 1870s there was a lightening in the atmosphere of the upper-class nursery, though it was still carefully ruled. Toy cupboards were better stocked with dolls and dolls' houses, clockwork toys, Noah's ark animals, puzzles and bricks. But the remoteness of some upper-class mothers continued. B.L. Booker said she met her mother once a day upstairs in the drawing room after tea, and Mary Lutyens wrote, 'Nanny was my life . . . Mother was a goddess. It was unthinkable that a goddess should bath me.' Mary accepted such detachment; Helena Wright, the birth control campaigner, did not. She was bitterly critical of her mother, who had been more bound up in her social life and charitable works than in her children. 'To me you were a shadow,' she wrote, 'a shadow with three characteristics: you were always "busy", and you were always either ill or worried . . . I don't remember that you once spent time actually playing with us in the nursery . . . Nurse Minter was our chief companion . . . Why didn't you get to know your children a little?'

Yet throughout the century some upper-class parents were very indulgent and tolerant of children's naughtiness, refusing to discipline them in puritan fashion. Emily, Lady Cowper (later Lady Palmerston) indulged her child Minny, whom Lady Bessborough described as 'by far the prettiest and most spoiled child I ever saw . . . she is the nastiest little thing . . . and rules the house rather unpleasantly.' Yet Minny grew

up to become the rather prudish and charming bride in 1830 of the reforming Earl of Shaftesbury. Ellen Weeton was governess in 1812–14 to
the wealthy Armitage family in Huddersfield, and reported that the
children were extremely spoilt, screaming dreadfully whenever she tried
to teach them, and flying into violent fits of passion. The girl, aged
seven, went on strike and refused to do anything. Miss Weeton tried
persuasion but said, 'the maddening child only smiled and tossed her
head.' In the end, 'notwithstanding that it is so repugnant to the present
mild system of education', she resorted to the rod. Then all the children
went on strike and discipline collapsed. The Brontë sisters looked after
difficult children when they were governesses in the 1840s. Anne was
expected to cope with what Charlotte called 'an unruly, violent family
of modern children' whose parents would not back her authority; in
desperation she once tied two little Inghams of Blake Hall to a table leg,
and was dismissed. Charlotte was actually stoned by a small Sidgwick
of Stonegappe Hall, though later the child came to love her.

The heiress who later became Daisy, Countess of Warwick, spent her
childhood in the 1850s in the stables, making friends with grooms,
stableboys and gamekeepers, learning to ride and jump on her white
pony and hunt. She said it was an idyllic, unintellectual life-style that
continued until she was eighteen. Beatrice Webb (then Potter) and her
sisters, daughters of a very wealthy industrialist, also had an unrestricted
childhood and were not simpering Victorian misses. They said what they
thought, all their lives, without reference to the feelings of anyone,
and their mother thought her husband 'far too acquiescent in his
daughters' unconventional habits.' Margot Asquith, who married the
Prime Minister in the early twentieth century, was a daughter of wealthy
chemical manufacturer, Sir Charles Tennant, and brought up in an
isolated Scottish castle in the 1880s. She said, 'We were wild children
and, left to ourselves, had the time of our lives.' There are many other
examples of parents who allowed their daughters great freedom, but
they were usually upper-class, eccentric and wealthy.

Middle-class girls often had a nursery and a nanny. The middle class
grew in numbers and affluence between 1822 and 1882. They could
afford more servants and from 1850 it was common for even a 'genteel
tradesman's family' to advertise for a nanny. But bourgeois mothers
took a much larger part in teaching their daughters than did aristocratic
mothers. This was partly because they could not afford private
governesses and tutors, but also because they wanted to see that 'proper'

values were instilled. In the 1860s there was a lively correspondence in the *Englishwoman's Review* on the efficacy of whipping one's daughters, and it was mothers who wrote in.

Writer Molly Hughes described a happy nursery childhood in the 1870s. She and her four brothers had few treats or toys, so made their own amusements, but there were plenty of books. There were few rules but these were strict: obedience was essential; there must be no fuss or argument about going to bed; there must be no rudeness to servants; and the children must make 'a clean plate' at dinner, even when they had been too lavish with the mustard. A special rule for Molly was that she must not cry in order to get something. The family went on outings to Kew or Richmond, and spent holidays with relatives in Cornwall. On Sundays they attended St Paul's Cathedral, and found the afternoons long and dull because they were not allowed games or toys and were allowed only to read religious books. Girls like Molly got their formal education at day or boarding schools, which will be described in the next chapter.

In contrast to Molly Hughes, Beatrix Potter (cousin of Beatrice Webb) had a lonely childhood in the 1870s. She led a sheltered existence in Kensington, with no awareness of the need for affection or fun. She had no playmates until the birth of her brother when she was five, and only a few toys – a black Topsy doll and a flannelette pig among them – and she was not sent to school or any classes. Her father qualified as a barrister but did not practise, having ample means to live. Beatrix was neither rebellious nor self-pitying, but found refuge in books. It was on holiday on a Scottish farm that she found delight, saying, 'I do not remember a time when I did not make for myself a fairyland amongst . . . all the common objects of the countryside.' She used to draw animals wearing coats or frocks, and bearing umbrellas or baskets. Peter Rabbit, Tom Kitten, Squirrel Nutkin and the host of creatures she later created, for the enduring delight of children, had their origins in those summer holidays. There is no easy explanation why, from her starved background, she produced such magic.

In families where there were children of both sexes girls could compare their own treatment with that of their brothers. It was usual for middle-class girls to share in the household tasks, but their brothers did not. Dorothea Beale, later Headmistress of Cheltenham Ladies College, said much of her childhood in the 1820s was spent on 'the inevitable sock-darning which falls to a girl's position in a family of so many boys'.

Not everyone approved of this: the conservative writer Sarah Ellis wrote, in her popular book *The Wives of England* (1843), 'I never could imagine why little girls were to fetch and carry . . . while boys sat still, and fancied themselves into lords of creation.' Molly Hughes complained that, 'I came last in all distribution of food at table, treats of sweets and so on. I was expected to wait on the boys, run messages, fetch things left upstairs, and never grumble, let alone refuse.' Educationist Helena Swanwick, born in 1864, mended her own clothes from the age of eight, and also helped mend the underclothes of 'men' in the family. She said she never could fathom why the boys were not expected to help. Suffragette leader, Emmeline Pankhurst, said as a young child she was puzzled why she had to make home attractive to her brothers since it was never suggested they make home attractive to her. Some women developed from their discontents a feminist viewpoint: others like Molly Hughes denied they ever felt any disadvantage, or dismissed their jealousies as trivial.

There are not many accounts of a Victorian nursery in a lower middle-class home, such as that of a minor civil servant or a teacher, but author Richard Church described his, in his autobiography *Over the Bridge*, as the most static institution human society has ever known. Unlike the upper-class nursery where children lived their lives separately from the parents, here the children and parents lived intimately together, in a narrow but secure setting, keeping themselves apart from other families and living an emotional life dependent on each other.

Girls from different strata of the middle class were segregated from each other, and girls from the lower middle class were not allowed to play with working-class girls. Stella Davies, born in 1895 and the daughter of a successful commercial traveller, recalled living in Edwardian Manchester in a large house, with a maid of all work, 'Fat Ellen'. A street of working-class houses with lots of children ran the length of their garden but, she said, 'We were not allowed to speak to them.' Next door lived a wealthy Manchester merchant who employed servants and a nursemaid to look after his children, but they too 'were not allowed to play with us.' Stella used to stand on the flat roof of their summerhouse, looking at both lots of children, and dream of a game of rounders. Novelist Phyllis Bottome, born 1882, and daughter of a Church of England clergyman, told how when young she made friends with a village child, Hannah, who told her not to tell anyone they were friends because 'they'll stop us.' She was right; the family nurse found out and stopped the friendship, and Phyllis's mother confirmed the decision by saying that 'Hannah might have things in her head that Phyllis might catch.' She meant lice, not ideas.

Working-class children were everywhere. In the bigger cities they dominated the pavements, alleys and courtyards, with their noise resounding above all else. More than a third of the population, at any one time, were under fourteen years of age, and half of these were girls. The philanthropist Octavia Hill, campaigning for open spaces for the poor at mid-century, commented that 'the children are crawling or sitting on the hard hot stones till every corner of the place looks alive, and it seems as if I must step on them if I am to walk up the Court.'

The respectable working class brought up their daughters according to high standards of good behaviour, and most girls were devoted to their mothers, recognizing their hard lives and sacrifices. Hannah Cullwick entered service in 1841, when she was eight, and since the house was near her home, said, 'There wasn't a day but I was up to see Mother, if it was only for a minute.' Mrs Burrows, born around 1850 in the Norfolk Fens, and daughter of an agricultural labourer, said, 'No mother in the world ever strove more earnestly for her children's welfare than my mother did.' Some autobiographers say their mothers showed them little affection. Faith Osgerby, born 1890 in East Yorkshire and daughter of a stonemason, complained that she was never cuddled or kissed, but constantly punished for trivial offences. Doris Francis, born 1908 in London, whose mother had been a domestic servant, recalled the jealousy she felt when she saw a friend's mother kissing her. Some girls told of parents who played with them, made toys for them, sang and told stories to them, though many rarely saw their fathers who had long hours of work. Regular heavy drinking was a male habit, and Doris Ponton expressed a typical view when she said, 'My relationship with my father was one of love when he wasn't the worse for drink, and fear when he was.' A pattern of life where parents had the time and inclination to play with their children required a standard of living above mere subsistence.

Most working-class girls had to help with the domestic chores, and resented it when their brothers did not. Hannah Mitchell, daughter of a poor farmer in Derbyshire in the 1870s, said that when she was eight she had to darn all the stockings, including her brothers', whilst they played cards or dominoes. This filled her cup of bitterness to the brim. Doris Francis was burdened with housework from the time she could hold a duster, having to polish all the brass doorknobs, clean all the family's boots, shop for groceries, do the washing-up, peel all the vegetables and do all the mending, including the socks. But generally speaking, boys did the heavier and dirtier tasks such as humping coal and water, sweeping the yard, turning the handle of the mangle. Some girls even remembered their childhood duties with affection. Alice Foley, born in Bolton in 1891 and later a Trade Union official, wrote of her care of the cobbled yard and 'petty' house (outside lavatory):

> When it became my responsibility much labour was devoted to its transformation. The wooden seat was scrubbed to faultless whiteness and the floor vigorously 'donkey-stoned'. The whitewashed walls were adorned with picture almanacs and scraps of verse, whilst within handy reach of the occupants I hung a neat pile of 'bum papers' culled from father's old racing handicaps.

Poor girls did not have the same toys and recreations as upper-class girls. The informal games of the street and field provided the enjoyments of their short childhoods. They made dolls from straw or rags, used an orange-box for a doll's house, old rope for skipping, hoops from barrels for hoop-la, made a see-saw from an old plank and some bricks, and a swing from rope hitched to a tree. Poor girls had many fewer possessions than rich girls, but all shared similar problems that arose from being female.

The taboos surrounding menstruation were so strong in the nineteenth century that there is little direct evidence of girls' own reactions to its onset. Helen Corke, born in 1882, is one who described how she felt. Daughter of a small shopkeeper and a strict Congregationalist mother to whom respectability was all, she came to puberty at fifteen. When her mother explained it, her reaction was one of revulsion:

> I hear what she has to tell me with impatience and disgust. What an odious, limiting state of things! Are boys, as well as girls, subjected? No, boys are not. This is, I object, unfair! For the first time I wish that I were a boy! My mother ignores this, and proceeds hastily to advise me of all the precautions and prohibitions relative to the

monthly period that she had received at my age.

Helen's reaction was perhaps typical of girls at all times. Menstruation was referred to by euphemisms such as 'turns', 'monthlies', 'poorliness', 'the curse' or 'being unwell', and for protection women wore a napkin (similar to a baby's napkin and made of soft material), or a 'clout' (an old rag), both of which had to be soaked in a bucket of salted water and then washed thoroughly or boiled. There were no disposable sanitary towels of the modern kind until the end of the century (and then they were not in general use), and no tampons. Girls with stomach cramps were advised to drink hot ginger tea or a little gin and water. Doctors strictly forbade the use of opium, laudanum and paregoric (a tincture of opium) during periods, which suggests some women used them, and instead advised women to avoid indigestible foods, sudden exposure to cold or wet, and 'mental agitations'. Menstruating women were still regarded as 'unclean'; John Eliotson, writing in 1840, said without comment, 'In this country, it is firmly believed that meat will not take salt if the process is conducted by a menstruating woman.'

There is almost no explicit allusion to menstruation outside contemporary scientific literature, and it is hard for modern readers to comprehend just how little doctors and scientists then knew about human reproduction. In the first half of the century it was believed that the menstrual flow came from 'an excess of nutrient in the female', and until the discovery in 1845 that eggs were ejected spontaneously they were thought to descend from the ovaries only as a result of intercourse. Furthermore, the discomfort many women felt elicited a full-blown attack by some doctors on their capacity to think rationally.

Early in the century children were regarded as innocent of sexuality, but by the 1860s doctors and 'purity publicists' knew that girls and boys masturbated. Writer Priscilla Barker, deeply concerned that girls should be pure and chaste, offered this cautionary example of its degenerative effect:

Another victim came under my notice whose infatuating habit betrayed itself in sweaty, clammy hands, stinking feet, and mouth always full of saliva. I felt compelled to question her, for her own sake, and she confessed that as a child living in the quiet country, her chief delight was to go and sit up in a tree for hours, to gratify her sinful pleasure, under the pretence of cracking nuts.

Others spoke of masturbation causing 'increasing numbers of hysterical cases among girls', and much earnest thought went into trying to prevent it. Strict supervision, especially at night, was a normal procedure of parents and teachers, but it is doubtful if this worked. Bridget Tisdall wrote of her girlhood before the First World War:

I remember masturbating, but never felt guilty as I was never caught. I also remember my dear grandmother telling me to go to sleep lying on my side, with my arms crossed and folded against my potential bosom. This seemed to me weird and very uncomfortable. However, I was always anxious to placate the adult loony bin, so did as I was told. I remember the rest of my body feeling very left out lying in the safe position. But there I would lie, longing to scratch my toes, spiritually truncated from the animal half of myself.

Some doctors said masturbation caused 'certain forms of insanity, epilepsy and hysteria in females.' A gynaecologist named Isaac Baker Brown said that 'the period when such illness attacks the patient is about the age of puberty' and that it continued 'to almost every age'. He cited the case of a woman aged twenty who suffered 'great irregularity of temper . . . culminating in a monomania that every gentleman she admired was in love with her. I quickly discovered that her symptoms arose from peripheral excitement [masturbation].' Brown ran a fifty-bed clinic in London in the 1860s, and told wealthy parents he could cure masturbation, which he called anti-social behaviour. His treatment was the removal of the clitoris. He was not the only practitioner of clitoridectomies at the time, though the number of girls operated on must have been very small. Brown's career came to an abrupt end when he was expelled by the Obstetrical Society for failing to tell his patients or their families the true nature of the operation. However, devices to prevent onanism (masturbation) were marketed in the 1860s and 70s, and as late as 1930 a medical catalogue offered for sale belts to prevent male and female 'self-abuse'.

Most parents thought it essential for young girls to remain virgins and innocent about sex until marriage. When Mrs Menzies (whose first name is unrecorded) was seventeen in 1870, she married an army officer and in 1917 she wrote:

> I was shot out into the realities of life after the manner of those days, in a condition of black ignorance of the facts of life that would be unbelievable to girls of that age today – happily for them. The fact that I did not have the faintest idea of what I was doing was a matter of legitimate self-congratulation to my parents as a proof of the success of the upbringing they had bestowed on me.

Helen Corke (b.1882) told how she discovered sex by watching the neighbours' cats mating, and was 'enlightened by her sensations'. Her knowledge became more accurate when she found a book called *Esoteric Anthropology* hidden in her mother's chest of drawers. It described in simple terms 'the whole sequence of coition, conception, generation and birth'. Novelist Phyllis Bottome gave a frank account of her response to being told the facts of life by her mother, when other children laughed at her belief that an angel brought babies:

> There unrolled before my horrified eyes an amazing and tragic picture of the life between the sexes. The pains of childbirth – the greater physical strength of men – their far from greater moral strength – the white slave traffic – nothing was spared me.

She became nearly frantic with rage and terror. Her initial response was that she would live her life as if it were not true. 'My future – the husband and twelve children I had happily intended to possess – I would arrive at in a different way from Nature's.' She went through a difficult puberty, at seventeen had a gynaecological operation, and did not marry until she was thirty-five.

An obsession with sex does not feature in working-class women's autobiographies, though some mention knowing little or nothing about it when they were girls. Charlotte Meadowcroft was enlightened by the cook, when she entered service at the age of thirteen in 1901. She wrote, 'I was shocked, and I remember thinking how crude and vulgar she was.' Yet Bessie Wallis, a miner's daughter born in 1904, insisted that in her community 'there was no mystery about sex'. There was in fact a good deal of pre-marital sex in the working class, as will be shown in Chapter 3.

Incest was almost a taboo subject in Victorian England. When Beatrice Webb published in 1888 her findings as a disguised 'plain trouserhand' in London, she did not mention her discoveries about incest among the poor, but in a footnote to her 1926 autobiography she said:

> In this essay I omitted the reference in my MS diary to the prevalence of incest in one-room tenements. The fact that some of my workmates – young girls, who were in no way mentally defective, just as keen-witted and generous as my own circle of friends – could chaff each other about having babies by their fathers and brothers, was a gruesome example of the effect of a debased social environment on personal character and family life.

Although it had always been socially taboo and a sin in the eyes of the Churches, incest became illegal for the first time in England in 1908. In that year Margaret Bondfield (who in 1929 became the first woman cabinet minister) visited a home for unmarried mothers in Bradford and was told of a number of cases of women having babies by their brothers or fathers.

Incest was not confined then, as indeed nor is it now, to the poor living in overcrowded conditions. Lord Byron was said by his wife to have had a daughter by his half-sister, and Virginia Woolf described how from 1888 (when she was six) to 1904 (when she was eighteen) she was sexually abused by her half-brother. Incest was one of the darkest and best-kept secrets of the nineteenth century, and remained so until very recently.

The pre-1914 woman was also generally in ignorance of the homosexual patterns of a man's world. Clemence Dane's heroine, Elinor Broome, in the book *Broome Stages*, stumbles on it when her eldest son explains why his younger brother has run away from school: 'Do you mean to tell me, Richard, that all over England fathers can know that there's a risk of their own sons, boys of ten and eleven, being frightened as John has been frightened, and that they let it go on? It's not credible! D'you suppose if women knew – d'you suppose that if I had known, I'd have let it happen?' But it is not clear what she could or would have done to stop it.

As puberty approached, upper-class girls were chaperoned very carefully, and working-class girls were hedged round with more restrictions than were boys. Becoming a young lady was a serious business involving, according to writer Naomi Mitchison,

> a difference of behaviour, which must no longer be silly or careless, a lengthening of skirts to ankle length and putting up one's long maiden hair. The last was, to me, fiendishly difficult; I didn't want to be bothered with hairpins, nor did I think I looked nicer with my hair bundled up behind.

Molly Hughes said her father told her in the 1880s that 'boys should go everywhere and know everything, and a girl should stay home and know nothing.' Helena Swanwick said of her teens in the 1870s, and many women would echo her ideas today:

> I resented the idea that I could not be allowed out after dark, even in frequented thoroughfares. When it was explained to me that a young girl by herself was liable to be insulted by men, I became incoherent with rage at a society which shut up the girls instead of the men.

In the period 1880 to 1914 more and more middle-class women wrote of the confinement, claustrophobia and belittlement they had felt when growing up. Constance Maynard said she and her sister were 'shut up like eagles in a henhouse', with her mother 'pat pat patting down all ambition'. Naomi Mitchison (then Haldane) said in an intellectual home in Oxford around 1900 she felt 'constantly netted by invisible rules'. Others hated the minutiae of social etiquette, flower arranging, giving directions to servants, producing articles for sale at church bazaars, and worst of all the social visiting. Kathleen Chorley, daughter of a rich family in Cheshire, said, 'The day was indeed a black one, on which we found that our mothers had had their cards reprinted and that our names figured below theirs on the disgusting little white slips. But we were drilled and disciplined.'

Yet the difficulty of generalizing about how repressed girls were is proved by Sara Burstall's experience. She said of her lower middle-class upbringing in London in the 1860s and 70s:

> The modern age does not need to be told about Victorian conventions. They were oppressive to many girls and women, but they did not oppress me, partly because we were poor, partly because we lived

in a rather Bohemian quarter where artists and actors abounded, but chiefly because of the principles of my parents.

Sara said her mother was 'a woman of great natural ability, of strong physique and independent mind' who never followed fashion or wore a crinoline. She had been a Chartist in her youth, and attended lectures at Birkbeck Literary and Scientific Institution in London, where women were allowed in from 1833, but she felt her life had been a failure and wanted better for her daughter. Her father was also a strong, independent character, very involved in the day-to-day care of Sara. For example, when she was a child, her mother often took her to the father's office, where the child was 'perfectly happy playing in a corner with filing cards.' Her mother's dreams for Sara were fulfilled when, after a good education, she eventually became Headmistress of Manchester High School for Girls and encouraged her middle-class pupils to widen their horizons. In the next chapter we will look at continuity and change in girls' education.

2

That Won't Earn a Gal a Living

EDUCATION FOR GIRLS

> Now, the education of girls, whatever facts it may teach them, does not tend to expand and develop their minds, but to cramp and confine them. Far from being encouraged to use their own faculties, any symptom of independent thought is quickly repressed.
>
> Marion Reid, *A Plea for Women* (1843)

For most of the nineteenth century, the majority of English girls had little or no formal schooling, and what they managed to get was not of an intellectual kind. Girls at all levels of society were educationally deprived, as compared with boys of their own class. There was no state-supported system of free schools until the 1880s, and parents were willing to pay more for the private schooling of their sons than for their daughters. Upper-class boys were tutored at home until they went away to boarding school, often at the age of nine, or at the latest thirteen, to toughen up for adult life. These 'public schools' were so-called because the education was provided outside the home. Boys later went on to university.

Up until the First World War, upper-class girls did not go to school at all, being taught at home by governesses and tutors until they 'came out' into 'society' at the age of seventeen. Some then spent a year at 'finishing school' abroad. Upper-class parents seem to have had no particular philosophy for raising their daughters, who would one day become the most powerful women in the country, other than to keep them innocent about sex and uncontaminated by contact with girls from the lower orders. They believed that 'breeding will out', and that those with 'blue blood' in their veins were so superior that they needed little else. Mary Wollstonecraft complained in *Thoughts on the Education of Daughters* (1787) of the stress on dancing, playing the piano, performing on the harp, and studying French and Italian, saying that girls did not learn enough 'to engage their attention and render it an employment of the mind.' Her opinion was confirmed by Lady Ailesbury, writing in 1810, who was worried about her granddaughters:

> I abominate the modern education of females. The drift of it is to make them artists and nothing else, which, if they were to earn their bread, might be useful. Mind and morals are never thought about.

The life of Mary Somerville (1780–1872) illustrates how difficult it was for an upper-class girl to get a sound education early in the century, even when she was a determined student. A brilliant girl who was destined to become world famous, she was the daughter of a naval captain, Sir William Fairfax. When she was ten years old Mary could not write, so she was sent for a year to a boarding school. There she was made to wear stays with a steel busk and an iron collar to keep her head up, and to learn Johnson's dictionary by heart. When she returned home she began to study all the animals and flowers she could find, and by the time she was twelve had read all the English books in the house and even one in French, with the aid of a dictionary. She then taught herself Latin. When she was fourteen a drawing master said to her, 'You should study Euclid's *Elements of Geometry*, the foundation not only of perspective but of astronomy and all mechanical science.' Her brother's tutor got her a handbook of algebra and a Euclid, and this is how she struggled to learn:

> Before I began to read algebra I found it necessary to study arithmetic again, having forgotten much of it . . . I had to take part in household affairs, and to make and mend my own clothes. I rose early, played on the piano and painted during the time I could spare in the daylight hours, but I sat up very late reading Euclid. The servants however told my mother, 'It is no wonder the stock of candles is soon exhausted, for Miss Mary sits up reading till a very late hour', whereupon an order was given to take away my candle as soon as I was in bed. I had, however, already gone through the first six books of Euclid, and now I was thrown on my memory which I exercised by

beginning at the first book and demonstrating in my mind a certain number of problems every night, till I could nearly go through the whole. My father somehow or other finding out what I was about, said to my mother, 'Peg, we must put a stop to this, or we shall have Mary in a strait-jacket [in an asylum] one of these days'.

Mary's brother had a tutor, but she had none. Mary had to do housework and sewing, which her brother did not, and she fitted in her studies when she could. Like many, if not most parents, her father believed that study was bad for a girl and might well drive her mad. In spite of his prediction, Mary took to rising at daybreak, and 'after dressing I wrapped myself in a blanket from my bed on account of the excessive cold – having no fire at that hour – and read algebra or the classics till breakfast time.' Mary went on studying alone for many years. Her first husband, Captain Samuel Grieg, did not sympathize with her intellectual interests and thought she should give them up when she married. According to Mary's daughter, he 'possessed in full the prejudice against learned women which was common at that time.' They had two sons, but Mary was widowed in 1807, after three years of marriage. In 1812 she married an educated liberal man, William Somerville, an Army officer who delighted in her scientific pursuits. He encouraged her to write her first and most famous book, *The Mechanism of the Heavens*, published in 1827. Mary found it hard as a woman to find time to be creative, even when she had a supportive husband and servants, for she had four more children by her second marriage, three of whom died in infancy. She wrote:

I rose early and made such arrangements with regard to my children and family affairs that I had time to write afterwards; not however without many interruptions. A man can always command his time under plea of business; a woman is not allowed any such excuse. At Chelsea I was always supposed to be at home, and as my friends and acquaintances came so far out of their way on purpose to see me it would have been unkind and ungenerous not to receive them. Nevertheless I was sometimes annoyed when in the midst of a difficult problem someone would enter and say, 'I have come to spend a few hours with you.' However I learnt by habit to leave a subject and resume it at once, like putting a mark in a book I might be reading; this was the more necessary as there was no fireplace in my little room, and

I had to write in the drawing-room in winter. Frequently I hid my
papers as soon as the bell announced a visitor, lest anyone should
discover my secret.

The book written under these conditions was published when she was
forty-seven years old. It brought Mary Somerville recognition from
every scientific body in the world, and it was followed by *The Connection of the Physical Sciences* and several other books. She was eventually
made an Honorary (not a full) Member of the Royal Astronomical
Society, and in 1879 – a few years following her death – a women's college in Oxford was named after her. She was the living proof that a
woman could excel in mathematics and scientific investigation, and her
work influenced the teaching of the physical sciences both in England
and America. She was not the only upper-class woman of her day to
make a mark in science. Lord Byron's daughter, Ada Lovelace, was an
exceptionally gifted mathematician who foresaw how a digital computer
would work. In 1843 she published, with extensive mathematical notes,
her translation of Menabrea's *Sketch of the Analytical Engine invented
by Charles Babbage.*

Throughout the century there were of course cultured men who
wanted intellectual discussion with the women in their families, and gave
them serious books to read. Macaulay wrote in 1837 that he had often
heard talking 'men who wish, as almost all men of sense wish, that
women should be highly educated.' Writer Charlotte Yonge, born in
1823 into a gentry family, had lessons before and after breakfast with
her father, a stern tutor. She loved history and learned languages easily,
but was not mathematical and these lessons often ended in tears.
Florence Nightingale, born in 1820, was educated by her father in her
teens to a high standard of classics and philosophy, and at the age of
twenty mastered mathematical principles by studying on her own. But
most upper-class women throughout the century were educated only in
ladylike accomplishments. Lady Muriel Beckwith wrote of her late Victorian childhood, 'signs of individuality in the young, if observed, were
firmly nipped in the bud . . . the child was only permitted to think under
supervision'; and in 1912 Lady May Harcourt engaged a French
governess to help one of her daughters with her reading, and wrote to
a friend, 'the other girls are full of drawing, elocution, fencing, dancing,
German, singing and skating. So education is in full swing.' Clearly, little had changed since Mary Wollstonecraft's day.

More important than any formal education, perhaps, was the influence of family culture that upper-class girls absorbed from adolescence onwards. Politics, 'society' and the intellectual élite were closely interwoven in England, and young upper-class girls met distinguished visitors from all walks of life, hearing erudite discussions on literature, philosophy and the arts, as well as politics. The outspoken Beatrice Webb won the guidance of social thinker Herbert Spencer, who provided her with reading lists and discussed her ideas. Mary Gladstone was tutored by the famous historian, Lord Acton, her father's friend, though her father the Prime Minister took no interest in her education.

What upper-class girls thus learned, albeit indirectly, were self-confidence, an ability to rise to any occasion, and an unquestioning belief in their right to social rule. They were told in the Church catechism to do their duty in that state of life to which it had pleased God to call them, and they did not expect to move out of the privileged state into which they were born. Beatrice Webb described this process perfectly, when she wrote, 'As life unfolded itself I became aware that I belonged to a class of persons who habitually gave orders, but who seldom, if ever, executed the orders of other people.' She said she had 'no consciousness of superior riches; on the contrary, owing to my mother's utilitarian expenditure (a discriminating penuriousness which I think was traditional in families rising to industrial power during the Napoleonic Wars) the Potter girls were brought up to feel very poor.' Yet she was always conscious of 'superior power'. Effortless superiority was as much the trade-mark of the upper-class woman as it was of the upper-class man, and it tended to repress any possible sense of shared experience with women of other social classes.

Many middle-class parents, too, were uninterested in an academic education for their daughters. In the first half of the century the emphasis was on religious teaching which emphasised the subordination of women. As the popular writer Sarah Ellis (a clergyman's wife) put it in the 1830s, 'The first thing of importance is to be content to be inferior to men, inferior in mental power in the same proportion that you are inferior in bodily strength.' For their sons schooling was a different matter. It was an investment in a boy's future, and from the 1840s an education at one of the reformed public schools became a passport to success in professional and public life. Many girls knew that their parents put more resources into the education of sons than of daughters, and were jealous. The suffragette leader, Emmeline Pankhurst, eldest of the ten children of a Manchester textile manufacturer, wrote in 1914 of the 1860s:

> The education of the English boy, then as now, was considered a much more serious matter than the education of the English boy's sister. My parents, especially my father, discussed the question of my brothers' education as a matter of real importance. My education and that of my sister were scarcely discussed at all.

The wealthy middle class imitated the aristocracy and educated their daughters at home, with governesses and nurses. Lower down the social scale it was common to have a nurse until the girl was about ten years old, then to send her for two or three years to a private day school, and from ages thirteen to seventeen to a fashionable boarding school. The average cost of boarding education was £130 a year, though some schools offered costs as low as £25 to £30 a year, according to a letter in the *Englishwoman's Domestic Magazine* which questioned the quality of education in such places.

Even the least expensive of these schools was beyond the means of most lower middle-class families whose incomes ranged from £100 to £300 a year. Here it was usual to send the girl to a private day school, where the quality of teaching varied a great deal, but which attracted those who wished to segregate their daughters from poorer girls. Such social pretension can be seen in the case of Elizabeth Harrison. At age five in the 1890s she expected to go to the state infants' school nearby, along with her friends, but her shopkeeper parents sent her to a private school in Preston, paying a penny a week so that she would be with other tradesmen's daughters. She found a different world and said, 'Nobody there wore clogs. The boys all had jackets and the girls did not need pinafores to hide their shabby frocks.'

The education of Mary Howitt, whose quiet Quaker home life was described in the previous chapter, was typical for an affluent middle-class girl early in the century, with a mixture of schooling at home, day school and boarding school. She was unusual in thirsting for knowledge and in making efforts to educate herself. When it was discovered that their nurse was a woman of many love-affairs, who had induced the nine-year-old girl to write an imaginary love-letter, her puritanical parents sent Mary and her sister Anna to a day school, though 'only on condition that they sat apart from the other children in order to avoid contamination with possible worldlings'. This proved impossible, and in 1809 the girls went to a Quaker boarding school near Croydon, where they found themselves 'the youngest, the most provincial, and the worst dressed.' While the other girls did fashionable embroidery, Mary and Anna were expected to make linen shirts for their father, button-holes and all. After a few months they were recalled to their home in Staffordshire, because their mother was ill, and when she recovered they went to another Quaker school in Yorkshire. When Mary was thirteen and Anna fifteen, their education was supposed to be completed and they returned home. Their father paid the master of the local boys' school to teach them Latin, maths and the use of the globe, but this instructor died soon afterwards, so the girls decided to teach themselves. Mary said, 'We studied poetry, botany and flower-painting. These pursuits were almost out of the pale of permitted Quaker pleasures, but we pursued them with a perfect passion, doing in secret what we dared not do openly, such as reading Shakespeare, the elder novelists, and translations of the classics.'

A contemporary of Mary's, also thirsting for knowledge, was Harriet Martineau, daughter of a Norwich manufacturer. She was first educated at home, then at ten she and her sister Rachel went to a day school where boys and girls were taught together, the teacher being a dissenting minister turned Unitarian. All the pupils learned French, Greek and Latin, and Harriet revelled in her studies. But when she tried to continue her studies at home, after she left school, her mother objected to her studying 'conspicuously' during the day. She had to sit in the parlour and sew, and be ready to receive company. Her serious study, such as reading Latin with her brother James or working at Italian with a cousin, was carried on before breakfast or late at night. Few girls, though, were as keen on educating themselves as Mary or Harriet.

Early in the century, girls' boarding schools provided neither an academic education nor comfort. Mary Wright (later Sewell) said of her school at Tottenham in 1811–12, 'The method of teaching was the same as at most other boarding schools of the day, just learning by heart and repeating word for word.' The only thing she had to show for a year's education was a piece of wool embroidery. Writer Elizabeth Sewell and her three sisters went to school in the Isle of Wight between 1819 and 1828. She said they were half-starved with cold, lack of nourishing food and insufficient sleep. The bad conditions at Lowood School in *Jane Eyre* were based on a school for the daughters of the clergy at Cowan Bridge in Lancashire, which Charlotte Brontë and her sisters attended in the 1820s; two of the sisters died after contracting tuberculosis there. Writer Frances Power Cobbe went to a fashionable school in Brighton in 1836 and said:

> The din of the large double classroom was something frightful, with girls reciting their lessons aloud in a babel of languages, while four pianos were being played at the same time and other pupils were trying to write exercises or learn things by heart. There was no solid instruction, no real mental training.

Frances Power Cobbe said the education of women was probably at its lowest ebb when she was a girl, being pretentious and expensive. Her parents paid £1,000 for her schooling, but Frances said her mother and governesses gave her a better education at home than the school did.

Things did not get much better later on. At the end of the century about 70 per cent of girls getting secondary education were in private day and boarding schools. Lady Peck, as the small Winifred Knox, gave a vivid account of being a pupil at a snobbish, dull boarding school in the 1870s. She first went as a day-girl to Edgbaston Ladies College, then to Miss Quill's boarding school in Eastbourne, and reported:

> The building was not well suited for a school. There were two big sunny rooms divided by folding doors on the ground floor; the bigger was used as the school hall for prayers, and for the studies of the two top forms; the small had been kidnapped by the all-powerful French colleague of Miss Quill, who was her intimate friend and the only good instructress on the staff. In what house agents would call the semi-basement was a large, low, dark room in which the three or four lower forms all had their lessons from their respective mistresses at separate tables. Such a noisy and distracting background was of course common form in the 1860s and 70s, but was a real shock to my sister and myself after our orderly desks in our separate form rooms in the Edgbaston school . . . [The rooms] were haunted by the smell of damp cobbles from the yard and of boiled cabbage and steamed pudding, that immemorial scent of English educational

establishments, from the hall. The dormitories upstairs had no cubicles or curtains for privacy of any kind.

Kathleen Chorley, daughter of wealthy Cheshire parents, spent four years at a better school in Folkestone. The headmistress, Miss Abbot, had more intellect and taste than Miss Quill, though the girls were taught no science, not even botany or physical geography, which Kathleen noted were two subjects 'generally considered sufficiently ladylike to receive some attention' and she said her education 'provided us only with a top-dressing, a sprinkling of soil in which an appreciation of the arts and intellectual matters might flourish without raising any dynamic issues in our minds.' The girls were not allowed to write letters to anyone but their parents unless they were left unsealed for inspection, and contacts with girls from dissimilar backgrounds were discouraged to the point where the school played competitive games only with three local schools deemed acceptable. The main aim of the school was to train girls for matrimony.

At the end of their formal schooling, most middle-class girls stayed at home to attend to family duties. They read novels from the circulating library, wrote letters or did embroidery in the morning, spent the afternoons shopping or visiting, and their evenings drinking tea or going to concerts and parties. This was the life of an unmarried young woman that Florence Nightingale described as 'listless and purposeless'.

For a very small number of middle-class girls, however, things began to change in the 1850s and 60s. New types of private day and boarding schools grew and flourished, in response to changing social and economic needs, offering a commitment to academic achievement and meritocratic values. There were two very different sources of support for these new schools. One came from wealthy business and professional men who wanted educated wives and daughters with the leisure and knowledge to pursue aesthetic and intellectual interests and be the standard bearers of culture. They rejected the idea that it was desirably feminine to be ignorant and to waste time on trivial pursuits. The other group wanted middle-class women educated to earn their own livings. The 1851 Census revealed there were half a million more women than men in England, so it followed that not all could find husbands to keep them. Almost the only career open to middle-class women at mid-century was that of governess, grossly overworked and shockingly underpaid; most were as ignorant as their pupils. The Governesses' Benevolent Institution pressed for training to raise the professional status of teaching, and for this purpose Queen's College and Bedford College were founded in London in 1848/9.

Queen's College trained Frances Mary Buss (1827–94) who later built up the famous North London Collegiate School. Asked by the Schools Inquiry (Taunton) Commission (set up to examine middle-class education) in 1865, 'You believe there is not such a distinction between the mental powers of the two classes, as to require any wide distinction between the good education given to a girl and that which is given to a boy?' she replied, 'I am sure that the girls can learn anything they are taught in an interesting manner, and for which they have some motive to work.' Frances believed in girls competing with boys on the same terms. She made dramatic changes in the curriculum, away from traditional accomplishments towards academic subjects. She accepted nonconformist, Jewish and Roman Catholic girls into her Anglican school. She also started another school nearby – the Camden – where fees were lower and bright girls could win scholarships to the North London Collegiate.

Molly Hughes was a pupil at the North London Collegiate in the 1880s and wrote, 'Marks were the life-blood of the school. The iron discipline made things easy for those in authority. Every moment, almost every movement was ordered.' The teaching was sound and thorough, but Molly thought it too often dull; Shakespeare was read with footnotes which mattered more in examination than the text. French was learned from grammars and some reading, but rarely spoken. Some poetry had to be learned by heart every day. Religious instruction was uninspiring. Yet Molly found a refreshing lack of snobbery in the school, and she was happy there. Poverty was no stigma, old clothes no disgrace provided they were clean and neat. There was no class in needlework, though Miss Buss held a 'Dorcas' meeting once a month when 'for two hours we sewed horribly coarse cotton of a dull biscuit colour and a queer smell into garments for the long-suffering poor.' Molly recognized the difficulties of having 'five hundred girls, all to be trained along Victorian lines of good behaviour but also a new and high intellectual level.' In 1885, when she was eighteen, Molly won a scholarship to the training college at Cambridge, and she later taught at Bedford College in London.

Queen's College also trained Dorothea Beale, daughter of a surgeon at Guy's Hospital. She became Principal of Cheltenham Ladies College in 1858, when it was at a low ebb, and turned it into a highly efficient school with an academic curriculum. She said, 'The school is the link between infancy and mature life, between home and the world, the secular and the spiritual. Girls must be prepared for life, taught to know the truth, feel nobly, and hence act rightly.' She did not think, as did Frances Buss, that girls should compete academically with boys. Nor did her successor, Lilian Faithful, who said, after attending in her mid-teens a boys' preparatory school of which her uncle was Headmaster, that she 'realized the innate and immutable intellectual difference between boys and girls'. Cheltenham was more snobbish than the North London Collegiate School and excluded all but the daughters of independent gentlemen or professional men. Other schools modelled on it welcomed girls of ability from the lower-middle class but drew the line at daughters of publicans and 'others engaged in unsuitable callings'.

In order to survive, the new type of girls' secondary school had to conform to what parents wanted. They were not founded by feminists, and they do not tell a story of steady progress towards sex equality. Reforming heads established some equality between the girls by the wearing of school uniform, and eventually had their own way, though as late as the 1890s parents said uniforms made their daughters look like charity school students. Up to the last quarter of the century, it was accepted that strenuous activity was for boys, not girls. In gymnastics, girls had 'a much modified course of exercises on account of their greater delicacy'. In the struggle to open exams and degrees to women on equal terms with men, the study of Classics, deemed 'immoral', presented problems. Dorothea Beale had religious and moral reservations, saying, 'There is a pestilential atmosphere in the Campania, and one needs to have one's moral fibre braced by the poetry of the Hebrews, and of England and Germany, if one would remain unaffected by writings saturated with heathen thoughts.' So strong was this feeling that the Headmistresses' Association in 1887 voted against requesting Cambridge University to open its degrees to women on identical terms with men. The university had no intention of doing so, anyway, although it did allow them into lectures and exams, with the examiners' permission.

Despite their many conservative features, the reformed schools did provide girls with different role models, and loosened family ties. They sent a vanguard of women into higher education and 'broke the mould' once and for all. Janet Howarth, who taught at Cheltenham, said that by the end of the century 'most middle-class girls looked forward to college and a career; the old, domestic graces faded into the background.' In 1894–5, when there was a government inquiry into secondary education, the Chairman, Sir James Bryce, reported that no change had been more conspicuous, in the thirty years since the Schools Inquiry Commission, than the improvement in girls' secondary education and the creation of colleges for women. Yet the number of pupils involved was small. There were only 200 of the new 'endowed and proprietory girls' schools' in 1894, each with a few hundred pupils.

Even more fortunate and adventurous than the girls who got a good secondary education were the tiny number who went up to university later in the century. Up to 1877 no British university accepted a woman as a student, and no examining body would award a degree to a woman. The universities were public bodies, under the direct control of Parliament which granted their Charters, and hence the law permitted them to exclude women. Opposition even to the idea that women were capable of intellectual study was widespread throughout the century. In the 1820s it was based on spurious anthropological 'proof' that women's brains were smaller than men's, and thus, it was said, evolution had passed them by.

The movement for higher education for women began in the 1860s, when women pressed to enter medicine. The pioneering figure was Elizabeth Garrett (later Anderson), the daughter of a wealthy Suffolk businessman. She left school at fifteen, but at twenty-three she heard a speech by Elizabeth Blackwell, an American and the world's first modern woman doctor. Elizabeth was inspired to become a doctor herself, and to specialize in the treatment of women and children. Her father was initially astounded then disgusted by her decision, but when he found that all medical schools and hospitals were officially closed to her, he paradoxically determined to help all he could. One of his friends, a male governor of the hospital, helped Elizabeth begin training as a nurse at the Middlesex Hospital, and to go to lectures and the dissecting room. When, however, she was placed first in an exam at the hospital, the male medical students protested and had her thrown out. She then applied for permission to matriculate at London University, this being the first step to a full degree. Despite the formidable support of Prime Minister Gladstone, Richard Cobden, the Russell Gurneys and

F.D. Maurice, she was turned down. It was a sign of changing times and attitudes to women's education, however, that she had such support, and that voting in the University Senate was so close – ten for and ten against – the motion being lost only when the Chancellor, Lord Granville, gave his casting vote against it.

Elizabeth continued to study, and in 1865 applied to take the examination of the Society of Apothecaries. Despite the terms of its non-discriminatory Charter, the Society had never contemplated the possibility that a woman would apply, and said it was impossible. Elizabeth's father threatened legal action. The Society, advised that he had a strong case, gave in. Elizabeth passed the exam with ease, and got from them a licence to practise. The Medical Council was obliged to put her name on the Register, and she opened a small dispensary for women and children in Marylebone. Within a few weeks between sixty and ninety patients appeared each consulting day. The Society of Apothecaries immediately passed a resolution that effectively excluded women from their exams. Elizabeth later took advantage of the opening of medical degrees to women by the University of Paris. Through influential friends she got permission to take her degree without residence in France. In 1870, after performing two operations and answering written and oral exams in French, she was awarded her M.D. diploma with credit. The following year she married the steamship merchant, James Anderson, with whom she had two children and a happy home life. In 1872 she founded the New Hospital for Women, which was renamed the Elizabeth Garrett Anderson Hospital after her death.

Sophia Jex-Blake, another strong-minded woman with a wealthy father, continued the fight for women to enter British medical schools, but she lacked Elizabeth Garrett Anderson's tact and charm, being headstrong, unruly and emotional. Doctors opposed to women in medicine argued that even if they possessed the necessary intellectual ability, 'can we deny that the general delicacy of females is a serious bar to an occupation which necessitates exposure at all hours and in all weathers?' Queen Victoria thought 'the possibility of allowing young girls and young men to enter the dissecting room together to be an awful idea'. An Edinburgh medical professor said that no decent woman, let alone one who called herself a lady, would wish to study medicine. Yet it was Edinburgh University which allowed five women, including Sophia Jex-Blake, to have a class of their own, for which they were charged double fees, and to matriculate in 1870. No one expected them to finish the course, and when all the women passed the exam it raised a lot of hackles.

The women now needed to attend an anatomy class, and solved this by going to the Extra-Mural School. When they went to take the exam at Surgeon's Hall in November 1870 they found a dense crowd outside. Sophia said it consisted of 'the lowest class of our fellow-students . . . the gates were slammed in our faces by a number of young men who stood within, smoking and passing about bottles of whiskey, while they abused us in the foulest possible language; not a single policeman was visible.' A friendly male student wrenched open the gates and escorted them into the exam room, but the rioters harassed them further by pushing sheep into the room. After the exam sympathetic men students escorted them home, the women receiving 'no other injuries than those inflicted on our dresses by the mud hurled at us by our chivalrous foes.' There was publicity and sympathy from the newspapers, but little else. Many such squalid ways were found to block women's route into medicine, and the bitter fight did not end until 1877, when London University opened its matriculation and other exams and degrees to women, for all subjects. Edinburgh University did not follow suit, and in fact did not admit women to graduation until 1894. In 1912 there were only 533 women physicians and the number remained small until the 1970s, when women gained almost half the places in medical schools.

Women's wish to study medicine provoked a far from subtle response from some doctors. From the 1860s onwards they solemnly declared, without evidence of any sort, that higher education would make it difficult for a woman to conceive and bear a child. Social thinker Herbert Spencer said educated women would not be able to suckle their babies. Preposterous as this sounds to modern ears, it scared the Victorians. Frances Power Cobbe said the medical profession occupied 'with strangely close analogy the position of the priesthood of former times, and it assumes the same airs of authority'. A good deal of scaremongering followed, and women educators had to defend themselves against the charge that they were wrecking the health of their female pupils.

Dr Henry Maudsley published an article entitled 'Sex in Mind and Education' in the *Fortnightly Review* in 1874, using menstruation as justification for his anti-feminism. He said women could never hope to match masculine accomplishments, because their physiology acted as a handicap, body and mind being 'for one quarter of each month . . . more or less sick and unfit for hard work'. The next issue of the journal contained a sharp rebuttal from Elizabeth Garrett Anderson, a medical doctor and married woman with children who was well placed to refute his arguments. On grounds of propriety she rebuked Maudsley for discussing menstruation at all, but then said doctors much exaggerated the amount it incapacitated women, since working-class women did not remain in bed during these times and continued to work hard. Yet Elizabeth, too, believed that adolescent girls should avoid fatigue during menstruation, and so encouraged the view that it was a form of weakness.

At the beginning of the twentieth century both male and female doctors used eugenic concerns about the quantity and quality of the race to argue that middle-class girls should be protected from rigorous exams and learn mothercraft in school. Headmistresses of the new secondary schools, however, introduced classes in domestic science only when the Board of Education threatened to cut off state funds if they did not comply, and always made it clear that this subject was for less intelligent students.

The pioneers of higher education for women in the 1860s were of two kinds: those who were content to see improvements without demanding that girls be measured by male standards (the separatists), and those who insisted that girls take the same exams as boys (the uncompromising). Women in the latter group were more likely to be accused of unladylike behaviour and to be stigmatized as 'unfeminine'. Emily Davies was the most famous of them. Daughter of an Evangelical clergyman, Emily had a puritanical upbringing and practically no formal education. No novels, card-playing or theatre were allowed. Emily ironed her own collars and cuffs: 'We were not much waited on, and did a great deal for ourselves', she said of her youth in Gateshead. When her father died she went to London with her mother and through her brother Llewelyn was drawn into educational circles. There is a story that one day she was mulling over with Elizabeth Garrett Anderson the great causes of the day. 'Well, Elizabeth,' said Emily, 'it's clear what has to be done. I must devote myself to securing higher education, while you open the medical profession to women. After these things are done, we must see about getting the vote.' Then, turning to Elizabeth's sister Millicent, who was only a young child, she said, 'You are younger than we are, Millie, so you must attend to that.' And of course when Millicent (Garrett Fawcett) grew up, she was to do just that (see Chapter 7).

Emily's first object, in 1863, was to gain admission for girls to the university local exams. After some skirmishing Cambridge University gave permission for a private and unofficial trial examination of girls to be held in London. Some girls were brought up from the provinces, and this meant housing them and finding chaperones. Cheltenham sent no candidates because Dorothea Beale disapproved. The girls acquitted themselves well, except in the all-important subject of arithmetic. Ten of Frances Buss's girls from North London Collegiate were among the casualties. She realized the problem was bad teaching, and in future her girls were drilled relentlessly. The next step was to get the exams opened to girls on a permanent footing, and after a three-year trial period Cambridge approved this. Oxford followed suit in 1870. These changes were opposed tooth and nail by the influential *Saturday Review*, which never ceased to say that 'an over-accomplished woman is one of the most intolerable monsters in creation.'

Fortunately, others disagreed with that verdict. Emily Davies persuaded the Schools Inquiry Commission of 1865 to include girls' schools in its examination of middle-class education. She knew that most female education was superficial and frothy, and that while there were endowments (scholarships) in plenty available for boys, there were practically none for girls. The Commission revealed a sorry state of affairs, including the fact that money intended for girls' schools was being diverted to those for boys. This led to an overhaul of the endowment system and the opening in towns all over the country of good, relatively inexpensive day schools. To Emily Davies's glee, the Commission's findings also led to the founding of colleges for women.

In 1869 a college offering advanced tuition for women, with Mrs Manning as Mistress and Emily Davies as secretary, was opened at Hitchin, some way from Cambridge. It was injudicious, Emily argued, to let young women loose in a university town. Five students entered in October of the same year. The strictest decorum was observed, so there could be no scandal. An older woman chaperone sat with the students if the lecturer was a male. There were no organized games, but students went for long walks, and in the evenings had cocoa parties in their rooms. Despite Emily's misgivings, the college moved to Girton, on the outskirts of Cambridge, in 1874. The women were allowed to take university exams unofficially and by courtesy of the examiners. In 1887 Agnata Ramsey, a Girton student, scored top marks in the classical tripos (the Cambridge University degree exam) and got a first-class degree. No man achieved higher than a second-class degree that year, so a *Punch* cartoon showed a woman being shown into a first-class railway carriage marked 'Ladies Only'.

Newnham college was founded in Cambridge in 1871. The first Principal was Anne Jemima Clough (b. 1820), daughter of a Liverpool cotton merchant and a 'compromiser' who adopted a protective, maternal attitude towards her students. She was constantly fussing over their health, diet, hours of sleep and exposure to draughts. Frances Grey said on her first day she got 'the comfort that a tired child receives from its mother'. She was introduced to Miss Clough and also the Vice-Principal, Eleanor Sidgwick (born Balfour) and lecturer Helen Gladstone. Despite their high birth and intellectual prowess, the three ladies were sitting together hemming dusters. Frances said algebra was for her 'an impenetrable mystery' but somehow she got through, and passed the classical tripos so well that she was appointed Lecturer in Classics at Westfield College, part of the University of London. And it was a Newnham student, Philippa Fawcett (daughter of Millicent, mentioned earlier) who in 1890 had a brilliant success in the mathematical tripos, being placed above the Senior Wrangler (the man with the highest marks). Colleges similar to Girton were established in Oxford in the 1870s, all of which prided themselves on offering a secluded, family-like environment. But the total number of women university students was still tiny. In 1939 there were 876 women to 4,147 men students at Oxford, while at Cambridge there were 509 women to 5,422 men students. Until 1923 women had no *right* to attend lectures at Oxbridge; they could attend only by courtesy of each individual lecturer, who had to be asked permission. Nor were women who studied at Oxford and Cambridge awarded full degrees. They left these ancient foundations with pieces of paper known as 'certificates of degrees' and with no letters after their names. In fact, both universities refused to admit women into full university membership until well into the twentieth century (Oxford 1920, Cambridge 1947). However, the lack of a full degree did not appear to hamper Oxbridge women in finding good jobs.

In 1878 London University admitted women students and granted them degrees, and every university founded after that date followed suit.

In 1837 there were only four universities in England, none open to
women; by the end of Victoria's reign there were twelve universities and
colleges which admitted women to degree courses. For the small number
of women involved, a university education in the late nineteenth century
was a new world. Lilian Faithful said of her days at Oxford:

> To women, more than to men, the delight of having three years in
> which it was right to be selfishly absorbed in intellectual pursuits was
> unspeakable, for claims large and small are apt to beset women at
> a very early age.

Yet it was only after the Second World War that English women broke
through in large numbers to higher education.

As the century progressed, God and the Bible were mentioned less and
less to justify the inferiority of women. The 'evils of competition' were
cited, and the view that women were 'better off without degrees' was
expressed without any apparent need to justify it. Men saw clearly
enough that women were trying to break into their world of work, and
their fear for their own future in overcrowded professions was enough
to sustain opposition to educated women. There was a tendency, on
slender evidence, to claim that educated women were free thinkers and
morally lax. Some linked higher education with lesbianism, and lesbians
were called inverts or freaks. Eugenicist Karl Pearson employed Alice
Lee to investigate the relationship between skull capacity and intellectual
ability in both men and women. She measured the heads of thirty-five
male anatomists attending the Anatomical Society meeting in Dublin in
1898, twenty-five male staff at University College, and sixty women
students at Bedford College, and found no such relationship existed. In
1914 the psychologist Hugo Munsterberg took a different tack when he
asserted that women were incapable of abstract thought, and therefore
unable to do scientific work. He ignored the earlier scientific work of
Mary Somerville and of his contemporary Hertha Ayrton, who was the
first woman member of the Institute of Electrical Engineers, and had
been awarded their Hughes medal for her original work on the electric
arc.

Little thought was given to the education of the majority of English
girls – the daughters of the labouring classes. Before the state system
was operative in the 1870s it was difficult for poor girls to get even an
elementary education – that is, reading, writing and some arithmetic.

In 1805 George III said, 'It is my wish that every poor child in my dominions be taught to read the Holy Scripture.' The Sunday School movement had been started in 1784 by Robert Raikes, but two women were mainly responsible for its rapid growth, Sarah Trimmer and Hannah More, both of whom wrote moral tales for the young. In Sunday schools both boys and girls were taught to read, with the Bible as primer, and girls also learned sewing and knitting. Children were not taught to write, for fear they might use that skill to compete for jobs with their betters.

There were also day schools run by religious bodies and aided, from 1833, by government funds. There was a competition between the Church of England and the Nonconformists to found schools. The 'British' schools founded in 1808 were run by the Nonconformist British and Foreign Bible Society. The 'National' schools founded in 1811 taught the principles of the established church; there were naturally more of these because the Church of England had more money. All the early schools were run on the 'monitorial' system. One teacher taught the lessons to the older children – the monitors – who then taught the rest. The system depended on rewards and punishments: money, medals and books for rewards, and a range of punishments for breaking the rules – confinement in a closet, suspension in a basket, the pillory, being handcuffed behind, being washed in public, wearing a fool's cap, and expulsion. The system had many defects, but gave a chance of learning to read and write to thousands of girls who would otherwise have been illiterate. The quality of teaching improved from 1846, when the pupil-teacher system was introduced as an alternative to the use of monitors. In his community experiments at New Lanark, Scotland, in the early nineteenth century, socialist millowner Robert Owen established schools where children were educated with kindness, and there were neither punishments nor rewards. However, his example was not followed by other schools at the time, and only became popular after the Second World War.

Industrial schools, run for the poor by charity and manufacturing interests, taught trades to boys and domestic service to girls. Lady McNeill visited one of the more progressive of such schools, run by educational reformer James Kay-Shuttleworth at Norwood in the 1840s, and wrote, 'We saw the boys making clothes and shoes, others working as carpenters, tinsmiths and blacksmiths, and a large body of little fellows, dressed as sailors, climbed rigging, drilled as soldiers, and practised at great guns. The little girls wash, iron, mangle, cook, learn to make clothes and knit.' These girls were learning early to accept their allotted place in life. According to Mrs Austin, in *Two Lectures on Girls' Schools and the Training of Working Women* (1857), working-class girls' education was intended to fit them to be better servants to the rich and better wives to poor men, and nothing else.

Some lower-class girls went to dame schools, run by women in their own homes. They were popular with parents because they taught useful skills, and cost only a few pence a week (though this was too much for the very poor to find). There was only one small class, with pupils of all ages, and knitting and sewing occupied most of the day. Mary Smith, daughter of a shoemaker in Oxfordshire, went to a dame school in the 1820s, from the ages of four to nine, and remembered that her mother was annoyed when she developed a passion for books:

> It was indeed a good school, thoroughness being the aim in the few things that were professed to be taught, as well as almost faultless discipline and good manners. A girl's education at that time consisted principally of needlework of various descriptions . . . Parents were prouder of their daughters' pieces of needlework than of their scholarship.

Mary used to stay in at playtime to read books, and eventually persuaded her father to arrange for her to have arithmetic lessons, which at her school were considered unsuitable for a girl. She later became a pupil-teacher and schoolmistress.

Poor girls who lived in towns and had neither money for fees, nor decent clothing, nor the freedom to attend school during the day, could go to a ragged school which met in the evenings. Frances Power Cobbe, who worked at Mary Carpenter's Ragged School for Girls in Bristol, said of these schools:

> They were specially designed to civilize the children; to tame them enough to induce them, for example, to sit reasonably still on a bench for half an hour at a time; to wash their hands and faces; to comb their hair; to forbear from shouting, singing . . . making faces . . . after which preliminaries they began to acquire the art of learning lessons.

Girls at ragged schools were scrupulously policed for bad language or signs of sexual knowledge, and often expelled for fear of 'moral contamination'.

In spite of these voluntary efforts, the general level of education for poor girls was very low in the 1840s and 50s; in 1851 the Registrar-General reported that 45 per cent of brides had marked the marriage register with a cross, being unable to sign their names. This rate of illiteracy was reduced as the century wore on, but some parents opposed education for their daughters even when it was available. In 1851 an inspector of a Parochial School Union was told by one mother that it was better for girls to work and earn, rather than 'waste time learning to cipher and know about things as don't concern them.' Social investigator Henry Mayhew found the London street sellers of the 1850s and 60s reluctant to educate their daughters, saying, 'What's the use of it? That won't earn a gal a living.'

Under the Factory Act of 1833 children working in textiles and aged between nine and thirteen were allowed to work an 8-hour day, as short-timers, provided they attended school for two hours daily. From 1844 the half-time system actually allowed children to start work at eight years old, but restricted working hours until the age of thirteen to six and a half a day, requiring them to attend school for three hours a day. Employers connived with parents to evade the legislation, by pretending children were older than they were. Gradually protection was extended, but each advance in the minimum age for half-time work, to nine, ten, eleven and eventually twelve (in 1901) was resisted by parents and employers alike. When a Lancashire Member of Parliament voted in 1899 to raise the school-leaving age from 11 to 12, angry mothers spat at him, because they wanted their daughters to leave school and start work as early as possible. However, the necessity of reaching the respective 'standards' fixed as the condition for half-time exemption and for school-leaving provided an educational incentive. Hilda Snowman recalled that as a 12 year old in 1913 she went to work in a textile factory in Bolton as a half-timer. Before going to work she had to collect and return the washing her mother did for others, help with mangling and the careful laundering of lace curtains, scrub and scour the stone-flagged floor and run errands. She said it was the custom in many households for the main wage-earners to eat first and the children last, and that 'small children never had an egg except on Easter morning. Other times we made do with the tops from the grown-ups' eggs.'

The establishment of a state system of free, compulsory, elementary education for all came about by stages, mainly between 1870 and 1880, but later in some areas. Sadly, it was not supposed or intended that children should enjoy their schooling, and the majority did not. The voluntary schools, overwhelmingly the responsibility of the Church of England but supported by state funds, still taught about half the elementary school children; in some areas they were the only schools available. Working-class girls were limited to elementary education – the three Rs (reading, 'riting and 'rithmetic) plus history, geography and nature study – to prevent them getting ideas above their station. School was meant to make workers more industrious, content and respectable, but to keep them in their place at the bottom of society. Teachers tended to be strict disciplinarians. Most children left school by the age of twelve, but before that girls attended less regularly than boys because their mothers kept them home to help with housework. For boys, truancy was an offence; the absence of girls was overlooked.

The education on offer was not attractive to most girls. Kate Edwards went to a family-run, one-room rural school in the Fens in the 1880s, and later wrote:

> School in them days was a place where you 'learnt your lessons' and teachers didn't do nothing but teach. It wasn't part of their job to look after children in any other way . . . Teachers in them days were cruel to children in any case, because they thought that were the only way to make them learn anything . . . it seems to me they must have despised us all as poor, ignorant creatures of a different sort from themselves, and treated us more like animals than children.

Because her mother kept her neat, clean and tidy, Kate was singled out by the schoolmistress for 'special duties', which meant doing all the domestic work in the teacher's home. 'At the end of the week, she gave me my pay, a quarter of an orange peel,' Kate wrote. When she left school her sister was told to take over her duties, but 'she was different from me and had a lot more pluck . . . she wouldn't do just as she were told as meek as I did, and she knew she ought to have been in school doing her lessons.' The sister refused to be exploited, but few were brave enough to defy their teachers in this way.

Education was little better in the cities than in the countryside. Grace Foakes said in her modern London board school in 1900 there were seventy-two girls in her class, and throughout her schooling she had the same classroom, teacher and desk. 'We were not allowed to walk about as children do today, and were not permitted to talk or ask questions. If you disobeyed, you sat with your hands on your head until told to take them off.' They learned arithmetic tables by rote, and if they misbehaved they were slapped hard or sent to the Head-mistress for the cane. Punishments were entered in a red book and counted against a girl's character reference when she left school. Without 'a good character' a girl could not get a decent job. Most of Grace's friends were as poor as she, and often came to school without boots or stockings. Even those with boots found the cardboard soles wore out quickly.

The schooling of working-class girls always emphasised domesticity. Christine Bremner said in *The Education of Girls and Women in Great Britain* (1897), 'the sight of small girls of eleven or even younger learning cookery, housewifery and laundrywork is becoming common, as if little girls could not be too early pressed into a narrow mould.' The 1902 Education Act made domestic subjects compulsory for girls (but not for boys), but girls said their lessons were unreal and useless. They received plenty of practice at home in bathing, dressing and otherwise caring for brothers and sisters, and their mothers taught them how to cook and clean. Some girls found ways to rebel against lessons they neither wanted nor cared about, and Grace Foakes was one of them:

If we did the housewifery course, we were taught to sweep, dust, polish, make beds and bathe a life-sized doll. We had great fun on this course, for it was held in a house set aside for the purpose, and with only one teacher in charge we were quick to take advantage when she went to inspect some other part of the house. We jumped on the bed, threw pillows, drowned the doll and swept dirt under the mats. This was the highlight of the week, and the one lesson we never minded going to.

Yet whatever the defects of the state schools, and however unpopular they were with some girls, at least by the end of the century a basic elementary education had become a right for all girls and not a privilege for the few. The private schools continued to exist and no one was forced to use the state schools, though poorer parents had no choice. Fee-paying schools remained largely the province of the middle class.

The slight possibility of secondary education for a working-class girl lay in admission to a grammar school. Schools which were independent but 'maintained' by the state were required by law after 1907 to keep a third of their places for scholarship children who paid no fees at all. But even in 1914 the odds against a child from an elementary school obtaining a free secondary education were forty to one, and many girls had to reject a place because the family budget could not stand the cost of books, uniform, sports equipment and other extras. Even in poor homes parents were more willing to make sacrifices for a boy's education. It was well into the twentieth century before large numbers of working-class girls had access to schools where they could take academic subjects and aspire to a university education.

Although girls were educated differently, according to their social class, they were equally ignorant about how their bodies worked, and about sex and reproduction, as the next chapter will show.

3

Thinking of England

SEX,
COURTSHIP AND MARRIAGE

The truth about how we came to have our beings must at all
costs – even at the cost of deliberate lying – be kept from us. We ate
the embryo of fowls for breakfast, but it was devoutly hoped that
we did not realise what we were eating.

Eleanor, Lady Acland, *Goodbye for the Present* (of the 1880s)

A pall of prudery lay over nineteenth-century England. The process
of 'civilising' sex by ignoring it had begun in the early decades as part
of a puritanical drive to change the manners and habits of both rich
and poor. Sexual love was no longer to be pleasurable or fun, but a
marital duty. Women's bodies, hidden in long, voluminous clothes,
were almost as much of a mystery to themselves as to men. Lady Acland
said, 'Nice ladies no more thought of showing their legs than did nice
chairs.' Sex was not a fit discussion in polite society, among women
friends or between parent and daughter. There was no talk of pubic
hair, the clitoris, or orgasm. The words were never spoken, let alone
understood by most people, though they were discussed in medical
journals. Methods of contraception were little known, and not considered respectable. There were no easily available books for women
to read about sexual intercourse and its consequences, and no discussion of adolescent sexual longings. Plays which mentioned sex in
explicit terms, including those by Shakespeare and the Restoration

dramatists, were 'cleaned up' by Dr Bowdler and his sister. Sexual activity did not decline, but nor was it talked or written about. When novels mentioned adultery, they gave no details of the sex act.

Respectable parents believed that ignorance of sex would keep their daughters pure, and girls who 'knew' were usually afraid to take risks that would spoil their hopes of marriage. How children were conceived and born was a mystery. A young married woman said that 'about a month before the baby was born [in 1880] I remember asking my aunt where the baby would come from. She was astounded, and did not make me much wiser.' What, then, did an innocent young unmarried woman think marriage would involve? The romantic had a hazy idea of loving and being loved, in a warm glow of cuddles and kisses. The more practical thought of escape from the control of parents, having a husband to maintain her, a home of her own, children (even if she didn't know how they would arrive) and freedom to make her own friends. All these things were possible, but first she had to find a suitable man, and in all classes there was restricted choice. Up to the age of twenty-one, women and men needed the consent of their parents to marry.

For an upper-class woman, more was at stake than choosing a man she found physically attractive. Throughout the century, marriage played a central role in mobilizing wealth and power. Parents generally wanted their daughters to be happy, gave them some choice of spouse, and tried to avoid misalliances, but courtship was carefully controlled, and a veto could be imposed, as when early in the century Lord Verulam prevented his daughter Katty (future wife of the 4th Earl of Clarendon) from marrying one of the Coutts Trotters. Some young people extricated themselves voluntarily from love affairs of which their parents disapproved, as when one of Lady Conyngham's sons in the 1820s fell in love with Minny Cowper (later Countess of Shaftesbury); Minny liked the young man, but he was already engaged to an heiress and she was afraid to encourage him 'because it would upset the marriage and put her [Minny] out of favour at Court'. The young man, too, was 'anxious not to annoy his Mother' (who was George IV's mistress and very powerful) so the relationship ended.

Presentation at Court, when a woman was seventeen, announced her marriageability. National 'marriage markets', in which parents and lawyers negotiated the terms, developed during the Season in London and Bath. The wealthiest and best-connected young people met at concerts, balls and parties in exclusive private clubs such as Almack's, and at house parties on great estates – some of which lasted for as long as a month. The guests went riding and hunting, and they danced, played games such as charades, and talked together. But always the unmarried women were chaperoned. Two examples show how things often worked. Lady Georgiana Cavendish (1783–1828), daughter of the Duke of Devonshire, met Lord Morpeth, heir to the Earl of Carlisle, at her coming-out party in June 1800. Her family considered him suitable, and he was invited in the autumn to a house party in their country mansion, Chatsworth in Derbyshire. Georgiana was 'standoffish' and no engagement was announced. The Duke, apparently afraid of losing a good catch, offered his daughter a dowry of £30,000 and the use of Londesborough House in London, if she married Morpeth. The bribe did not take effect right away, and Georgiana held out until Christmas, but then she suddenly agreed. It was a happy and successful marriage.

Half a century later, Lord Stanley's daughter, Blanche (1829–1921) met the Earl of Airlie during the London Season. He fell in love with her and visited her Cheshire home, Alderley Park, later in the summer. Blanche did not want to marry him, complaining to her mother that she 'should so like to be desperately in love'. But when Airlie proposed she said she had 'no great objection' and the matter was settled. This too was a happy marriage. Charlotte Brontë spoke for many women when she said it was 'romantic folly to wait for the awakening of what the French call *une grande passion* [which] is *une grande folie*', and that 'no young lady should fall in love till the offer has been made – the wedding ceremony performed and the first half year of wedded life has passed away.' As the century progressed, an upper-class woman looked for both money and affection, but up to 1914 it was normal for her to marry a man from her own social circle, or one from an excessively rich 'new' family.

But some aristocratic women let their hearts rule their heads. In the 1820s Lady Charlotte Harley, daughter of Lady Oxford, married Anthony Bacon, the Senior Major of the 17th Lancers. Neither had any money, so their marriage was reckless, but their devotion to each other was legendary. They were never apart, and as a superb horse-woman Lady Charlotte rode with her husband in his campaigns. When

Bacon did not get command of the 17th as he hoped, he sold his commission and entered the service of the King of Portugal, his wife going with him. In the 1850s, the daughter of wealthy Lord Vernon chose an unambitious marriage to the Rector of Sudbury, near Derby, a village on her father's main estate. She had a happy and busy life, producing fourteen children as well as running the household, dispensing medicine to villagers, and teaching in the local school. In 1875, Lord Maynard's heiress, Daisy, turned down the chance to marry Queen Victoria's son Leopold, and instead married Lord Brooke, heir to the Earl of Warwick, who was comparatively impoverished. This became a marriage in which the partners lived comfortable but separate lives; for some years Daisy was the mistress of the Prince of Wales.

Middle-class women usually married men of whom their families approved, and whom they met at family gatherings, parties, balls and concerts. Great connections of wealth and title were not at issue, but women preferred to be allied with men of similar religion, intellectual interests, philanthropic concerns and worldly goods. Harriet Martineau (1802–76) thought the middle class placed a high emphasis on romantic love, and despite her advice that women should not wait for *'une grande passion'*, Charlotte Brontë turned down three proposals of marriage because she found the men physically repugnant, before eventually marrying her father's curate in 1854. Helen Bourn, having warned Thomas Martineau (brother of Harriet) that esteem for his virtues and a deep admiration for his mental qualities was all she could give him, agreed to marry him in 1822. They had a child in 1823, but sadly both Thomas and the baby died the following year.

A few middle-class women eloped from home or boarding school, to marry romantically against their parents' wishes. Mrs Arbuthnot said in her *Journal* that 'Lancaster was as full as it could hold with people collected to hear the trial of Mr Wakefield for running away with Miss Turner.' The heiress Ellen Turner, daughter of a wealthy Cheshire manufacturer, was 'beguiled from school' by Edward Gibbon Wakefield in 1816. They eloped to Gretna Green to wed, then travelled to Calais without consummating the marriage. There they were overtaken by the irate parents. Wakefield returned to England and was arrested and sentenced to three years' imprisonment, during which time his marriage was annulled by Act of Parliament. After spending her youth as a petted semi-invalid, Elizabeth Barrett (1806–61) eloped at the age of forty with fellow poet Robert Browning. They had managed to meet fairly frequently, with the cooperation of her servant who was her chaperone, and they knew each other's work intimately. Elizabeth's father did not want her to marry, and he never forgave her.

Writer Ann Richelieu Lamb described in 1844 the problem for a middle-class girl of meeting and getting to know men as friends, before considering them as husbands:

> It is difficult . . . to speak of friendship between persons of opposite sexes; to so low an ebb have matters come, that they can scarcely be on terms of acquaintanceship apart from the tie of matrimony, or bond of relationship. Women are so schooled about catching husbands, that the simplest species of civility from a man is converted into particular attention . . . Thus men are terrified from the presence and society of women, by the vision of an action for 'breach of promise', or there rises before them the startling question of some prudent parent, or brother, as to *intentions*, keeping them in a perpetual trepidation, rendering the intercourse between the sexes of the most restrained, artificial and embarrassing description . . . Young persons . . . cannot meet a few times, without some love affair being gossiped about, given out as a hint, that if they are not in love they ought to be so, or else it is very imprudent.

Also in the 1840s, Mrs Jeune, wife of the new Master of Pembroke College, Oxford, wrote, 'The society here strikes me as ponderous and wanting in ease . . . There seems no lack of young ladies in Oxford, but if they always sit so unnoticed as they did, in an innocent row last night, the young men are in little danger from their charms.' Mrs Jeune obviously thought a young woman could take some initiative to attract a partner.

By the 1860s middle-class girls were becoming more flirtatious and sexually assertive. The journalist Eliza Lynn Linton writing anonymously in the *Saturday Review* of 14 March 1868, trenchantly accused young women of behaving like courtesans:

> The Girl of the Period is a creature who dyes her hair and paints her face . . . the imitation of the *demi-monde* in dress leads to . . . slang,

bold talk, and general fastness . . . no one can say of the modern English girl that she is tender, loving, retiring or domestic . . . the legal barter of herself for so much money, representing so much dash, so much luxury and pleasure – that is her idea of marriage.

Eliza started a lively magazine controversy, and a cultural fad that took the form of 'Girl of the Period' products and jokes. The article caused a sensation because it seemed an accurate, if exaggerated, account of the current marriage market.

Middle-class men and women could meet in the second half of the century when taking part in popular sports. Roller-skating was a social craze around 1875, and since chaperones often could not keep up with their charges, flirtations thrived on the asphalt. Lawn tennis then became popular, with tennis parties providing opportunity for young people to meet and show off to each other. Women got a craze for cricket in the 1880s, though men wanted it to remain a man's game; golf mania then superseded cricket for women in the 1890s. But it was the bicycle, which also arrived in the 1890s, that most emancipated women and made courtship easier, since they rode bicycles without chaperones. *Hub*, a popular cycling magazine, reported in 1898 that many of the thousands of young women riding about were 'self-supporting young women who owned a wheel'.

By the end of the century there were many more ways for 'young ladies' to meet men; whether they had happier married lives as a result is debatable. Marriage was still the life plan of most of them. There was considerable discussion in newspapers and periodicals about the proper time to marry. Prudence and postponement were the key words used. A prospective husband had to be able to pay for the trappings of a bourgeois domestic life and the raising of children. The cost of education was one reason why middle-class families had fewer children.

Most working-class women, too, wanted to find a husband, for reasons of status and respectability. In the countryside couples generally waited until they had a house and some possessions before marrying, but the system of poor relief before 1834 was more generous to married couples than to single men and women, and this was said to encourage early marriage among the poor. Where cottage manufacturing developed, young women could earn adult wages and they worked, ate and drank with the men. At Aston Clinton in Buckinghamshire, where the straw plaiting trade provided work, men and women courted as they worked, and when they were ready to marry they announced it without getting the permission of their parents. One young strawplaiter just said she was ready to draw her money from the bank. 'So am I, too,' added her young man. 'We're both a going to draw out, and we're going to be married on the plait money. Ain't we, Mary.'

Women who lived in towns and worked in factories also courted independently, with little interference from parents, since they had money of their own and a voice in family affairs. Of women textile workers it was said, 'They had their father to keep, but they would not be dictated to by him.' Women liked to save up some money before they got married, and this determined the length of an engagement. Early in the century it was said that

A young woman, prudent and careful, and living with her parents from the age of sixteen to twenty-five, may in time, by factory employment, save £100 as a wedding portion. She is not then driven into an early marriage by the necessity of seeking a home.

Young people tended in their early teens to begin taking an interest in their appearance, their clothes and each other. They often had brief, casual friendships known as 'getting off' or 'clicking', the result of chance meetings on country walks, on street corners, in parks or on the 'monkey parades' (the well-established spots where young people strolled in the evenings). They also met in Sunday school, church or chapel, or places of entertainment. It depended whether a young woman was looking for a respectable and approved relationship or a bit of fun.

Women grew up with widely differing knowledge about sex, and it was not simply a matter of class, though upper- and middle-class daughters were more strictly guarded. Annie Besant, the birth-control activist, said when she married in 1866, 'My ignorance of all that marriage meant was as profound as though I had been a child of four instead of twenty. My dreamy life . . . kept innocent of all questions of sex, was no preparation for married existence.' She left her clergyman husband in 1873. Marie Stopes, born in 1880 and also an advocate of family planning, was the child of a university graduate mother who lectured on women's rights, but told her daughter nothing about sex. Marie went to university and married at the age of thirty-one, in 1911. It was not until two years later that she discovered (from a book) that she and her husband had not consummated the marriage. By 1917 their marriage was annulled and she wrote the book *Married Love* to help others avoid her problems. She received 5,000 pathetic letters from people of all social classes, asking advice on sexual matters. Evelyn Powell (born 1901) had a mother remarkably ignorant of the facts of life. She was the wife of a stockbroker at Westcliff-on-Sea. Before her marriage she had worked for 'fallen girls' without knowing what they were, and at the age of eighty she asked her daughter what a miscarriage was. A student teacher said that when she went to training college at the age of twenty (in 1900),

> I should have liked them to mention sex but they seldom did. I had never heard a dirty story, did not know of their existence. Each girl thought the others knew more than she and was afraid to talk for fear of showing her ignorance. Once when the science lecturer was absent the education lecturer took her place and to the amazement of the girls she unwove the story of the human embryo to a silent, thirsty class. I was grateful for that lecture, but I was still puzzled. What did my mother mean when she said, 'Now I have warned you against men. You've been warned so you can safely go anywhere.' That was all my mother ever told me.

Yet evidence of a middle-class girl's intense sexual longings comes from the diary of Frances Grenfell, who married clergyman and author Charles Kingsley. Before marriage, Fanny wrote about Charles kissing her: 'My blood boils and bounds as I recall it.' In 1842 she wrote how she longed passionately for the man she called her husband, and lay in bed imagining 'delicious nightery' when they would lie in each other's arms 'and I will ask you to explain my strange feelings'. Sometimes those feelings became so strong that she hardly knew what to do with herself. She longed to wring her hands, roll on the floor, scream, run until she dropped. She consulted a doctor because her heart 'stops beating every five minutes in a strange way'. After they married, for unspecified reasons Fanny and Charles postponed sex for a month, but then found themselves perfectly physically attuned. We do not know how many other women felt as Fanny did, because few wrote about it.

Not all well brought-up unmarried women were like Fanny, remaining 'filled with longings'. Madeleine Smith's trial for the murder of her lover (and subsequent acquittal) caused a sensation in 1857. She was nineteen when in 1854 she met twenty-six year old Emile L'Angelier, a shipping clerk who was far beneath her socially, but they soon had a sexual relationship in which they pretended to be married. Madeleine wrote over sixty letters to Emile, and it was their discovery in his rooms, after his death, which led to the trial. She never described love-making in any but general terms, never referred to the genitals, never used any expression that could have been termed vulgar. When she was menstruating she said she was 'ill'; for intercourse she coyly used the word 'love', underlined:

It was a punishment to myself to be deprived of your loving me for it is a pleasure, no one can deny that. It is but human nature. Is not everyone that loves of the same mind? Yet, I did feel so ashamed of having allowed you to see (any name you please to insert).

Elsewhere she wrote, 'You are a naughty boy to go and dream of me – and get excited.' Such admissions and expressions are startling from someone in her station of life, since she was no believer in free love and her view of relations between men and women was conventional. She originally wanted a romantic adventure, as a temporary escape from her boring life, and then found that sex was fun. Later, she wanted to marry someone of her own class, but could not persuade Emile that the fun was over, and he threatened to tell her parents all. He later died from arsenic poisoning. In one of the most sensational trials of the century Madeleine, who had purchased quantities of arsenic 'to use as a face-wash for her complexion', and was more than likely guilty of murder, was acquitted, though the verdict was the Scottish one of 'not proven'. Public sympathy for her was overwhelming: newspapers, legal reviews and even religious bodies maintained her innocence or defended her for taking righteous revenge against a depraved fortune hunter and seducer. After this case however, prudent women felt that they should not write love letters.

Knowledge and practice of sex varied considerably among working-class women, too. In many country areas it was the custom to marry only when the woman was pregnant, known as 'proving'. Mary Paley Marshall wrote of her native Lincolnshire village in the 1860s, 'It was not uncommon for young couples to put off marriage till the birth of the first child was expected.' The same applied to Moss Ferry, a semi-industrial village near Manchester, around 1900: 'It was accounted no shame for a child to be begotten out of wedlock – the shame was when there was no wedding to follow. That was something almost unknown – something that didn't stand thinking about,' wrote Margaret Penn. The official figures show that throughout the century well over a third of women were pregnant when they married. But there were also many illegitimate babies, so some men were escaping their customary obligations. More will be said about this in Chapter 9.

Working women tended to be very silent about lovemaking during courtship, but Bessie Wallis said she warned her elder brother, aged fifteen, who was a pit-boy in a Yorkshire mining village around 1900,

> 'You'll be in trouble with Pops if you land a lassie with a bairn! 'I don't care,' was Danny's reaction, 'the lasses egg us on. They get what they ask for. The only pleasure a lad gets is to lay a lass. Anyhow, they like it!' I worried a lot about Danny and the girls. I knew just how much he hated the pit. Girls were his only escape. What I did not realize until much older was that the bodies of these undernourished boys were barely capable of achieving an orgasm, let alone making a child. To most of the boys it was play. They just enjoyed handling the girls and exhibiting their mastery over them.

Another section of the working class was puritanical about sex, and their daughters learned about it only by keeping their eyes and ears open, or from warnings from parents not to allow men to be familiar with them. One woman wrote to the Women's Co-operative Guild, 'I was married at twenty-eight (around 1900) in utter ignorance of the things that vitally affect a wife and mother.' Another said, 'We were as innocent as the grave.' In Nellie Boulton's house in Stoke-on-Trent, the sexes were kept rigidly apart. Nellie was born in 1909, one of thirteen children, but the girls never went near their brothers' bedroom and she said, 'I'd never seen a man in the nude. I'd got seven brothers but I didn't know they'd even got ankles.' Stella Morgan, of the same generation, came from Southport, 'a narrow-minded place', and could not remember ever seeing her father 'without a tie on, let alone anything else missing. I'd never seen a man in bed and at home smalls would never be seen on the [washing] line, and underwear would certainly never be mended in front of father.'

Most respectable working women were determined to maintain their virginity up to marriage. Mrs Layton said her fiancé made 'improper suggestions' to her in the 1870s, after they had been engaged for two years, and she was disgusted and ashamed:

> From that moment I lost all respect for him, and in spite of all his protestations of regret and promises that it should not occur again, I told him I would never forgive him and broke off the engagement there and then.

Maggy Fryett said in her courting days in an isolated village around 1910 she had no intention of 'proving' herself:

> Well, if you go a' courting they want that, don't they? He used to say, 'What you got under your apron? I got to see if you're any good. I ain't going to buy a piggy-in-a-poke.' But I wouldn't let him touch me. I were too frightened.

Some women learned about sex in the workplace, though that did not necessarily mean they indulged in it. Jokes and sex play were a regular part of the work environment, either between men and women or between women and girls, and though some found this offensive, many were not uncomfortable (except in cases of actual sexual exploitation). Much depended on local culture. Some communities enforced strong sanctions against those who went in for illicit sex. In a mining village near Sheffield, if a woman misbehaved the colliers made an effigy of her and paraded it through the streets on a barrow to be pelted.

But the difficulty of generalizing about working-class attitudes towards sex can be illustrated by what Mandell Creighton (later a Bishop) said in 1874 of his living of Embleton in Northumberland, comprising five villages and a number of farms. Sexual morals varied from one village to another, he said, though all the people were strong-minded and independent. The farming community indulged freely in fornication and adultery, with neither shame nor apology, and with no great expense when illegitimate children arrived. On the farms there was always plenty of milk, food and work, and a new member of the family was not a burden. But in the nearby fishing village of Craster illegitimacy was unknown, the attitude towards fornication being very austere.

A sexual double standard existed in all classes, because many men had relationships from an early age and were not castigated for illicit sex as women were. This was to come under increasing attack. Naomi Mitchison said that in 1900,

For instance, my mother told me that if anyone proposed marriage (no other proposal would conceivably have been a possibility) I must ask whether he had ever had anything to do with another woman and if he had I must refuse him. This was straight feminism of the period, an attack on the double standard of men and women, which was still, of course, socially accepted.

Up to the First World War, most feminists supported pre-marital celibacy for both women and men, challenging the conventional view that male sexuality was uncontrollable and needed constant outlet. But it is clear that in each social class some women wanted and claimed sexual and emotional freedom, some wanted it but were afraid to claim it, and others were perfectly content to be celibate for part or the whole of their lives.

In the first half of the century, upper-class weddings were quiet, private ceremonies, celebrated within the family circle and taking place soon after the marriage settlement was drawn up. Engagements rarely lasted more than six weeks. Nearly all the wealthy married by private licence, to avoid public attention. This was a big change from the rowdy, public betrothals that were common in previous centuries. But as marriage became more sentimentalized, with the stress on love rather than on practical dynastic considerations, upper-class weddings turned into social extravaganzas. The rituals of giving away the bride in white, the family reception, and the honeymoon, all symbolized the idea of conjugal love. Blanche Stanley had seven bridesmaids for her 1851 marriage to the Earl of Airlie, and Jane Carlyle wrote of the occasion:

> I saw a trousseau for the first time in my life, about as wonderful a piece of Nonsense as the Exhibition of all Nations. Good heavens, how is any one woman to use up all those gowns and cloaks and fine clothes of every denomination? And the profusion of coronets! every stocking, every pocket handkerchief, everything with a coronet on it!

Queen Victoria described the wedding in 1852 of Lady Constance Leveson-Gower, daughter of the Duke and Duchess of Sutherland, to her cousin, the Duke of Westminster, in the Chapel Royal of St James's Palace:

The Chapel was full of relations, 120 in number. The lovely bride had a white satin dress on with lace flowers, held by a little chaplet of orange flowers. It reminded me so much of our own dear marriage . . . Constance had eight bridesmaids in white, wearing white bonnets. I had not witnessed a marriage in that spot since our one.

On this occasion the private festivities in London were prolonged, and were followed by two days of feasting and celebration amongst workers on the Grosvenor estates in Flintshire and Cheshire. This became normal practice on large estates.

Most middle-class folk could not afford the big white wedding. Charlotte Brontë was married in 1854 in a black satin dress, white bridal mantle and a white bonnet trimmed with green leaves. She and her husband had a honeymoon in Ireland. Clara Alcock said of a mid-Victorian middle-class wedding in Manchester that 'the church was not very full' and there was no public celebration, but the marriage was followed by 'a grand breakfast' for friends, after which the couple left for a honeymoon in Paris. Workers in factories were often given treats to celebrate the owners' family weddings. It was not until the middle of the twentieth century that the big white wedding became universal, though a Herefordshire blacksmith's daughter, married in 1910, had a fashionable gown, 'a reception in a marquee', and a seaside honeymoon.

In the working class, the rites of the old 'big wedding' had passed away by the nineteenth century; no longer was there the fetching of the bride, the 'treating' of fellow workers, the public start to the new household, the mock battle for the bride in places where parents encouraged early marriage. The poor could not afford a special licence, so they had the banns called on three successive Sundays in their local parish church. The couple walked to church on their wedding morning, accompanied by a handful of friends, and then returned to work in the afternoon. A Lincolnshire woman remembered that 'labourers, etc. all got wed in meal breaks, many at 8 am in the morning. The girl then went back to the kitchen and the man to the field.' Any celebration and merriment took place in the evening, when they and their friends had finished work. The bride's dress was of pretty but serviceable material, with a bonnet or hat to match, and these became her 'Sunday best'.

Whatever a woman's social class, and however grand or modest the wedding ceremony, getting married marked a major transition in her life. It entailed the right, and duty, of mutual sexual access. Church and state counted the inability or refusal to perform the sex act as among the few grounds for the annulment of a marriage. Whether or not women enjoyed marital sex is not easily provable, since few expressed an opinion, but after a week of marriage Queen Victoria wrote to Lord Melbourne, the Prime Minister, in 1840, 'I never could have thought there was such happiness in store for me'. She clearly enjoyed sex. Well-documented cases of adultery by upper-class married women, throughout the century, suggest there were plenty of women with hearty sexual appetites. Fanny Kingsley, as mentioned earlier, enjoyed her married sex life and said so. Some marriage manuals discussed women's sexual needs, and Dr Elizabeth Blackwell in the 1870s stressed in two books that female sexuality was as strong as that of males.

Yet an ideology about women emerged in the 1840s and 50s which virtually denied women's sexuality, and the majority of women accepted the judgement. Journalist Eliza Lynn Linton said that a wife's first treat, and her greatest, was when her husband began to leave off fervid love-making and became a tranquil friend. A mid-Victorian mother told her daughter, 'After your wedding, my dear, unpleasant things are bound to happen, but take no notice. I never did.' And Lady Hillingham famously wrote in 1912:

> I am happy now that Charles calls on my bedchamber less frequently than of old. As it is, I now endure but two calls a week and when I hear his step outside my door I lie down on my bed, close my eyes, open my legs and think of England.

Some women gained moral superiority over men by asserting their own lack of sexual passion, and others claimed to be frigid to avoid having more children. Few actually ran away from their husbands or screamed for help. The middle class continued to use double beds (twin beds not being considered 'nice' until the 1930s), as did the working class, therefore – in George Bernard Shaw's words – combining the maximum of temptation with the maximum of opportunity. And the consequence for most women was continual pregnancies.

Queen Victoria made no bones about disliking childbirth, which she called 'the shadow side of marriage'. In a letter to her pregnant daughter, dated 15 June 1858, she said:

What you say of the pride of giving life to an immortal soul is very fine, dear, but I own I cannot enter into that; I think much more of our being like a cow or a dog at such moments, when our poor nature becomes so very animal and unecstatic . . .

The following January, after a difficult and dangerous labour, the princess bore a son. The Queen thought women's pain in childbearing was increased by a sense that their husbands did not understand or participate in their anguish. Her resentment led to her being among the first to use chloroform as an anaesthetic, for her eighth and ninth deliveries, thus making it respectable for other women.

Most women feared pregnancy and childbirth, which could cause tearing, uterine prolapse, and ulcerations. These and other 'female troubles' such as anaemia, vaginal infections and venereal diseases (often passed on by their husbands) weakened women and could make intercourse unpleasant. Childbirth might cause the death of the mother: toxaemia, haemorrhage and puerperal fever were notorious killers. More than one in 200 women died in childbirth then, in comparison with one in 60,000 in England today. By the early nineteenth century, doctors were using forceps for difficult deliveries, but the baby or mother were sometimes injured through inexpert use of the instrument. For most complications doctors could do nothing, and because they were ignorant of the principles of contagion they often infected women with germs from other patients. Midwives, used by poor women who could not afford a doctor, ranged from the able, clean and moderately expensive to the ignorant, slovenly and cheap. In general, mother and baby did best if the birth took place outside a hospital.

Upper-class women were generally healthier than the poor, because they were better fed and housed. They had a life expectancy six years longer than other women, though they suffered similar birth-induced complaints. A study of forty-eight of them by Judith Schneid Lewis (see Bibliography) shows that five died in their twenties, whereas fourteen lived to be eighty or more and had an average of nine children. Pregnancy was not so restrictive for them as it was for middle-class women; it was a cause for pride, not hibernation, and they remained publicly and frivolously active up to the time of giving birth. Throughout the century they went when pregnant to royal drawing rooms, balls, salons, or fox hunting in the countryside, not letting their condition curtail their pleasures. The Queen commented in March, 1870:

And now one of the new fashions of our very elegant society is to go in perfectly light-coloured dresses – quite tight – without a particle of shawl or scarf . . . and to dance within a fortnight of their confinement and even valse at seven months!!! Where is delicacy of feeling going to? Sybil St Albans danced a quadrille under these circumstances.

Soon after giving birth, aristocratic women resumed their hectic social lives and handed over the child to a wet-nurse, either to free the mother from that responsibility or because she was unable to suckle. The number of wet-nurses dropped during the century, but many famous people used them, such as Catherine Gladstone, wife of the Prime Minister, Lady Amberley and Jennie Churchill. There was a curious belief in the transference of characteristics by breast milk. Margot Asquith, born in 1864, wrote, 'My second sister, Charlotte . . . was the only member of the family who was tall. My mother attributed this – and her good looks – to her wet-nurse, Janet Mercer, a mill-girl from Innerleithen, noted for her height and beauty.' Good health she could have got from the milk of a healthy wet-nurse, but not good looks!

In middle-class circles, pregnancy was too indelicate a subject to discuss. In 1881 author Maria Ewing wrote to a friend's pregnant wife, 'Naturally there were many enquiries for you. We got through the delicate subject very well, considering a gentleman was present.' Voluminous clothes hid the increasing size of the mother-to-be, who tended to stay in virtual hiding until after the birth.

Some doctors believed that lower-class women had an easier time in childbirth than the rich, because they got more exercise, ate less rich food and were therefore healthier. Neither statistics nor personal accounts bear this out. Women who worked outside the home had to fit pregnancy and childbirth into their hard lives. They often worked up to the time of delivery and returned to the factory after a brief confinement. Stella Davies said her grandmother was too shy to tell the overlooker she was in labour, and gave birth at the mill. An Act of 1891 required women to stay away from factory work for four weeks after giving birth, but women could not afford to lose their wages and the law became unenforceable. Working women's own views on pregnancy and childbirth were graphically presented, for the first time, in a 1915 book called *Maternity*, published by the Women's Co-operative Guild and containing 160 anonymous letters. All referred to incompetent or lackadaisical doctors or midwives. One began, 'I do hope I shall never see the young women of today have to go through what I did.' The birth usually took place at home, with no pain relief, the common practice being to pull on a towel knotted round the end of the bed when the pains came. A doctor was called only in extreme need, since his fee was more than a man earned in a week. One woman said, 'I had to do without common necessaries to provide doctors' fees, which so undermined my health that when my baby was born I nearly lost my life.' Another said, 'The doctor's bills grew like mushrooms, so I had a midwife the next time.'

Almost every letter spoke of lack of food, overwork before confinement, and excessively quick return to household chores after the birth, as the prime causes of stillbirth, miscarriage and lifelong disablement of the mother. One woman who had had seven living children, three stillbirths and four miscarriages, wrote, 'I looked after my husband and children well, but I often went short of food myself, though my husband didn't know it. He used to think my appetite was bad and that I could not eat.' Lack of money to pay for help made matters worse. One woman said, 'I used to do my own ironing and knead my bread in bed, unknown to the doctor. Now I am suffering from not being able to take care of myself.' And these were the wives of skilled manual workers, living in considerably better conditions than the very poor.

The Women's Co-operative Guild persuaded Parliament to include maternity benefit in Lloyd George's National Insurance Act of 1911. The benefit was thirty shillings, which covered the cost of a doctor or midwife but left nothing over for extra food. So the Guild demanded provision of fully-equipped maternity and infant welfare centres, home-help services, free extra food for needy mothers and 'pure milk' depots. Local authorities were given discretion to provide these services, and during the First World War many were pressured into doing so.

Perhaps the most important change that has occurred in women's lives since the nineteenth century is control over the number of children they bear. The large family is popularly thought to be typical of the Victorian age; it is portrayed in thousands of photographs of family groups, with children lined up by sex and age. But this impression is deceptive. Many people had no children at all, because they were infertile; others had a few children because they were sub-fertile. And there is clear evidence that many people were limiting their families from mid-century onwards.

Family limitation was first practised by the middle class and by textile workers, generally through *coitus interruptus*, and was not adopted uniformly by all groups. The *Saturday Review* said in 1871 that there was 'a decided diminution among [middle-class] women in desire for children' and Dr Acton referred in 1875 to 'the spirit of insubordination in wives to fulfil their conjugal duties.'

But large families did not disappear. Farm workers and coalminers went on having larger families than other workers. If the poor had been 'provident' they would have had few or no children, and been better off financially. But, being human, they wanted them, and until it was clear that most of their children would survive infancy the idea of limiting their families was incomprehensible. The first census of family size, in 1911, showed that in general working-class families were a third larger than those of the middle class. Eugenicists became anxious, since they wanted only 'quality' families to increase, but people made their own decisions as to how many children they had. In all classes, the very large family of ten or more children became statistically insignificant between the late-Victorian and inter-war periods.

Contraception was written about openly after philosopher Jeremy Bentham advocated the sponge method in 1797. Richard Carlile published in 1825 *Every Woman's Book: or, What is Love*, which recommended partial withdrawal, the sponge and the condom. By the following year the book was in its fourth edition. In his book *Moral Physiology*, the socialist Robert Dale Owen in 1830 advocated complete withdrawal. Charles Knowlton's *Fruits of Philosophy* (1834) recommended the douche, and George Drysdale's *Elements of Social Science* (1854) described five techniques of contraception. His book ran to thirty-five editions and was translated into ten European languages.

In 1877 Annie Besant and Charles Bradlaugh re-issued Knowlton's pamphlet, and were prosecuted for publishing obscene literature. The publicity surrounding their trial brought knowledge of family planning to almost everyone. It is often said that this was the time when middle-class families ceased to be so large, but census evidence suggests it was earlier. One hundred types of vaginal pessary had been developed for uterine disorders, and doctors found they were being used for contraception. The vaginal cap became popular with the vulcanization of rubber in 1843. At the end of the century the condom was popular, but middle-class women preferred the sponge, the douche or the vaginal cap, methods over which they themselves had control. In 1905 the popular magazine *Myra's Journal* had what the *Lancet* described as a 'filthy advertisement' – it was a picture of a condom. Family planning was almost certainly practised initially by people for whom religion had lost its compulsion, since all the churches disapproved. Doctors officially disapproved, in spite of the fact that the 1911 Census showed they were the group making most use of contraception. Charles Knowlton's treatise, *Fruits of Philosophy*, which advocated the use of birth control on social, economic and medical grounds, and contained details of contraceptive techniques, began to sell at the rate of 250,000 copies a year after Bradlaugh and Besant were prosecuted for publishing it in 1877. Public opinion on the matter changed to the point where, in 1895, an article in the conservative *Saturday Review* said, 'The only woman at the present time who is willing to be regarded as a mere breeding machine is she who lacks the wit to adopt any other role, and now she is the exception rather than the rule . . . For the first time since her creation woman has begun to doubt the morality of producing children under unfavourable conditions . . .'

Few working-class women said that for birth control they used the Dutch cap or the sponge, or that their husbands used condoms. Some thought contraception was not respectable, and others said their husbands regarded it as unnatural. The lack of privacy in small houses without bathrooms made it difficult for women to feel comfortable about inserting the sponge or cap, or douching. It is believed that withdrawal was the main method of contraception, and this continued up to and after the Second World War, though some distrusted this method, one woman saying she could not reckon on being able to 'push him out of the way when I think it's near.' Women who decided to limit their families said they were influenced by relatives. Ada Hayhoe, born 1890, said, 'My mother had fourteen children and I didn't want that. So if I stayed up mending, my husband would be asleep when I come to bed. That were simple, weren't it?' Hannah Mitchell said of her mother-in-law, 'Poor soul! Childbearing and cooking for twenty years – she must have been worn out before she died a comparatively young woman. So I was determined not to begin where she left off.' Jessie Stephen, an active trade unionist, ended up teaching her own mother about birth control when the latter was forty-two years old.

The only method of family limitation many women knew was abortion. There were many folk remedies for it. A Sheffield patholo-gist said, 'The news is handed from woman to woman by word of mouth, like any of the other household remedies or cures which every woman knows.' There were also advertisements for abortifa-cients in many newspapers. A typical one read:

Ladies only/ THE LADY MONTROSE MIRACULOUS FEMALE TABULES/ Are positively unequalled for all FEMALE AILMENTS. The most obstinate OBSTRUCTIONS, IRREGULARITIES ETC. of the female system are removed in a few doses.

Most of the remedies legally available from the chemist – Epsom salts, aloes, castor oil, pennyroyal – produced nothing but nausea, but diachylon could also be bought. One woman in Dudley, whose doctor was called after she collapsed, and who then aborted, said she got the prescription from a friend in Manchester: 'Hickey-pickey, bitter aloes, white diachylon – one pennyworth of each.' According to the *British Medical Journal* of 1905, home-made pills based on a lead substance were being used for abortion. These could lead to insanity or death. In Nottingham they were known as Mrs Seagrave's pills, in Sheffield as Nurse O's pills. In 1900, Faith Osgerby's mother took gunpowder to abort a child, and Margaret Perry's mother induced an abortion by drinking gin, soaking in hot baths, and jumping off the water copper. The case histories of women who suffered from botched, self-induced abortions were tragic, but one woman said, 'Can we wonder that so many women take drugs, hoping to get rid of the expected child, when they know so little of their own bodies, and have to work so hard to keep, or help to keep, the children they have already got?' Another woman said she'd rather 'swallow the druggist's shop and the man in it than have another kid.'

It was not only the lower orders who used drugs for abortions. In 1847, Henrietta Maria Stanley (1807–95), wife of the second Lord Alderley, who had borne nine children in seventeen years, found herself pregnant again. Her husband was appalled by the news, saying he hoped it was not the start of another flock, 'for what to do with them I am sure I know not'. His wife wrote back, 'A hot bath, a tremendous walk, and a great dose have succeeded . . . I am reassured for the future by the efficacy of the means.' This was a pious, aristocratic Victorian lady.

An Act of 1803 made it illegal for anyone to assist a woman to procure an abortion, but the law was not broken if the woman sought her own miscarriage. The law was tightened in 1828 and again in 1837, and by an Act of 1861 self-abortion became an offence. Prosecutions followed, and doubled between 1900 and 1910, but this did not stop women having abortions. According to some doctors 20 to 25 per cent of pregnancies ended this way. Ethel Clark talked of 'the joy of a miscarriage which helped a woman back to happiness again' in her village of Woolaston, Gloucestershire, in 1900, and as late as 1938 a government committee found that 'many mothers seemed not to understand that self-induced abortion was illegal. They assumed it was legal before the third month [before quickening] and only outside the law when procured by another person.'

Some of the wealthy got surgical abortions by paying doctors to perform them. Abortions by 'irregular practitioners' for non-medical reasons were not approved, but doctors felt they had a legitimate right to terminate a pregnancy 'on therapeutic grounds', in the interests of the health of the woman. Such a quandary arose, for example, when a woman's pelvic passage was distorted to such an extent that a natural birth was impossible. A Caesarian operation meant almost certain death for the mother, because doctors did not know how to prevent infection. The first Englishwoman to survive a Caesarian was Jane Foster of Lancashire, operated on by Dr James Barlow in 1793. The majority of doctors knew that an abortion was less dangerous for the mother than a Caesarian. In order to justify the operation, doctors went to great lengths to deny that the foetus had real life, though they did not approve of repeating the abortion procedure for any woman. It is not known how many 'therapeutic abortions' there were, but no doctor acting in consultation with colleagues was ever prosecuted for performing one.

Concerning women's health in general, prior to the First World War, more married women than unmarried women died under the age of forty-five. The difference was not simply that so many women died in childbirth. In 1913, Mrs Pember Reeves was shocked to realize that working-class wives in Lambeth, who looked as if they were 'in the dull middle of middle age' were in fact young. They were undernourished, and they sacrificed their own interests to those of their children, expecting to be ill from anaemia, headaches, constipation, rheumatism, varicose veins and toothache. Few got medical help, because of the cost. The National Insurance Act of 1911 provided access to a doctor for all insured workers, male and female, but not for their dependants. Yet as time went on women were less fatalistic about pain and early death. They demanded help from the government in campaigns which drew attention to their plight, and received unprecedented attention from politicians worried about the poor physical condition of army recruits in the Boer War.

Real benefits had come to most women by the end of the century. In 1800, the average life expectancy of women was forty-four years, by 1910 it was fifty-two, and by 1920 almost sixty. The average working-class family had declined to five children in the 1890s, and would go down to three by 1920. By 1910, women who had faced high rates of death in childbirth now risked only a 1 in 1,000 risk, either at home or in hospital. Many fewer babies and young children died than had done a hundred years earlier. The legal status of wives had changed, too, as will be seen in the next chapter.

4

Angels in the House

MARRIAGE
AND DOMESTIC LIFE

Marriage is the cement of society . . . and . . . the only way for a
woman to rise in the world.

Mary Wollstonecraft,
A Vindication of the Rights of Women (1792)

Marriage with its one-sided obligations, is not a thought-out rational
system of sex relationship, but . . . the last citadel of the less
intelligent kind of conservatism.

Mona Caird, *The Morality of Marriage* (1897)

There were loud and continuous arguments throughout the nineteenth
century about the virtues and vices of the traditional patriarchal family,
dominated by the father and bolstered by law. Supporters saw it
as a bulwark against a hostile and rapidly changing world. Marriage
sanctified by religion was a sacrament, binding two people together
for life. The man was protector, chief breadwinner and head of the
household. The wife and children were expected to be obedient and
submissive to his rules.

By marriage, husband and wife became one person in law – and
that person was he. He had almost complete control over her body,
and their children belonged to him. Unless a marriage settlement
arranged things differently, the husband was entitled to all his wife's
property, and he could claim any money she earned. Indeed, as soon

as a woman accepted a proposal of marriage, her property belonged entirely to the man. It was argued that 'were she permitted to give away, or otherwise settle her property, he might be disappointed of the wealth he looked to in making the offer.' The ironic thing was that in the Church of England marriage service a man promised to endow his wife with all his worldly goods, yet in practice it was the wife who forfeited her property to him.

There were supposed to be some advantages in the wife's diminished and demeaning legal position. If she committed a crime in her husband's presence (except murder and high treason) the law presumed that she was coerced by him and was therefore innocent. Her husband was responsible for her debts and was obliged to support her as long as she lived with him. He could not ill-use her 'beyond reasonable chastisement' – although that could mean actually beating her – and he could not lock her up with impunity (that is, without being liable for punishment). The law assumed that any child she had during marriage was her husband's, however improbable the circumstances (such as his absence at the time of conception), unless he could prove adultery with a specific man.

This patriarchal family was regarded by many people as the essential building block of a civilized society. The Victorian family – by which was meant the affluent middle-class family, of course – won for itself a reputation as a noble institution upon whose continuance depended all that was fine and stable in Britain.

Opponents of the patriarchal family saw matters in a different light. The radical Mary Wollstonecraft, for example, thought marriage the best possible arrangement for providing stable emotional relationships and for bringing up children. But she called for improvements in married women's legal status, to make them more equal partners with their husbands. She said that upper-class men required of women only 'virtue' and physical beauty, and that women needed to gain some self-respect and behave as if they had spiritual and intellectual needs. She also attacked the double standard of sexual morality which allowed men to indulge in sex before marriage and to be unfaithful to their wives afterwards, yet required women to be virgins when they married and not thereafter to have sex with other men. Mary was not calling for sexual liberation for females; she wanted men to control their sexual impulses as they required women to do. For her championship of women's rights, Mary was denigrated as 'a hyena in petticoats', and because of her unconventional life some women were afraid of her ideas, believing the one stemmed from the other. Yet many of her beliefs appealed as much to women of conservative disposition as they did to radicals. They were taken up by other women writers, and formed the backdrop to debate in the next hundred years on 'the woman question'.

Despite the legal constraints of marriage, it was the life-plan of most women, who avoided the unmarried state like the plague. 'Being married gives one one's position, which nothing else can,' wrote Queen Victoria to her daughter in 1858. This seems a surprising statement from the hereditary ruler of the greatest empire the world has ever known, but the Queen had a knack of saying what her middle-class subjects would approve of, even when her own life did not fit the model. Beatrice Webb said of her upper-class upbringing in the 1870s and 80s that 'marriage to a man of their own or a higher social grade was the only recognized vocation for women not compelled to earn their own livelihood'. And of her pre-1914 girlhood Elizabeth Delafield, the *Provincial Lady* diarist, wrote that she 'could never remember a time when she had not known that a woman's failure or success in life depended entirely on whether or not she succeeded in getting a husband. It was not even a question of marrying well, though mothers with pretty and attractive daughters naturally hoped for that. But any husband at all was better than none.' The folklore at that time included the idea that 'women who want to get married and can't often turn queer as they grow older.' It was not a pleasing prospect.

Many women who left a record of their feelings actually welcomed marriage as an emotionally satisfying and indeed emancipating experience. Even those we would call feminists were often ambivalent in their attitudes towards a husband and family. Freedom is a relative concept, and for many women marriage meant release from a childlike and humiliating dependence on parents. It offered the possibility, on however unequal terms, to create a home and family of one's own and, surprisingly, the chance to go about and make separate friends, even ones of the opposite sex. Everyday married life was based on the personalities of the spouses, and how much affection or hostility they felt for each other. As John Stuart Mill pointed

out in his famous book, *The Subjection of Women*, men did not
want solely the obedience of women. They also wanted their love.
And in practice many wives were not at all dominated by their
husbands, who would have echoed the Beadle in Dickens' *Oliver
Twist*, who when told that 'the law supposes that your wife acts under
your direction,' replied, 'If the law supposes that . . . the law is a
ass – a idiot. If that's the eye of the law, the law is a bachelor,
and the worst I wish the law is, that his eyes may be opened by
experience.' Justice Colin Blackburn warned a grand jury in 1871,
'The law supposes that everything is in the property of the husband,
and that the wife is under his control. But in point of fact, in the
lower positions of life that possibly may not be the case at all.'
Nevertheless, if it came to a showdown, real legal power resided with
the husband.

All married women were hampered by some legal restraints, but
there were vast differences in women's experience of marriage, depending on their social class. In the upper reaches of society wives often
had an astonishing amount of freedom. At the lower levels the key
role of wife and mother, and the emotional dependence of husband
and children, often amounted to matriarchy within the home and
sometimes beyond it. It was middle-class wives who were most con-
strained by marriage law. The gilded cage of bourgeois marriage
was approved by those who idealized its comfort and security, but
hated by those who found it claustrophobic and frustrating.

Upper-class wives were usually protected from the harshness of
common law, which assumed that all husbands were kind, wise,
caring, responsible, hard-working and fair – and conversely, that
all women were childlike or imbeciles. Of course, many husbands were
far from being paragons of virtue. Wife-beating occurred at all levels
of society, and there were greedy and selfish men of all classes who
appropriated their wives' earnings when they could, often using their
children as pawns to exact wifely obedience. To protect them from
such husbands the English rich found ways to give their married
daughters separate incomes which the husband could not touch. A
system of private law, known as equity, was developed. Marriage
settlements laid down inheritance rights, jointure (a type of widow's
pension) and the pin-money and paraphernalia (money for her own
use) a wife was to receive. There were also trusts, by which trustees
held money for the sole use of the wife, and constructive trusts which

a woman could handle without trustees. The main reason why wealthy fathers used private law in this way was to prevent their sons-in-law dissipating the family money, but the effect was to give the woman some financial independence. It became common for even modestly wealthy families to provide for their married daughters in this way, and it was estimated in the middle of the nineteenth century that ten per cent of English wives had a private income.

Many wealthy men left their whole fortunes, or the bulk of their estates, to daughters, nieces, close female relatives or women friends. Of Fanny Pierrepont, who married in 1802, Lady Louisa Stuart commented that she 'would not have much less than £30,000, an old steward of the Duke of Kingston's having bequeathed her fifteen after his wife's death,' and she said with justice, 'she therefore is a good match for anybody'. Lady Louisa, who was herself a great heiress, saw nothing strange about the 'old steward' so disposing of his wealth. On the death of the 5th and last Duke of Ancaster in 1809, the property was finally divided between his two nieces (sisters of the 4th Duke). The daughter of Lord Perth inherited his vast Drummond estates. In 1811 Barbara Ashley Cooper inherited all the estates of the 5th Earl of Shaftesbury which did not pass with the title to his brother (the unpleasant father to the humanitarian 7th Earl). Barbara married in 1814, and in 1838 her husband was created Lord De Mauley in acknowledgement of his wife's descent and the family's wealth. In 1814, Coghill's and Huck's estates in Hereford-shire and Oxfordshire respectively descended to the owners' two nieces, who remained spinsters. Frances Anne, only daughter of Sir Harry Vane-Tempest and of Anne, Countess of Antrim, inherited from her parents all their large estates in Durham and the North of Ireland. When in 1819 she married Charles William Stewart, half-brother of Lord Castlereagh, she insisted that he added *her* surname, Vane, to his own. This became a fashion. In the 1820s Frances Mary Gas-coyne married into the mighty Cecil family, bringing a Liverpool fortune with her. A condition of the marriage settlement was that the family change its name to Gascoyne-Cecil. In 1831 John Ward married an heiress and had to change his name to Ward-Broughton-Leigh to signify her being the heiress of her mother (maiden name Broughton) and of her father (named Leigh). In the 1850s the last Lord Maynard left all his immense fortune and lands to his young granddaughter, Frances, who later became Countess of Warwick.

At the age of twenty-two, Lady Mary Douglas-Hamilton, only child of the twelfth Duke of Hamilton, inherited on his death in 1895 the huge fortune of £35,000 a year. In addition she had a personal fortune of about £450,000 and also an annuity of £7,000. Had she been a boy she would have held ten British and two Scottish titles. In 1906 she married the Marquis of Graham.

Women who controlled such vast fortunes as these (albeit through trustees) were persons of consequence in their own right, and marriage did nothing to change that. They did not feel dominated or oppressed; they were often not fully aware of the legal disabilities they *did* have, because they were not subjected to them unless something went seriously wrong with the marriage. The need to give all married women property rights was not obvious to this élite group of women, and few took part in the campaigns to reform the law. As the Duchess of Manchester remarked in the 1860s, 'I hear much of women's rights but I only know that I have no wrongs.'

Women of immense wealth could behave as they pleased, and generally did, subject only to the customs of their own class. They travelled frequently, at home and abroad, with or without husband and family. They handed over the care of children to nurses and governesses, and housework to a bevy of servants. They controlled the employment of staff, farm bailiffs, grooms and gardeners in their town houses and country estates, and employed architects and craftsmen for the design, building and furnishing of their homes. They decided which local tradesmen would supply the large quantities of food and drink consumed in their households. They appointed clergymen to livings, and were the patrons of artists, sculptors, singers, writers, actors and budding politicians.

These great ladies, or *grandes dames* as they were then called, decided who was 'in' and who was 'out' of 'society', that small but closely connected group which made its own social laws. They had an intricate system of card leaving and calling, and the women decided whether or not to call on a newcomer, whether cards should be left, and whether further introductions would be made. In circles where an introduction served as a social endorsement, this meant women had the power to exclude anyone they disliked. Lady Dorothy Nevill wrote in 1919, of the 1850s:

The social power wielded by great ladies (such as Lady Jersey and Lady Londonderry) seems almost inconceivable today. Their easy leisured arrogance was taken more or less as a matter of course, and they would have been much astonished had it aroused any criticism; small wonder, when they were brought up to think they were the very salt of the earth.

Their social power may have declined somewhat, but was still strong at the end of the century. In the 1890s Lady Warwick (who called herself a socialist) gave the following snobbish advice to novelist Elinor Glyn, who was newly married into the aristocracy, about entertaining in the country:

Army or naval officers, diplomats or clergymen may be invited to lunch or dinner. The vicar may be invited regularly to Sunday lunch or supper if he is a gentleman. Doctors and solicitors may be invited to garden parties, though never, of course, to lunch or dinner. Anyone engaged in the arts, the stage, trade or commerce, no matter how well connected, cannot be asked to the house at all.

In fact, outstanding theatre people *were* received in great houses, though it was more common in London than in the country. Actresses Sarah Bernhardt and Lily Langtry were invited everywhere, as favourites of the Prince of Wales. And indeed some aristocrats married actresses.

Consuelo Vanderbilt, the American heiress who married the Duke of Marlborough, said that in 1900 duchesses were still treated with respect and reverence, and they had an aura of glamour. Crowds used to gather to admire Georgiana, Countess of Dudley, who was considered a great beauty, when in the 1870s and 80s she went riding in Rotten Row in a barouche. By the 1920s the women stars of silent films, and then the 'talkies,' had supplanted duchesses as objects of public awe and adoration.

Upper-class English wives had an astonishing amount of sexual freedom. Before marriage they had to remain virgins, but after producing an heir or two they expected to pursue extra-marital relationships, and there were certain unspoken understandings which allowed them what we might call 'emotional space'. Absolute discretion had to be observed, of course, and it was considered unforgivable to humiliate a spouse publicly or draw attention to love affairs. Their own peers gossiped endlessly about each other, but they did not like people lower down the social scale to talk about them. Thus, the early nineteenth-century Lady Melbourne well understood why her daughter-in-law Caroline Lamb had a passion for Lord Byron, but she could not understand why Caroline caused a scandal by cutting her wrists at a public function when Byron brought the affair to an end. Lady Melbourne herself had four children, three of whom (including the future Prime Minister who inherited the title on the death of his elder brother) were almost certainly by men other than her husband. But she was always the soul of discretion.

The moral lead on what was acceptable behaviour passed early in the century from the upper class to the rising middle class. Being influenced by evangelical Christianity it had consequently more puritanical notions. The aristocracy was persuaded to reform its outward conduct, at least, and it became unfashionable for men to flaunt their kept mistresses. Manners became more refined in public, and language was cleaned up. But the upper classes continued privately to practise their own code of sexual morality, as in the case of Lady Londonderry, who had a dramatic love-affair with the Tsar of Russia when her husband was the British ambassador to the Court of St Petersburg in the 1840s. She added the fabulous jewellery he gave her to the Londonderry family collection, without anyone batting an eyelid.

Queen Victoria disapproved of these goings-on and wrote about them in her diaries. The hope that her son would not join in was futile: the Prince of Wales led 'the fast set' and from around 1865 was the most unfaithful husband in Europe, though at the same time he was devoted to his wife and scared of her tantrums. All the Prince's later love affairs were with married women in society whose husbands were blind or complaisant. Yet, despite the generally tolerant attitudes of spouses, some upper-class women were ill-treated by their husbands (they will be discussed in Chapter 6). And as well as the 'semi-detached' or unhappy couples, there were a minority of aristocrats who favoured the type of companiable marriage extolled by the Evangelicals. For example, the famous reforming Earl of Shaftesbury and his wife had a close and loving relationship, as did Prime Minister Gladstone and his wife.

At the other end of the social spectrum were the working-class wives who made up the majority of English women. There were infinite differences between groups, based on where they lived (town or country, a 'good' or 'bad' area), which church or chapel they attended (if any), local customs, how much regular income they had, and the number of children in the family. The working class itself used the terms 'respectable' and 'rough' to describe the greatest division of all, between those who were thrifty and prudent, sober and industrious, and those who were hard-drinking, pleasure-loving and uninterested in saving for a rainy day. Mary Hollinrake said of her home town of Todmorden, Lancashire, in the early twentieth century, 'There were untidy families, even dirty and feckless ones, and there were respectable, upright families who knew they were the salt of the earth.' Mary made it clear that she belonged to the latter. Respectable women guarded their reputations and looked down on those who were less respectable or 'no better than they should be'. The sexual morals of the respectable were strict, whereas those of the rough were extremely free, as social investigator Henry Mayhew made clear in his lengthy reports on the life of the London poor in the 1840s. Rough women rarely envied the dull lives of the respectable, who sacrificed pleasure for duty, though they envied their ability to keep out of debt.

Within the working class, relations between husbands and wives depended on personality and strength of will. It was unimportant to these women that their husbands legally owned their property, since they rarely had any real property, though a drunken or bullying husband who forced his wife to give him her own earnings was unfortunately common. Working-class women were realistic about marriage, expecting to work hard both inside the home and outside, either regularly or casually, to earn or add to the family income. They married between the ages of twenty-three and twenty-six, though one in twelve married before the age of twenty. They wanted affection and support, a home of their own and children, and most did the best they could for their families, within their means.

There are more descriptions of working-class homes from the viewpoint of children than from their mothers, and more information available about the latter part of the century (because more writing has survived). A striking point is the great variation in the numbers of people in any one home, and the extent of what we would now regard as overcrowding. Many people had no space for possessions, and no privacy or quiet. Mrs B. (whose name was not given in full), the

respectable wife of a skilled factory worker in Stockport, with five
children, told the Factory Inquiry Commission in 1833 that they lived
in four rooms with two beds, four chairs, a table, boxes for their
clothes and a few cooking utensils. Their diet was plain but wholesome,
with lots of porridge, milk and potatoes. Mrs Layton, born in Bethnal
Green in 1855, was one of fourteen children living with their parents
in three rooms, one so dark it could not be used. The poor made
children's cots from packing cases, and stored clothes in orange boxes.
Even in Edwardian times, carpets were found only in very affluent
homes. Eleanor Hutchinson described the two rooms in Paddington
where her family of eight lived around 1900 as 'a clean, tidy and cosy
home.' The front room contained a double bed, a chest of drawers,
a square table, a few chairs and a small iron bedstead which folded
up during the day. The back room was the living room cum kitchen,
with a sideboard, a fitted cupboard for provisions, a table and chairs,
and also a double bed where the four boys slept. Amy Gomm, born
in rural Oxfordshire in 1899, was one of a family of ten living in a small
cottage. She reckoned people were used to what they had, and did not
feel particularly disadvantaged, but by modern standards it was not a
comfortable life. In cramped homes those who worried less about
respectability used the street for extra space. Mothers sat on doorsteps
on warm evenings, breast-feeding their babies, with children skipping
in the road, and playing marbles or hopscotch. The corner shops and
pubs supplied local news and gossip. Women had an informal network
of support from relatives, friends and neighbours, who shared joys and
sorrows, lent a loaf of bread, or looked after the baby for an hour.

Robert Roberts described, in his book *The Classic Slum*, growing up
in Edwardian Salford, a world of smoky chimneys, reeking gasometers
and grimy terraced cottages. He observed the local matriarchy, an inner
ring of grandmothers known irreverently as the 'old queens'. Wielding
great influence behind the scenes, they represented an ultra-
conservative bloc in the community. Mothers and daughters kept up
a female connection and let the sons move out into another female
grouping when they married. A grandmother reigned supreme as long
as she kept her own home, but if she went to live with a son or
daughter, her influence declined.

When social investigator Mrs Pember Reeves reported on respectable
mothers' lives in Lambeth in 1913, she found conditions similar to those

described by Mrs B. of Stockport in 1833 (see above). The wives spoke well of their husbands, though their children seemed to fill their lives. One woman said, 'My young man's that good ter me I feel as if somethink nice 'ad 'appened every time 'e comes in' ('young man' was the usual term for the husband). Other women just said, 'E's all right', though one said, 'E's a good 'un. 'E ain't never kep' back me twenty-three bob [shillings], but e's that spiteful Satterday nights I 'as ter keep the children from 'im.' To manage a husband and six children in three rooms, on a pound a week [20 shillings], as many of these women did, needed stamina, wisdom and loving kindness.

It is difficult now to imagine the dirt, decay, disease and desolation that was common in nineteenth-century English towns, where by 1900 over three-quarters of the population lived. Whether a woman was respectable or rough, there was no escape from crowded living and a polluted environment. Even where industrial pollution was not severe, house fires produced a pall of smoke over the area, and streets and rivers were polluted by excrement from humans, horses and other animals. Despite outbreaks of cholera in towns, sanitary reform was opposed by taxpayers who wanted to avoid increases in the local rates. From 1848 the central government encouraged local authorities to establish drainage schemes and water-supply systems, but they were slow to do so. The poor shared non-flushing lavatories (usually called privies) until late in the century when water was brought to many homes. The respectable taught their children to relieve themselves in a closet or pot. The rough sent them out to the nearest alley, lane or field. Toilet rolls were an unheard-of luxury, and until newspapers became cheap even that was not an alternative. Public baths were available in some towns from 1846, providing a cold bath for one penny, and a warm bath or shower for two pence (both charges included a clean towel). Such baths were much used when available, but otherwise the numbers of the 'great unwashed' remained high.

An enormous effort had to be made by the hardworking housewife who struggled to keep her house and clothes clean. Washing day was an ordeal for everyone. The clothes had to be soaked overnight, water carried to the house and then heated, and the clothes agitated in a tub with a dolly (a wooden implement with three legs and a stout handle), then rubbed, boiled and starched. They were finally dried outside (if there was fine weather) or round the fire. The public washhouse movement launched in Liverpool in 1842, by a poor woman called Catherine Wilkinson, was very popular. The washhouses had sinks and hot water, and it was cheap to use them. The idea was taken up by Lord Shaftesbury, and the movement spread rapidly to other towns, but there were never enough washhouses for everyone. When running water and gas were installed in working-class homes, so that women could have a gas boiler to heat water and a gas stove instead of cooking over an open fire, it was comparative bliss. But of course there were no vacuum cleaners, washing machines or refrigerators.

Food was another problem for the poor. Unscrupulous shopkeepers added cheaper ingredients to many foods, thus making profit by endangering people's health. Alum and chalk were added to bread, to whiten it. Tea was sold mixed with hawthorne and elm leaves. Chocolate was enriched with Venetian lead, which caused children to vomit. Milk was diluted with water that was often polluted. Most of the food people ate was illegally adulterated up to the 1880s, though things improved after the passing of the Adulteration of Food, Drink and Drugs Act, 1872. Public analysts were appointed to implement the provisions of the Act. From the 1840s there was a working-class co-operative movement which aimed to provide food and household goods of better quality and at lower prices than elsewhere. It eventually moved into production as well as distribution, and with its retail shops, factories, ships and tea plantations the Co-operative Wholesale Society grew and thrived. But Co-op shops were the preserve of the respectable and thrifty, out of reach of the very poor because they would not give credit. So those who most needed cheap goods had to shop at corner stores which were more expensive because they gave 'tick' and took the risk on bad debts. People's diets and health improved somewhat towards the end of the century, when incomes rose.

Country women had problems, too. The air may have been cleaner than in towns, but wages were lower, housing no better, and food just as adulterated. Agricultural labourers in the North of England earned more than those in the South, because of the competition for labour from the mines and factories, but rural wives had harder lives than townswomen. They were isolated, hidden and inarticulate. Those who did not work outside the home saw only their families and an occasional neighbour or the village midwife. Relations between husbands and wives were described by outsiders as 'a kind of dogged companionship' and their lives as dull, tame, and colourless. If the husband was a confirmed drunkard (and that was not uncommon) his wife's life was almost impossible, since the man often deposited his wages at the ale-house and drank his way through them. Yet there are some accounts of happy family relations among country dwellers. James Bowd wrote in 1889, 'I was as fond of my Wife as a Cat is of New Milk', and Mrs West said of her farm labourer husband, 'We've been very happy together, and never had a word amiss. He just takes things as they come.' They were living, man and wife and five children, on twelve shillings a week, when most working-class women considered twenty shillings barely adequate.

The handling of the family budget gave women a dominant role in the home, though this also led to the woman taking responsibility for making ends meet, and putting her family's needs before her own. Mrs Burrows, brought up in rural Lincolnshire in the 1850s, said her father had a tumour in the head and never worked for sixteen years. Her mother's life was one of 'loving sacrifice' in which she 'worked like a slave to keep a home over our heads', never asked for or received charity, and never once ran into debt: 'Scores of times I have seen her sit down to a meal of dry bread, so that we might have a tiny mite of butter on our bread, yet she never complained.' Mrs Layton, married to a railwayman in London in the 1880s, said, 'No one outside my door ever knew how often I was hungry or how I had to scheme to get my husband nourishment.' Women usually gave their husbands the best food, either because they depended on them as the main breadwinners, or to keep them in good humour, or because it was the 'done' thing. Some husbands may not have realized this was happening; others took the best food as of right. Getting into debt was not socially acceptable to the respectable, but there were hard times when most families had to resort to some form of credit, or the pawnshop. In the depression of 1884 there was a large increase in the number of wedding rings pawned.

Social investigator Anna Martin, who had great sympathy for the working-class women, wrote perceptively in 1911 that an important psychological reason why they handled the family finances, and indeed often opposed state intervention in family problems, was that

The women have a vague dread of being superseded and dethroned. Each of them knows perfectly well that the strength of her position in the home lies in the physical dependence of husband and children upon her, and she is suspicious of anything that would tend to under-mine this. The feeling that she is the indispensable centre of her small world is the joy and consolation of her life.

This is probably as true today as it was then, judging by the way women take full responsibility for the domestic chores and child care (even when they have full-time jobs outside the home) rather than insisting on sharing the burden equally with their husbands.

Between the upper and lower classes were the middle classes, who numbered about a quarter of the population. The men worked in business and the professions, and their prestige and income varied con-siderably. At the top were a small group of wealthy businessmen, lawyers and government servants who had incomes of £1,000 or more a year and lived as stylishly as the upper class. By 1867 roughly 10 per cent of middle-class families earned over £300 a year, 41 per cent earned between £100 and £300 (lower professions and smaller businessmen), and 49 per cent earned under £100 (small shopkeepers, clerks, schoolteachers). By comparison, highly skilled workmen earned between £50 and £73 a year. Obviously, it was difficult for those on the smaller incomes to keep up middle-class appearances, though they claimed the status.

There were two very different middle-class ideals of 'the perfect wife' or 'true womanhood'. One was held by men, the other by women, and they were incompatible. Yet both ideals continued side by side down the century, with most women pretending to be as men wished them to be, but at the same time developing their own identities. Men's idea was of a decoratively idle, sexually passive woman, pure of heart, religious and self-sacrificing. The most popular image was of an 'angel in the house', an ivy-like wife who was also a doting and self-abnegating mother, clinging to her husband on whom she was totally dependent. There is hardly an example of a novel written by a man before 1860, in which the principal woman character is not insignificant both in mind and body. Harriet Martineau quarrelled with Charles Dickens about his portrayal of women as 'viz. to dress well and look pretty, as an adornment for the homes of men'. It was women authors such as Jane Austen, Charlotte, Emily and Anne Brontë, and George Eliot who portrayed women of independent mind and strong passions. George Meredith was the first male writer to show he knew more of the female character (for instance in *The Egoist*, 1879), and what he did for fiction, Ibsen did for drama. They analysed women as people in their own right, not simply as adjuncts to men.

The number of wives who were decorative and idle was very small, since few were wealthy enough to employ servants to do all their housework and child care. Florence Nightingale complained that her mother was one such 'perfect lady', who could have organized an army, but preferred to do nothing. Yet the ideal of most middle-class wives was to organize their households as efficiently as their husbands organized their businesses, thus making a substantial contribution to the family's well-being and solvency, and also to become the morally superior partner in the marriage. In the period 1800 to 1840, in Evangelical Christian circles in particular, women established the home as their own sphere, claiming moral authority over religious and sexual matters. Most women believed what Sarah Lewis wrote in her influential book, *Women's Mission* (1839), that they needed to guard the citadel of respectability, to control men's passions and eliminate male profligacy. They had also to establish peace, love and unselfishness, not only for themselves and their children, but also for 'the poor, the ignorant, the domestic servant'. In short, women (particularly middle-class women) were to regenerate society (a mission which will be addressed later, when women's involvement in politics is considered). It was a tall order, but women accepted the challenge so as to justify their lives.

Household management grew in importance. As Isabella Beeton said in her *Book of Household Management*, published in 1861: 'As with the commander of an army or the leader of an enterprise, so it is with the mistress of the house. Her spirit will be seen through the whole establishment.' The middle classes expanded rapidly in number, as a result of industrialization. Many of the new recruits and their wives were born into the rural classes, and when they became middle class by occupation, moving to the towns to live, they were often unsure how to behave correctly. For them there was a growing number of books and magazines concentrating on practical and home-based subjects. In particular, the handling of servants was a problem for those with no prior experience of employing them. Isabella Beeton's book was intended for the upper middle class. The 1,172-page book gave information for 'the mistress, housekeeper, cook, kitchen-maid, butler, footman, coachman, valet, upper and under housemaids, lady's maid,

maid-of-all work, laundry maid, nurse and nurse-maid, monthly, wet and sick nurses etc.' and showed aspiring middle-class women how their betters conducted themselves. The book cost 7 shillings and 6 pence, (or more than half what an agricultural labourer earned in a week at that time) and more than 2 million copies of it were sold by 1870.

Most middle-class women took a large share in looking after their children, mending clothes and nursing the sick. Their houses were badly planned, with the kitchen in the basement, the dining room on the ground floor, the drawing room on the first floor, and the bedrooms on the second and third floors. By 1814, water-closets were in general use in gentlemen's houses, but in many homes a cesspit for effluvia persisted to the 1850s – it might be in the yard, or inside the house, even below the living-room floor (the contents had to be carried away in buckets by 'night men'). Running water, when it came, rarely ran above the basement; it was later piped up to the kitchen sink but had to be carried upstairs. Until around 1870 the bath or wash basin were portable affairs which had to be filled and emptied by maids. Houses were frequently plagued with mice, rats, bugs and flies. Even Buckingham Palace had need of bug destroyers. Yet there was such reverence for the home in Victorian society that housewives had considerable self-respect. Women were proud to be efficient housekeepers, and proud to be 'the power behind the throne' exercising indirect influence through their husbands. Popular conservative writers such as Sarah Ellis explained to them in detail *The Trials of Everyday Married Life* and how to deal with recalcitrant husbands. Women imposed their wills by sheer force of personality, by manipulative charm, by plain meanness or by claiming to be ill – invalid or hysterical women could wield formidable powers.

Yet many women were irked by their subordinate legal status, and the fact that their husbands controlled their property and their earnings. The campaign to reform the marriage law was a middle-class movement for the very good reason that these wives needed the reform, and they were articulate, affluent and informed enough to do something about it. They knew that the upper class had devised a private system of law to give rich married women control of their property, and they wanted similar protection for all women to be provided under public law. As the Manchester feminist Lydia Becker (1827–90) said:

What I most desire, is to see the married women of the middle classes stand on the same terms of equality as prevail in the working classes and the highest aristocracy. A great lady or a factory woman are independent persons – personages – the women of the middle classes are nobodies, and if they act for themselves they lose caste.

The reality of the law on property was sometimes made clear in unexpected ways, to people who had never questioned it before. Harriet Grote, wife of the banker and historian, was one day robbed of her watch and purse. When she appeared in court she was astonished to hear the purse described as belonging to Mr Grote. When the legal reason for this was explained to her, she was so indignant that she became a supporter of women's rights. Similarly, Millicent Garrett Fawcett, wife of a Liberal Member of Parliament and leader of the women's suffrage movement, had her purse snatched by a young thief in London in the 1870s, and he was charged with 'stealing from the person of Millicent Fawcett a purse containing £18.6d, the property of Henry Fawcett'. She recalled, 'I felt as if I had been charged with theft myself.'

Cases such as the following show just how bad things could be. A woman in the North of England whose husband had failed in business set up a fashionable millinery establishment, from the proceeds of which she kept herself and her husband and saved a fortune. When the husband died, he left a will by which he bequeathed his wife's property to his own illegitimate children. She was left in poverty. Yet another case was where a woman deserted by her husband had set up a successful laundry business and put her savings in a bank. Her husband heard she had done well, went to the bank and asked that his wife's stock be paid to him. Next time she went to the bank she found herself penniless.

A separate but related issue was a husband's right to his wife's earnings. This was a moral issue, but no more than an irritant to most women. For example, Elizabeth Gaskell said her husband banked the money she earned, once writing that 'William composedly buttoned up in his pocket' the cheque she received from *Household Words* for 'Lizzie Leigh'. Yet Elizabeth had remarkable independence and it is clear from her correspondence that she had the *disposal* of her earnings. The right to their earnings was a burning issue for women who had to keep themselves when their husbands deserted them. The successful writer Charlotte Elizabeth Phelan (afterwards Tonna), born in 1790, explained how her first husband, from whom she was separated, tried to get her large earnings for himself. Only the fact that she wrote under her Christian name, and not her husband's name, enabled a sympathetic judge to decide in her favour. Mrs Glover, who was abandoned by her husband in the 1840s, was less fortunate. She went on the stage in order to keep herself and her children, and became a celebrated actress. Eventually, her husband applied to the theatre manager to have her salary paid over to him. The manager refused and the case went to court, but the judge (expressing his regret) said the husband was entitled to the earnings since that was the law. It was said at the time, 'For the robbery by a man of his wife's hard earnings there is no redress.' For abominations such as these nothing but a change in the law would help, though Elizabeth Gaskell feared that even legislation could not protect a wife's property, writing to her friend Tottie Fox on Christmas Day, 1856, ' . . . a husband can coax, wheedle, beat or tyrannize his wife out of something and no law whatever will help that I can see.' Defenders of the *status quo* said, 'Why complain? Not one husband in a thousand ever takes advantage of the power it gives.' That was almost certainly true, and to some extent it explains why so few women took an active part in pushing for change. But reformers such as Caroline Cornwallis argued, 'No law can be good or wholesome which gives a bad man the liberty to do with impunity what a good man's conscience would prevent him from attempting.'

The unlikely heroine who began the campaign for reform was Barbara Leigh Smith (later Bodichon), the then unmarried daughter of a Radical Member of Parliament. She had a private income of £300 a year from her father, so she was not a dependent victim, but she was much moved by the plight of women less fortunate than herself. She published in 1854 her *Brief Summary, in Plain Language, of the Most Important Laws of England concerning Women*, pointing out how severely legally handicapped married women were. She let the facts speak for themselves, and they roused enormous interest, since most women appeared unaware of their true legal situation. A petition for change was sent to both Houses of Parliament in 1856, signed by 3,500 women including Elizabeth Barrett Browning, Jane Carlyle, Elizabeth Gaskell, Mary Howitt and Harriet Martineau.

Seventy other similar petitions were signed by 24,000 women.

Barbara Leigh Smith knew there would be difficulties, writing that 'Respect for the law, as something like revelation, is very general in England; women, especially, have a vague feeling that the law is often cruel, no doubt, but that it is in some mysterious way very right, and certainly unchangeable.' Change is what Barbara had in mind, but she and her supporters had no idea what bitter passions they would arouse, and how much personal abuse they would suffer when they asked for legislation that struck at society's notion of man and wife as one flesh. 'Is there a plague in England or Egypt worse than the strong-minded woman?' screamed the influential newspaper, the *Saturday Review*, and referred to them indelicately as 'a species of vermin'. It went on to say there was 'a smack of selfish independence' about the reform 'which rather jars with poetical notions of wedlock'. Needless to say, critics did not think it selfish for a husband to take possession of his wife's property and earnings.

A Reform Bill was presented to Parliament in 1857, by men sympathetic to the women's cause, but it failed to pass. This was a bitter disappointment, and it was to be many years before the issue was raised again. The Attorney-General said such a reform would tend to 'the placing of the women of England in a strong-minded and independent position which so few chose for themselves.'

Continuous pressure in the 1860s, by both men and women, led to the passing of the Married Women's Property Act of 1870, a halfhearted measure which gave a married woman the right to her own earnings, and to her personal property as an heiress, but gave rights in other property to her husband. Thus, the legal fiction of the unity of man and wife was kept firmly in place. Yet this measure was an advance on previous law. What led to later change was the fact that, as things stood, a married woman could not be sued for debt. To plug this loophole, in 1882 a further Act of Parliament gave a married woman 'all real and personal property' which belonged to her at the time of the marriage, or was acquired later. Middle-class husbands could by this time see considerable advantage in their wives holding separate property. For example, a husband's creditors could not claim for his debts against property held by the wife, and this became a family insurance against possible business disaster.

The 1882 Married Women's Property Act was far from perfect, and could not solve all the problems that married women faced, if it came to a showdown with their husbands. The practical applications of separate property rights are still being worked out in the late twentieth century. Yet these early reforms were some of the greatest achievements of the Victorian women's movement, in recognizing married women as independent persons, and subtly changing the power relationship between husbands and wives. Mary Wollstonecraft would have been pleased that some progress was being made towards making wives and husbands more equal, though there was still a long way to go.

5

Time of Their Own

WOMEN'S INTERESTS
AND ENTERTAINMENTS

The married woman can call but a very small portion of each day
her own . . . I hope I shall never incline to regard it as a misfortune.

Charlotte Brontë to her friend Ellen Nussey, 7 September 1854,
after her marriage to her father's curate, Arthur Nicholls

Whatever their social class, and however many servants they employed,
few women in nineteenth-century England were completely idle. Few,
on the other hand, however hardworking, had no time at all to do
as they pleased. Women spent their leisure time in a variety of pursuits,
depending on the kind of person each was, but women of all social
classes were preoccupied with dress. In the upper and middle classes
the variety and complexity of their clothes showed rank and position.
Every cap, bow, streamer, ruffle, fringe, bustle, glove and other
elaboration signalled some difference in status. It was said that
jewellery was 'a badge that women wore like a sergeant-major's stripes
or field marshal's baton'.

For the sake of being in fashion, a small waist and a straight back
were considered important, and even young girls were put into stiff new
stays. The scientist Mary Somerville complained of having to wear
stays at school, early in the century, and educationist Jane Ellen Harrison went through similar torture in the 1850s. Women endured having
their waists compressed, by tight lacing, to measure twenty-four inches,

or less. Corsets, which functioned as brassières and girdles in one, were made of whalebone stays and a wooden or whalebone busk (a stiff slat of about an inch wide running down the centre of the corset to keep it flat). By tightening the laces which held the corset together, women could achieve the very small waist that was the ideal of beauty. Doctors warned that tight lacing was producing stomach ulcers, gallstones, dislocation of the ribs, headaches, dizziness, curvature of the spine, lung disease and sickly offspring, but few women took any notice. Some young women still at school turned the wearing of corsets to their advantage; according to Cecily Steadman, a pupil at Cheltenham Ladies College in the 1870s:

> There was a minor ailment that gave some trouble, and that was the addiction of some girls to slight fainting fits. This was, I think, partly the consequence of measures taken in the hope of securing an eighteen-inch waist, and . . . some young people certainly contrived to accomplish a good deal of unconsciousness, and even to make it correspond to a surprising degree with unpopular homework.

In 1869 and 1870 the readers' advice columns of the *Englishwoman's Domestic Magazine* were filled with letters about the difficulties and advantages of tight lacing. One astonishing letter said:

> When my sisters were, the one sixteen, the other nearly two years younger, my mother considered it was time that their figures, hitherto unrestrained, should be subjected to some control and accordingly she laced them rather tightly in stiff new laces, both day and night. They tried the usual expedients of cutting laces, and so forth, at first, but were entirely frustrated by mamma procuring a steel belt, fitted with a lock and key, to be worn at night outside the corset.

Apparently, these girls were persuaded to accept tight lacing when they were given tiny-waisted riding-habits, but it was six months before they could fit into them.

Not everyone favoured tight lacing, however. The novelist Charlotte Elizabeth Tonna said that when she was young, early in the century, her clergyman father had absolutely forbidden her to wear stays; she never had, and to this she attributed her lifelong good health. The feminists Barbara Leigh Smith and her friend Bessie Rayner Parkes travelled in Europe on a sketching tour in 1850, when they were in their early twenties, and they joyously abandoned their corsets in favour of flowing dresses. Barbara once drew a diagram of the Venus de Milo, comparing her bust measurement with those of pigeon-chested Victorian women who had, she felt, sacrificed both health and natural grace to support an unnatural ideal. Working-class women wore tight lacing and stiff corsets only when they were dressing up for a night out or a special occasion, and on Sundays to go to church. When working in factory, field or home, they wore loose, comfortable clothing that did not impede their movements. At the end of the century, fewer women used tight lacing, but good corsets were still regarded as essential to preserve the figure, and bust-improvers were occasionally worn to give an hourglass look.

Fashionable dress came more and more to emphasise the ideal of women's dependence and weakness, as clothes became ever more constricting. At the beginning of the century, fashionable women wore Empire dresses which flowed in loose, soft lines from a high waist. The ideal of feminine beauty and deportment, for women of 'the quality', was extreme slimness, a pale complexion and slow languid movements. By the 1820s the fashion magazines showed tighter waists, more confining corsets and puffy skirts, aimed at the 'Perfect Lady' who was distinct from the 'Great Lady' of lineage, since she had roots in commerce and represented the affluent middle-class woman who was anxious to be ladylike. A note of sedate respectability was the mark of the new gentility. By the 1840s hair was often looped over the ears, as if to protect women from coarse sounds. The bonnet became more and more a shield to the face.

When Victoria came to the throne in 1837, wasp waists, moulded bosoms and rounded skirts were the rule. Underpants were not worn by women before the 1840s, and were at first slit at the crotch and down the inseams so that they did not resemble trousers, then a male prerogative. In the following decades affluent women continued to wear extravagant clothes which immobilized the body and used many yards of costly fabric. The sewing machine was invented in the 1850s and high fashion gradually ceased to be the luxury of the few. Crinolines came into being in 1856. At first no more than a skeleton petticoat of hoops, it was improved by using watch-spring in place of wire, and came to resemble a huge parrot cage. It was welcomed as a relief from the heavy layers of petticoats that women had previously worn, but was later criticized because it was difficult to sit down in it, and indecent when bending over. Lady Dorothy Nevill reported on the danger of standing too near a fire when wearing a crinoline:

> Somehow or other my voluminous dress caught fire, and in an instant I was in a blaze, but kept my head, and rolling myself in the hearthrug, by some means or other beat out and subdued the flames . . . None of the ladies present could do much to assist me, for their enormous crinolines rendered them almost completely impotent to deal with fire, and had they come very close to me, all of them would have been in a blaze too.

The period 1866 to 1880 was the golden age of the dressmakers' art. Never before or since has the Englishwoman's costume been so complex. Extravagant clothes were as complicated as art and craft could make them; utility, comfort, convenience, did not count. Bosoms were flattened and the rear was exaggerated under shaped horsehair or steel bustles. Fashions changed around 1887, getting rid of the bustle and simplifying skirts, but the sheaths and tubular skirts of the last decade of the century were still constricting. Sleeves varied dramatically down the century, but whether they were tight off the shoulder, puffy legs of mutton, layered pagoda frills or closely fitted, it was difficult for a woman to move her arms in them. 1896 saw the collapse of the inflated sleeve, and ladies' dresses became fluffy and frilly, undulating in waves around their feet. There was, however, an important 'alternative' dress reform movement co-existing with these complex, inconvenient fashions.

Fashionable dress was a sign of wealth and class importance. The height of fashion was worn by women who had servants to help them dress and keep their clothes clean, who walked on soft carpets, and who were rarely troubled by dirty pavements or the rain, because they travelled everywhere by private carriage. Even so, in those days when washing-machines were unknown, elaborate dresses were not usually washed, they were only sponged and pressed. The best dresses were protected by thick underwear and careful wearing and storage, but after being worn for some time even these were not sweet-smelling, and became progressively more rank as they were passed on to the second- and third-hand markets.

Lower middle- and working-class women dressed more practically than the well-to-do, of necessity. For everyday they wore shorter dresses, stouter shoes and layers of clothes to keep them warm. A new pair of shoes cost about six shillings, or the equivalent of a week's wages for many women. Their clothing was often bought second-hand, and often the poorest wives wore patched and mended clothes so that the men of the family (whose clothes were more expensive) could dress respectably. Some of the young factory girls who wanted to be more fashionable bought 'one-shilling crinolines' (cheap ones, but still quite an expense) or clubbed together for fancy accessories, such as ostrich feathers for hats, which they could all share. They were then criticized by middle-class moralists for dressing garishly or above their station, but smart clothes were obviously important to most women. Servants sometimes got cast-offs from their mistresses. A song of 1870, called 'The Lasses' Resolution to Follow the Fashion', said:

> The servant girls follow the fashions,
> As well as the best in the place:
> They'll dress up their heads like an owl, boys
> And will think it no shame or disgrace.
> They will bind up their heads with fine ribands,
> And a large bag of hair hangs behind;
> And when they do walk through the streets, boys,
> No peacock can touch them for pride.

Reformers first attempted to introduce healthier and more comfortable clothes in 1851, advocating the costume invented by Amelia Bloomer in America. The outfit was ridiculed because of its daringly trouserlike design. Fast ladies wore knickerbockers. In the 1880s the Rational Dress movement introduced the divided skirt, cut to clear the ground, and recommended abandoning corsets. Few women were brave enough to adopt these ideas, but loose, flowing, pseudo-medieval dress had been introduced into Bohemian circles by the Pre-Raphaelite painters and their models, and some women began to wear plainer dresses. The real change in women's fashions came in the 1890s, when an even simpler style of dress was introduced for middle-class women who rode on railways and omnibuses, walked on pavements, worked in offices and schools, and took more exercise.

Women's hobbies and leisure pursuits varied down the century according to their social class, their incomes and, of course, their personalities. As far as upper-class women were concerned, sexual laxity was not their only vice in the Regency period. Gambling was then at gigantic levels. Card games of chance, and games of dice, were played in all the leading clubs for high stakes, in an atmosphere of excitement and insecurity. Fortunes were won and lost in a night. Women were as addicted to gambling as were men. Georgiana, Duchess of Devonshire, married to one of the richest men in England, ran up such huge gambling debts that for a long time she dared not tell her husband, but he eventually rescued her with ill-grace. Heavy drinking accompanied the gambling, and was an accepted part of life. Aristocratic women in the Regency period enjoyed hunting, racing, horse breeding, cockfighting and dog fighting as much as did their menfolk. The love of breeding horses and hunting, such expensive hobbies that they are known as 'the sport of kings', continued down the century, and exists to this day. Some upper-class women enjoyed amateur theatricals, and reading novels and poetry. Byron had a host of such admirers.

Aristocratic women also liked to dance, but only with acceptable partners, so masked balls which hid identity fell into disfavour. A powerful group of patronesses, including Lady Castlereagh and Lady Jersey, took over the club Almack's (which had started as a set of subscription dances open to anyone who could afford to buy tickets) and began to apply strict criteria for entry and behaviour. It was said that even the Duke of Wellington was turned away for being five minutes late for a function there. Almack's became the most fashionable club in London, and to become a member was the ambition of every woman who wanted to be in 'society'. Up to 1813 English country dances, Scottish reels, minuets and gavottes were the main dances performed, but at the end of the Napoleonic Wars the French quadrille and German waltz were introduced, and fashionable London went crazy over them. Stuffy opposition to the waltz crumbled altogether when Tsar Alexander of Russia waltzed at Almack's in 1828.

Invitations to state balls at Buckingham Palace and other royal entertainments were much sought after throughout the century, as was the attendance of a member of the Royal Family at a dinner or other function in a private home. This could immediately 'make' a hostess's social reputation. The royal seal of approval, which put women on the inside track of society, continued to be a matter of supreme importance throughout Queen Victoria's reign, and continues so to this day, as can be seen from the constant jockeying throughout the world for invitations to functions attended by British royalty.

Throughout the century the upper class went to spa towns (also known as watering places) to relax and enjoy themselves and to 'take the waters' as a medicinal cure for their excessive eating and drinking habits, for they worshipped their stomachs. Cheltenham was a social and cultural centre which attracted both British and European nobility, ranging from Queen Victoria to French kings and Russian Grand Dukes. Bath had the most elaborate pattern of entertainments, with its own code of conduct, courtesies, privileges and round of events. Jane Austen gave detailed descriptions of the town and its social conventions in her novels *Northanger Abbey* and *Persuasion*. Bath's popularity waned as sea-bathing and the Prince Regent's enjoyment of Brighton increased. But 'taking the waters' in Bath and Cheltenham, as well as in Buxton, Scarborough and Harrogate, remained a popular (and necessary) thing for the rich to do.

The upper classes spent holidays in grand houses with friends or family, or they went abroad. Switzerland, France, Germany and Italy were the most favoured countries, though some romantic souls ventured to Greece, and a few invaded Turkey, Portugal, Hungary and the Middle East. Lady Dorothy Nevill was a noted traveller, and said later of her journeys on the Continent in the 1840s, 'You then saw the country through which you passed in its everyday, natural state, the people living their own lives in repose, unspoilt as yet by a constantly moving herd of travellers'. Lady Dorothy disliked the advancing tide of newly-rich people who wanted a share of the privileges she enjoyed.

Upper-class women set the fashions in clothes, manners, habits and hobbies, never doubting their superiority and right to lead, and most English people accepted their leadership without question. At the end of the century Lady Ottoline Morrell, daughter of the sixth Duke of Portland and in fact a critic of her class, said the unquestioning, unimaginative arrogance of aristocratic life had a power of impressing itself on her as 'The Thing'. And the American heiress Consuelo Vanderbilt, who had married the Duke of Marlborough, said it was difficult not to feel oppressed by upper-class assumption of superiority. By the end of the century Margot Asquith (the later Prime Minister's wife) and her set of friends called the 'Souls' gave society a slight shift of emphasis and made intellectual and artistic interests matter more. The Marchioness of Ripon (Gladys de Grey) was the first aristocratic patroness of Covent Garden Opera. Once a year she invited all its stars to a party as her personal guests, along with other titled friends, and she gave musical parties at her house, inviting performers such as the singers Melba and Caruso. She also helped to make the visit of Diaghileff's Russian ballet to London a success.

The 'middling sort' of English women were considerably influenced by the lifestyle of their 'betters', and they copied them as far as their purses allowed. Charlotte Brontë spoke for them when she wrote in the 1840s, 'I love high life. I like its manners, its splendours, the beings which move in its enchanted sphere'. At the top end of the middle class people merged with the fringes of society, which some tried desperately to enter. At the bottom they merged with the prosperous working class from which many of them had been recruited. The middle class was intolerant of infiltrators, and guarded its boundaries very carefully. There were infinite gradations of status, expressed not only in dress, style and location of house, number of servants, and possession of personal transport in the form of a riding horse, a carriage and pair, or a pony and trap, but also in the intangible rules about who spoke or bowed to, called on, dined with or intermingled with whom. It was the people immediately below and immediately above a particular layer who caused the most trouble in this respect.

Despite their aping of upper-class fashions, the middle class was very different from the aristocracy. For example, the latter tended to be irreligious. Religion was useful for keeping the masses in order, but there was little need, in their opinion, for *them* to have a personal saviour. They attended church to set a good example, and they appointed the clergy for political or personal rather than religious reasons. But religious belief really mattered to the middle class, even though religious observance was riddled with divisions and petty snobberies, and critics said that the women went to church only to show off their clothes. Those who lost their religious faith often went through agonies of conscience, as can be seen from the writings of George Eliot, for example. The Church of England was at the top of the religious hierarchy, though in some country villages in the North there was a Roman Catholic squire. Paradoxically, large numbers of the working class were Anglicans or Catholics. The Quakers and Unitarians came next to the Church of England, followed by the Congregationalists, the Baptists, and the Methodists. In Anglican parish churches and some fashionable chapels, upper- and middle-class members rented pews where they could be separated from other worshippers.

The middle classes were the money-making section of society, and their vices were not those of the fashionable world or the sporting gentry. The women generally had no opportunity to indulge in extramarital love affairs, and few men or women wasted their money on gambling or drinking. The social lives of most women consisted of exchanging calls, visits and parties with friends of their own station in life. The more worldly went to dances and parties in local assembly rooms, and some had space in their homes for dancing and amateur theatricals. They supported the straight theatre, musical concerts, opera and ballet, and liked spectacular shows and firework displays, though the more puritanical had no time for dancing or play-acting. The music which played so large a part in family life was the singing of ballads, hundreds of which were published every year. The middle class crowded to hear travellers tell of far-off lands, and found lantern lectures as enthralling as we find the cinema. They enjoyed panoramas (a series of large pictures painted on canvas which was unrolled before the audience), dioramas (a more elaborate form of a panorama) and cosmoramas (a kind of peepshow). The dioramas were sometimes called dissolving views. A child of ten who saw one of them in 1840 wrote fifty years later, 'I can still recollect the feeling of awe and wonder as I watched a storm over the painted mountains give way to sunshine.'

Shopping was always a source of entertainment for women. A wealthy woman went shopping in her carriage; the middle-class woman took public transport or a cab, or walked. The shops were open every day but Sunday, and remained open until there appeared to be no probability of further custom. The Victorian woman could buy anything she liked in London, and provincial shops followed the fashions as soon as they could. The world sent its wares to London: silks and spices from the East, teas from China and India, wool from Kashmir. Most shops were small, with bow-fronted windows, until the end of the century when some larger department stores were opened. There were drapers selling flowered brocades, shawl shops, the lace-man and the embroiderer, the bonnet shop, the glove shop, the stay-maker, the grocer and the tea merchant, furniture shops, dairies, the apothecary, the china warehouse and the sweetmeat shop. Outside the shops were street vendors of all kinds, selling everything from bread and milk, fruit and vegetables, to baskets, brooms and brushes.

Whereas the upper-class woman filled her life with grand social events, the ordinary middle-class woman occupied much of her leisure time at home with needlework and knitting. She took pride in fine plain sewing. Patchwork was popular, and often a family affair, as a letter of 1850 indicated: 'Mama, Louise, Barbie and I finished the setting together of my patch bedcover. I am so pleased!' Berlin-work, a form of fancy embroidery, was fashionable in the middle of the century, and magazines gave instructions for making mats, chair seats and sofa backs. Fringe making was a ladylike occupation, together with bead-work on velvet. There was a lot of crochet work, making of antimacassars and doilleys, and also popular were netting and tatting. Both were done with a small shuttle. Purses were netted in silk and lined in a contrasting colour. Tatting produced a fine crochet effect, and was used for cuffs and collars and the 'falls' which trimmed the sides of a stylish cap. A woman of independent mind with a taste for politics might find sewing intolerably boring, but a surprising number of what we would now call feminists seemed to enjoy it. Harriet Martineau, for example, boasted that she could make shirts, and writer Dinah Mulock insisted that the neatest needlewomen were 'ladies whose names the world cons over in library lists and Exhibition catalogues.'

The middle-class woman spent several hours a week in regular letter-writing, especially to family members living at a distance. It was a less expensive pastime after the Penny Post was introduced in 1840. Writing letters to friends was an important and positive safety valve for many women. But how were they able to write special confidences about their marital relations to their friends and relatives if, like Elizabeth Gaskell or Jane Carlyle, their husbands read all their letters before they sent them? Elizabeth and Jane both waited until their husbands were away from home and then wrote in secret to their sisters-in-law. Later in the century Henrietta, wife of T.H. Huxley, poured out her troubles to her sister-in-law Lizzie in the United States. When in 1899 Elspeth Thomson married the writer Kenneth Grahame (author of *The Wind in the Willows*) she found a husband set in his bachelor ways who could not adjust to a wife. For advice she wrote to Thomas Hardy's wife Emma, who responded by telling the wrongs she in her turn had suffered.

Sketching and drawing were popular, but reading was the major interest for most women. Florence Nightingale said in an autobiographical sketch, *Cassandra* (1852), that she believed all middle- and upper-class women indulged in day-dreams; they were 'women's plans and visions . . . indeed, their very life, without which they could not have lived,' and their dreams were fed by what they read. Circulating libraries brought the latest novels to those who could not afford to buy them in monthly parts. An enormous number of novels were written especially for women: society novels, tales of mystery, highly coloured romances. Characters of independent mind were much admired: females in Jane Austen's works took risks and did not always suffer. Charlotte Brontë's Jane Eyre was passionate, proud and independent. Emily Brontë's Catherine Earnshaw in *Wuthering Heights* did not give a fig for the conventions of the day. Up to the 1840s there were annuals such as *The Keepsake* and *The Album Wreath*, handsomely bound books edited by fashionable women such as the Countess of Blessington and the Hon. Caroline Norton, which sold by the thousand. Contributors included Elizabeth Barrett Browning, Thackeray and Dickens. For more general reading the monthly magazines such as *La Belle Assemblée* had big sales. *The Englishwoman's Domestic Magazine,* edited by Samuel Beeton, first appeared in 1852 and soon had a huge circulation; comparatively inexpensive, it was aimed at a middle-class market. These magazines published stories, poems, reviews of current books, critical notes on concerts and plays, and articles on travel, music, painting and science. The subjects were set out at length and seriously discussed. *Eliza Cook's Journal* dealt with movements for social reform, the housing problem, sweated industries, child factory labour, ragged schools, public health and hygiene. Only one subject was avoided by the magazines, and that was religious doubts arising from the new discourse in science.

This discourse centred on the publication of Charles Darwin's *Origin of Species* (1859), which undermined the belief that God had created the world in six days, suggested to some that a Creator had not been involved at all, and also challenged previously held ideas on the age of the world. Creationism versus Darwinism (the evolution of the species and the survival of the fittest) continues to be a burning issue for some Christians to this day.

Improving books like *The Young Wife's Companion* were also immensely popular. Discerning editors realized that middle-class women were cut off from family networks, as affluence and better transport enabled them to live in outlying suburbs. It was difficult for them to make close friends from whom they could ask personal advice, and they were often insecure about what was normal and acceptable behaviour. These magazines raised standards of housekeeping and child-rearing because their advice was solicited, welcomed and followed. Of course, the magazines also persuaded women to purchase new things. Women were, then as now, the target for advertisers who realized their power as consumers. Women were not slow to accept the wonders of technology. Laments in the 1850s that the sewing machine would destroy handicraft failed to impress women who hated sewing and mending, and they welcomed innovations such as gas lighting, gas cookers, and piped water as emancipation from boring chores. Those who thought women should stick with the old ways were regarded as conspiring to keep them in domestic bondage.

The sensational fiction of the 1860s recorded family patterns in which hatred and contempt were so deep-rooted that accommodation among its members was impossible. Marriage was portrayed as a cage, and heroines expressed hatred for husbands, parents and siblings. Stories of domestic murder were common, and women lined up at Mudie's Select Circulating Library for bestsellers such as Mary Braddon's *Lady Audley's Secret* (1862) and Rhoda Broughton's *Cometh Up as a Flower* (1867). Reviewing this sensational fiction in 1864, Justin McCarthy noted that 'The institution of marriage might almost seem to be . . . just now upon its trial.' Women in these novels who went off the rails invariably came to a bad end, but sinners got a good run for their money and were rarely wholly unattractive characters. Against this background, Ruskin's famous essay 'Of Queen's Gardens' (1864), which sentimentalized women, portraying them as angels, seems a kind of desperate propaganda.

The coming of the railways in the 1830s made travel much easier and cheaper, and it was enjoyed by almost everyone. The Queen loved it, and Lady Holland so relished her trips she had the Great Western trains slowed down to twenty miles an hour to suit her convenience. Travel abroad by the middle classes was well established by the 1840s, France and Germany being well within their means. The family seaside holiday became fashionable after Queen Victoria bought a house in the Isle of Wight in 1845, so that her children could play on the sands. The wealthy travelled in upholstered first-class railway carriages, the less wealthy in comfortable second class. There was also plenty of accommodation in the cheap third class, for the lower middle and prospering artisan classes who would be the railway companies' steadiest customers. New railway lines were built in all directions, and coastal villages set out to attract holiday makers, allowing private speculators to build rows of houses to let as the lodgings that most families wanted. They bought their own food, which was cooked by the landlady. Landladies were notoriously dishonest; one diarist wrote, 'We should be tolerably comfortable here, save that Mrs T— is undoubtedly cutting at our ham.' Hotels and boarding houses provided food, and were patronized by the more affluent, but Jane Carlyle for one had many complaints about their poor service, calling one in Ryde during the 1840s 'the dearest hotel in Europe,' and saying, 'I had to make tea from an urn, the water of which was certainly not as hot as one can drink it; and the cream was blue milk, the butter tasted of straw, and the cold fowl was a lukewarm one, and as tough as leather.' Her next complaint was from Carlisle, where she said, 'I have fallen among bugs! My neck was all bitten infamously.' This was a common complaint from travellers, since the hotel-keepers' attitude was that bugs were inevitable, and clients must protect themselves as best they could.

The bathing machine, which came into use at the end of the eighteenth century, was an essential part of the bathing ritual. A changing hut on wheels, it was pushed into the sea with the bather inside, who then descended the steps, at the sea end, sometimes under an awning. The bather was then 'dipped' by a bathing-woman, a strong matron with bare legs and hitched-up skirt. The women wore sacklike bathing dresses that had a peculiar tendency to ride up and reveal bare bottoms as the women sported in the waves. In what we consider an age of prudery, it is startling to discover that many people bathed in the nude, at the seaside or in lakes. In 1858, the wealthy Rothschild family was at Scarborough, a high-class seaside resort, and one of the daughters discovered nudity 'in the full glare of the day and sunshine.' She noted in her journal, 'Here is complete absence of costume as in the garden of Eden before the fall of man, and hundreds of ladies and gentlemen look on, while the bathers plunge in the foaming waters, or emerge from them.' She thought it scandalous, and that the police should interfere, but the latter wisely left the bathers alone. In 1857 the puritanical Marquis of Westmeath tried to introduce into Parliament a bill to prevent women from bathing nude, but it got nowhere, and the practice was common up to the 1870s, when Victorian prudery finally introduced what the Revd Francis Kilvert described in 1876 as 'the new-fangled fashion for bathing in drawers'.

Upper- and middle-class women of energetic temperament managed to get plenty of exercise. Riding was the most popular form, and those who did not own a horse could hire one inexpensively. Women rode side-saddle, and the riding habits they wore were extremely impractical, if not dangerous. The skirt was so voluminous that if the rider took a fall, it was likely to get entangled in the stirrups and drag her along the ground. Skating was popular throughout the century, and the fact that ice could be artificially manufactured by the century's end made the sport possible in summer as well as winter. Also, as a writer in *The Ladies' Treasury* remarked, 'the attractiveness of skating is due to opportunities it affords of a little quiet flirtation'. The game of croquet reached the height of its vogue in the 1860s, though in a story of 1850 there is a reference to a young woman who took all eyes at afternoon parties because 'she played a fierce game of croquet'. In the 1890s drawings of young women energetically rowing on a river suggest that layers of petticoats did not deter them. Skittles, or ninepins, was another popular pastime, but the most elegant sport was archery, popular for 'its eminent gracefulness, and for its being adapted to every age and every degree of strength, for by altering the strength of the bows it may be practised from childhood to green old age.' Archery meetings were favourite social events, as much enjoyed by spectators as participants. Lawn tennis became popular from the 1870s, and many middle-class homes had their own courts so that they could hold tennis parties. When the safety bicycle arrived in the 1890s it was popular with women of all social classes, since it was not very expensive to buy, and it was acceptable for women to cycle around the countryside without chaperones.

A major concern of nineteenth-century middle-class moralists was to tame the pastimes popular with ordinary people. It is difficult for us today to regret this, considering the brutal and callous nature of much of it, though we should note that concern about cruelty to animals was expressed far earlier than concern about cruelty to children. Throughout the Regency period, men and women of both the upper and the lower orders (but not the middle classes) chose leisure activities that were cruel or sensational. They watched bare-fisted boxing, wrestling, cock-throwing, cock-fighting, and bear- and bull-baiting. They also liked the pantomime, circuses, early music hall in the form of a 'free and easy' (where drinking was the main activity) and visiting the pleasure gardens. Vauxhall Gardens and Cremorne Gardens in London, which offered dancing, drinking, refreshments, a maze, a miniature zoo and endless other amusements, and where large numbers of prostitutes congregated, were still popular at mid-century. Sexual permissiveness, drink and riot were associated with popular festivals, fairs and other recreations, these being lightly policed and little regulated. Some clergymen felt that the 'common people' required such intervals of relaxation from their hard lives, but others felt manners and morals had sunk too far. However, in the long war against blood sports it was the activities of ordinary people that were suppressed. Bear- and bull-baiting were considered pointless and cruel, and were the first to go. Next were contests that were a focus of gambling, like cock-fighting and dog-fighting. Those that could be defended as a way of killing edible species (such as shooting game) or keeping down pests (such as hunting foxes or badgers) survived as predominantly upper-class sports to the present day.

Respectable working men and women distanced themselves from the rough poor and from their noisy and vulgar celebrations and pastimes, concentrating on family and church or chapel activities and the more middlebrow concert halls and theatres. In country areas they were generally more concerned than the gentry to control alehouses, discourage idleness and present sinners to church courts.

In the towns, poor people were free from the suffocating atmosphere and pressures of small communities. There were lots of entertainments, and the freedom to do as one pleased unless it was illegal. However, the radical tailor, Francis Place, made an extensive study of popular manners and was convinced that a virtual revolution had taken place by the end of the 1820s. He said drunkenness, improvidence, uncleanliness, theft, gambling, violence, promiscuity, coarse language and an addiction to obscene songs were by then confined to an underworld of the poor. But in fact fairs were commonplace throughout the century, and audiences were rowdy and riotous.

The penny theatres or 'gaffs' of London, which existed between 1830 and 1890, were for young working-class men and women. There were cheap circuses or penny equestrian shows, and sometimes plays performed by strolling actors. The shows were performed in regular playhouses, saloons and fairground booths. In terms of total audiences for theatre, the middle-class West End theatregoer was in a minority, far exceeded by these working-class audiences. Moral reformers objected to 'the worldly-wise little factory girls' who came to be entertained at the penny gaff, though some with little common sense believed the women did not 'take' (understand) the jokes or *double entendres*.

The rapid expansion of cheaper music-hall entertainment in late Victorian London, soon to become a prototype of the modern mass entertainment industry, put an end to penny theatres. The emphasis in the 1840s was on drinking at 'free and easy' music halls, but later on music halls were advertised as family entertainment, and by the 1890s many did not sell alcohol at all. As early as the 1860s men would take their wives to certain music halls without the women feeling demeaned. 'I think the model music hall is the Canterbury Hall, where you see artisans and small shopkeepers with their wives and families . . . it is quite a godsend to the wife and family to get out of their dull homes,' said author Frederick Guest Tomlins to the Select Committee on Theatrical Licences and Regulations, in 1866. But a few years later Thomas Wright described 'the roughs sitting in the gods' (the galleries of theatres) as 'those who came with unwashed faces and dirty attire, who brought bottles of drink with them, who would smoke despite the notices . . . and were the most noisy.' The females, he said, were generally accompanied by infants who were sure to cry and make a disturbance at some interesting part of the performance. By the 1880s many theatres had raised their prices so as to exclude the very poor.

The attitude of a respectable working-class woman towards the rowdy music hall can be seen from these comments by Mrs Layton:

> The Co-operative Women's Guild altered the whole course of my life. When I look back and think what my life might have been without its training and influence, I shudder. I was living in a house with two other families whose only ideas in life were work and sleep, and, for recreation, a visit each evening to the public house or a cheap music hall. They tried very hard to induce me to go with them, and possibly if I had not been connected with the Guild, when my baby died I might have fallen a victim to the drink habit.

Public houses were intended for men, though women were there as barmaids and entertainers. Women who drank alone in pubs were regarded as whores, unless they were very old. Some women bought drink from the off-licence of the pub and drank at home. A minority of women, strong-willed and determined, decided to join their husbands in their drinking, as Kathleen Dayus's mother did in Birmingham around 1910:

> 'Mine's a pint!' she called out to Dad. Everyone stopped talking . . . they all knew what Mum was like when she was in one of her moods . . . Dad came over to her and gave her a pint . . . She tipped her head back and drank it down. Dad was always giving in to her when she was in a bad mood . . . Today I realise why she was like she was. It must have been a terrible ordeal for her and the rest of the women who had to live in one room and two bedrooms and bring up thirteen and even more children.

Down the century poorer women read, or had read to them, first the street ballads, broadsheets and chapbooks sold by pedlars, which were often sensational but some of which contained socially-conscious material, then unstamped journals such as Cobbett's *Twopenny Trash*, popular Sunday newspapers and penny novelettes. According to a contemporary, in 1828 *Bell's Weekly Messenger* was 'a most entertaining newspaper, full of accidents – charity sermons – markets – boxing – Bible societies – horse-racing – child murders – the theatres – foreign wars – Bow-street [police] reports.' In the 1840s and 50s the weekly magazines the *London Journal* and the *Family Herald* dominated the mass market, selling three-quarters of a million copies per week between them. They cost a penny a copy. In the 1850s the elimination of the stamp tax made newspapers competitive. There were public libraries and inexpensive reprints of new novels, as well as special interest magazines. By the 1890s, when many more women could read, penny magazines such as *Forget-Me-Not* were rivalling the penny novelettes in popularity, and the *Daily Mail* newspaper, started in 1896, had a section for women readers.

English people of different status took their pleasures separately, in the company of their social equals, and that also applied to seaside holidays. In 1813 cartloads of both the middle and working classes came on summer Sundays to Poulton-le-Sands, later known as Morecambe. They were visitors out for the day from nearby towns like Lancaster. Blackpool in 1824 had visitors from all social classes, but after 1835 the rowdy day trippers (and the overnight stayers called 'padjamers') who arrived by train, bringing their own food and spending little except on drink, drove out the better class of visitor. From the 1870s and 80s, when a rise in real wages made holidays possible for many workers, Blackpool became the working-class playground of the North. Southend was the workers' paradise in the South, and Rhyl was that of North Wales. The differences between resorts were striking. The higher-toned had expensive hotels, classical concerts, art galleries and museums; the lower-toned had cheap boarding houses, brass bands, donkey rides, beach entertainments and catchpenny amusements. Each social class amused itself in its own way, and women enjoyed their outings and holidays just as much as men.

The more respectable type of day tripper – both women and men – went on excursions organized by Thomas Cook from 1841. Cook was the secretary of a temperance association, and he began what was to become an enormous tourist industry by providing transport from Leicester, by train, to a temperance demonstration in another town. The success of this led him to organize trips to London for the Great Exhibition of 1851, and to Paris for the Exhibition of 1855. He then persuaded respectable working women and men to save for holidays through their savings clubs.

Despite the appalling physical conditions of their lives, the rough working class who had no money to spare for newspapers or holidays were by no means all dejected or downcast, and the women were often as raucous, riotous and roistering as the men. They expected a short life, but strove for a merry one if they could get it. Beatrice Webb said of the Whitechapel tenants of a housing block she managed in 1885, 'They seem light-hearted enough, in spite of misery and disease' and of casual workers she said they were 'drunken, thieving and loose in their morality' but also 'generous hearted and affectionate'. She was uncomfortable among the street crowds, saying their 'ceaseless, sensual laugh, coarse jokes and unloving words' depressed her, as did 'the regular recurrence of street sensations, quarrels and fights; the greedy street-bargaining and the petty theft and gambling'. She called it a 'monotonous and yet excited life' and thought the bright side of East End life was the sociability and the generous sharing of small means.

To be a respectable working-class woman meant not living a riotous life, not drinking or gambling or using bad language, not going in for rough sports and pastimes, and not getting into debt. Respectability meant having a good self-image, dressing modestly and keeping up reasonable appearances. The lives of these women seemed drab and colourless to outsiders unable to understand the satisfaction and sense of moral superiority it gave those who kept their distance from the roughs. They approved of organized religion, and Christianity provided an ethical framework for life. Church or chapel services, especially emotional ones such as those of the Methodists, and activities such as Bible classes or the temperance movement's Band of Hope, were very important in the lives of women who eschewed music halls, pubs, dance halls and other places of entertainment. Salvation was especially high drama, climaxing in the moment of redemption – the sinner saved, the taking of the true path of righteousness, the coming of Christ and the acclamation of the congregation. To be counted among the saved brought many women happiness, a cheerful conviction that in God's providence there was a place for everyone, however humble, and that each individual was part of God's plan for the universe.

In the nineteenth century, married women's interests and activities, both inside and outside the home, varied tremendously according to their social class and personality. What cannot be denied is that wives of all social classes found some room to follow their own inclinations, within the narrow limits imposed on them by law and custom, unless they found themselves in impossibly unhappy relationships with their husbands. Then their lives could be sheer hell, as will be shown in the next chapter.

6

Punch and Judy

HOLY DEADLOCK,
SEPARATION AND DIVORCE

I do not ask for my rights. I have no rights. I have only wrongs.

Caroline Norton, *Letter to the Queen* (1855)

The notion that a man's wife is his PROPERTY is the fatal root of incalculable evil and misery.

Frances Power Cobbe (1878)

The inferior position of married women was made crystal clear in the laws of nineteenth-century England. The laws were made only by men, since women could not be members of either the House of Lords or the House of Commons, and they could not even vote for a parliamentary candidate who might change the law to their advantage. In the law courts to which a woman might apply for redress of her wrongs, the judges, magistrates, barristers, solicitors, legal clerks, jurors and police were all men. When a woman appeared in court – as plaintiff, victim, witness or defendant – she stood alone in a man's world. Justice was administered according to a male view of her rights, and of how she ought to behave. It seemed appropriate that justice was portrayed as a blindfolded woman, since her scales were so tilted in favour of men. Nonetheless, few married couples seem to have spent time worrying about the law, as long as they chose to live together and make the best of good times and bad. When husbands and wives fell out, however, it rapidly became clear that the man had the upper hand. Conflict in marriage could erupt into extreme discord and even violence, whatever the social class of the combatants, as the following cases show.

The unfortunate Nellie Weeton demonstrated the hell of being married to a harsh and selfish man. After working for some years as a governess, she had saved for and bought a cottage which brought her an income of £75 a year. In 1814 she married Aaron Stock, owner of a small factory in Wigan. Nellie had a daughter in 1815, but the following year she wrote, 'My husband is my terror, my misery. I have little doubt he will be my death.' Two years later she wrote, 'Bitter have been the years of my marriage, and sorrowful my days', and in June 1818, 'Turned out of doors into the street. In the anguish of my mind I broke out into complaints; this was my only fault . . . My principal ground of complaint is being kept so totally without money, at times when he is angry with me.' Nellie objected to having no access to her own hard-earned income, for when she married that income passed to her husband. After a reconciliation, Aaron Stock gave his daughter by a previous marriage charge over the house, did not generally allow his wife to speak when sitting with him in the parlour, and constantly threatened to turn her out again. He had her arrested on the grounds that she had struck him, and if her friends had not arranged bail she might have been sent to a house of correction. She managed in 1820 to get a deed of separation by which her husband allowed her £50 a year – less than the income she had brought to the marriage. She had to agree not to live within three miles of Wigan, and was allowed to see her child only three times a year, because legal custody belonged to the father. Her husband put so many obstacles in the way of even these few meetings that in 1823 Nellie said she had not seen her child for twelve months. Only when the daughter was grown up were she and her mother reunited.

Another abused wife was Caroline Norton (1808–77), a society beauty with no personal fortune who at age nineteen married into the aristocracy. Her husband George, a brother of Lord Grantley, was a jealous and vindictive bully who beat her. He was also a lawyer and well aware of his legal rights as a husband. Caroline wrote of her early married life:

> The treatment I received as a Wife would be incredible if, fortunately (or unfortunately) there were not witnesses who can prove it on oath

. . . We had been married about two months, when, one evening, after we had all withdrawn to our apartments, we were discussing some opinion Mr Norton had expressed; I said (very uncivilly) that 'I thought I had never heard so silly or ridiculous a conclusion.' This remark was punished by a sudden and violent kick; the blow reached my side; it caused great pain for many days, and being afraid to remain with him, I sat up the whole night in another apartment.

This kind of behaviour continued for nine years, and on several occasions Caroline left her husband and took refuge with her mother and sisters. She returned because Norton begged her to, and because she could not legally take her three sons away from their father. George Norton was constantly short of money, and Caroline earned substantial sums of money from literary work – editing fashionable women's magazines and writing poetry, plays and novels – which she spent on household expenses. At the end of 1835, when Caroline was visiting her relatives after a painful quarrel with her husband, he sent the children to stay with his cousin, who refused to allow Caroline to see them. Norton then brought an action against Lord Melbourne, the Prime Minister, for 'criminal conversation' with Caroline (a euphemism for adultery), hoping for a money settlement and grounds for divorce. It was a farcical case, though Caroline had long been friendly with Melbourne. There was no real evidence at all, and although Caroline was not allowed to appear in her own defence the case was soon dismissed.

When the Nortons finally separated, George refused to tell Caroline where the children were living. He evaded a court order which said he must allow his wife access to them, by taking them to Scotland where they were not subject to the jurisdiction of English courts. Caroline, who was the granddaughter of the playwright Richard Brinsley Sheridan, was socially well-connected and she had no intention of having her sufferings overlooked. She began a campaign to change the law on child custody, writing in 1837 a pamphlet called *The Natural Claim of a Mother in the Custody of her Child as affected by the Common Law Right of the Father*, which included evidence she had collected of cases worse even than her own. Her main supporter was Serjeant Talfourd, a Member of Parliament of progressive outlook, who had long been disturbed by the terrible cases of misery and injustice he had seen in the courts, where badly treated women were deprived of their children through no fault of their own. His first Bill passed the Commons but was thrown out by the Lords. Caroline was determined to get the Lords to consider a second Bill more objectively, and she wrote another pamphlet, *A Plain Letter to the Lord Chancellor on the Infant Custody Bill*, protesting against laws which gave a father undivided custody over his children when parents were separated. She signed the pamphlet with a man's name, knowing this would carry more weight with male readers, and sent it to each member of the House of Lords. Its logical presentation of facts and clear arguments had the effect she hoped for: the Lords passed the Bill, and it became law in 1839. It was a limited measure – giving a court power to grant a mother access to her infant children, and custody of those under seven years of age (though these rights were forfeit if the woman had committed adultery) – but it removed one of the chief reasons that had previously coerced a wife into remaining under the roof of a cruel or vicious husband. The writer Harriet Martineau described the Act as the first to strike a blow at the oppression of wives under English law.

Caroline still had a long struggle to see her children regularly, and one of them died before she finally won her fight:

> Mr Norton yielded – simply so far as the law would have compelled him . . . I saw my children in the most formal and comfortless manner. His cruel carelessness was afterwards proved, on a most miserable occasion. My youngest child, then a boy of eight years old, left without care or overlooking, rode out with a brother but little older than himself, was thrown, carried to the house of a country neighbour, and died of lock jaw, consequent on the accident. Mr Norton allowed the child to lie ill for a week – indeed to be at death's door – before he sent to inform me . . . Lady Kelly (who was an utter stranger to me) met me at the railway station. I said, 'I am here – is my boy better?' 'No,' she said, 'he is not better – he is dead.' And I found, instead of my child, a corpse, already coffined. Mr Norton asked my forgiveness then, as he had asked it often before . . . and then he buried our child, and forgot both his sorrow and his penitence.

Caroline's trials and tribulations with her husband were to continue. When separated from her, he successfully claimed a legacy left her by her father, which had not been legally secured to her separately, but was unable to get his hands on a legacy properly settled on her by her mother, so he stopped paying her the maintenance allowance he had agreed to make voluntarily. He kept property left by his wife in their home, including gifts made to her by her own family. He even subpoenaed her publishers under common law to hand over her earnings to him, and confiscated them for his own use. Caroline wrote later:

> My husband has taught me, by subpoenaeing my publishers to account for my earnings, that my gift of writing was not meant for the purposes to which I have hitherto applied it . . . It was meant to enable me to rouse the hearts of others to examine into all the gross injustices of these laws, to ask the nation of gallant gentlemen whose countrywoman I am, for once to hear a woman's pleading on the subject . . . I deny that this is my personal cause – it is the cause of all the women of England . . . Meanwhile my husband has a legal lien on the copywright of my works. Let him claim the copywright of this!

By 1855 Caroline had not received any money from her husband for three years, and she did the only thing she could in the circumstances – she ran up bills for food and clothes and told creditors to sue her husband for payment.

The astonishing thing is that, despite the fact that all her problems arose from the man-made laws relating to married women, Caroline Norton denounced the 'wild and stupid theories' of equal rights for women, asserting that by her actions she put forward 'no absurd claim of equality', and said 'I, for one (I with millions more), believe in the natural superiority of man as I do in the existence of God.' It is not credible that she really felt inferior to her vicious husband, but she knew better than to say so outright, for fear of alienating the male Members of Parliament whose help she needed.

The Infant Custody Act of 1839 gave women separated from their husbands some right to see their children, but a mother could be excluded altogether from the guardianship of her children, in favour of someone appointed by her husband. In 1840 the Lord Chancellor considered the following case. G.H. Talbot, a Roman Catholic, married a Protestant woman. They had two children, John and Augusta. By a deed of separation between the parents it was agreed that Augusta should remain with her mother until the age of ten. The father died, having by will appointed a Roman Catholic priest to be guardian of his children, who were then made wards of court. The mother remarried a Mr Berkeley, a Protestant. The guardian put John in the care of his uncle, the Earl of Shrewsbury, who refused to allow him to visit his mother. The court was asked to decide whether Augusta might continue to live with her mother, and whether John could visit his mother. Lord Cottenham said the mother 'had no right to interfere with the testamentary guardian', but since the girl was delicate and the late father had wished her to stay with her mother until she was ten, he would leave her there. As for the boy, the mother should have access to him only at Lord Shrewsbury's house, and in the guardian's presence.

The father of a legitimate child was legally the sole parent, even though the law imposed on the mother, under criminal and other penalties, liabilities and obligations almost equal to those of the father. The *Westminster Review* of January 1872 reported a painful scene in the Court of Justice when the Revd Henry Newenham applied for custody of his two daughters, Adelaide and Edith, who were under the care of their mother, Lady Helena Newenham, and her father, Lord Mountcashel. The older girl was nearly sixteen (the age at which she was legally a free agent) so she was allowed to exercise her free choice and stay with her mother, but the judge ordered that the seven-year-old girl should be 'delivered up to her father'. The child was brought into court by an officer, screaming and struggling, and exclaiming, 'Don't send me away. Will mamma ever see me again? Grandpa, grandpa, where are you?' Mr Justice Fitzgerald assured her that her mamma would see her often, and when the child asked, 'Will it be every day?' he said, 'yes.' But Lord Mountcashel said, 'Knowing what I know, that is impossible. He is a devil.' However, the child was handed over to her father, who carried her out. The newspaper report of this case touched the hearts of many mothers who had been unaware of the law. Only with the passing of the Guardianship of Infants Act of 1886 was the situation changed. This stipulated that the welfare of the child should be taken into full consideration, and thus undermined the father's assumed right to custody. The Act also permitted the mother to be sole guardian to her children when her husband died.

In theory, a married woman's body belonged to her husband, and he could enforce his right to her domestic and sexual services by a writ of habeas corpus. For example, Mrs Cochrane lived with her husband on apparently good terms for three years after their marriage, but in May 1836 she took their children and went to live for the next four years with her mother. Her husband lured her back to his house, ostensibly to discuss a separation, but then refused to let her leave. Mrs Cochrane asked for the court's protection, but the judge ordered her to stay with her husband, saying that providing he was not cruel he had the right to confine her, and that 'there could be no doubt of the general dominion which the law of England attributes to the husband over the wife.' Not all judges agreed, however. In 1852 Mrs Sandilands left her husband, and the latter applied for a writ of habeas corpus against his son-in-law, with whom she was living. The husband's lawyer argued that she could not be considered to have a will apart from that of her husband, any more than a child can have a will apart from that of its parents. But the judge, Lord Campbell, refused to accept this argument, saying that although a parent had a right to custody of a child, the husband had no such right to the custody of his wife.

An Act of 1884 gave a woman certain rights over her person, in that it removed the danger of a prison sentence if she refused to return to live with her husband; his remedy was to try to get a legal separation on the grounds of her desertion without reasonable cause. But the Act did not wholly dispose of a husband's right to keep his wife in his home by force. Not until 1891 was that right struck down, by the Court of Appeal, in the case of Mrs Jackson. She had gone to live with relatives during the absence of her husband in New Zealand, and refused to rejoin him on his return. Mr Jackson abducted his wife outside church one Sunday morning, and imprisoned her in his home. His lawyer said he had to right to do so, 'as long as it was not in a violent or cruel manner'. This the Appeal Judge, Lord Halsbury, deplored, saying that 'such ideas were tainted with the ideas of absolute dominion of the husband over the wife [and] were marked by the absence of a due sense of delicacy and respect due to a wife whom the husband had sworn to cherish and respect.' The court ruled that Mr Jackson was not entitled to imprison his wife to enforce conjugal rights.

Even so late in the century, not everyone agreed with this ruling. Mrs Jackson was booed and jostled by her neighbours on her return to the home of her relations. The *Times* newspaper, reporting the judgment, declared that 'One fine morning last month marriage in England was suddenly abolished.' And astonishingly enough, some women disagreed: for example, Eliza Lynn Linton wrote an article in *The Nine-*

teenth Century, saying that the court's decision was 'a triumph for promiscuity and a deadly blow to the foundations of social order and
morality.'

A husband had the right under common law 'to give his wife
moderate correction . . . by domestic chastisement', and to restrain his
wife physically in order to 'prevent her going into society of which he
disapproves, or otherwise disobeying his rightful authority.' Wife-
abuse was not confined to any one level of society. The novelist Susan
Ferrier, who moved in upper-class circles, wrote to a woman friend in
1818, 'I maintain there is but one crime a woman could never forgive
her husband, and that is a kicking.' Charlotte Brontë described 'the
drunken, extravagant, profligate habits' of a curate in the Church of
England, whose wife came to Charlotte's father for advice. She said
he 'treated her and their child savagely'. Mr Brontë, like most people,
disapproved of such behaviour and advised her to leave her husband
for ever and go back to her parents' home. In many cases, families
intervened to stop brutality to wives, but material considerations could
sometimes prevail over moral ones. In the 1850s 'that fox-hunting
thug', the Revd Lord John Beresford, handled his wife Christina so
roughly that her brothers came to take her away from him. When they
arrived, however, they heard that John's brother, the Marquis of
Waterford, had broken his neck out hunting, and John had succeeded
him. The brothers had second thoughts, and persuaded Christina to
accept the beatings and also the glory of being a Marchioness living
in the magnificent family seat at Curraghmore. Christina attempted to
make up for her own ill-treatment by beating her brood of children.
Her son, Lord Charles Beresford, swore he carried permanently on his
backside the mark of the gold coronet on his mother's hairbrush.

Typical of attitudes towards wife-beating lower down the social scale
were those of costermongers in London in the 1860s who, according
to social investigator Henry Mayhew, considered the wife 'as an inexpensive servant, and the disobedience of a wish is punished with blows.'
The law had by that time begun to provide some protection against
domestic abuse. Under the 1854 Act for the Better Prevention of
Aggravated Assaults Upon Women and Children, magistrates could
deal immediately (instead of sending them to a higher court) with cases
where women, or children under the age of fourteen, had suffered
actual bodily harm as a result of an assault. But prevailing attitudes

1. A Yorkshire village tombstone graphically tells the story of child mortality in the Victorian age

2. A satire on the early nineteenth-century fashion amongst women of the *beau monde* for spending more time with their children, and even breast feeding

3. A housewifery lesson in one of the new board schools in 1893. These lessons were not open to boys

4. Some of the first Girton students at Hitchin in Hertfordshire, 1870

5. Almack's, the most fashionable mixed club in London, during the Regency period

6. The Regency 'pedestrian hobby-horse' or 'velocipede' was traditionally for gentlemen. It was the safety bicycle of the 1880s that liberated the 'New Woman'

7. Toxophily was one of the most popular sports amongst well-bred Victorian women

8. *Clara: 'Yes, dear, I've got the last one down, and it's perfectly delicious. A man marries his grandmother — fourteen persons are poisoned by a young and beautiful girl — forgeries by the dozen — robberies, hangings; in fact, full of delightful horrors!'*
The sensation novels of the 1860s, portraying family relationships of extreme hatred and contempt, were immensely popular

9. Finding a good position in domestic service could be difficult and private registries grew up for the better class of servant

10. Towards the end of the century, with the advent of the typewriter and the telephone, white-collar occupations opened up for women

11. Before 1842, women and girls worked underground in the coal mines, not at the face but 'hurrying' the 'tubs' to the pit shaft

12. Ellen Grounds, aged 17, a 'pit brow lassie', photographed by Arthur Munby in 1866

13. The doubling room of Dean Mills, near Manchester, in 1871. This was a 'model mill' in which women were allowed to bring in their own meals

14. The women's day room in the Westminster Union workhouse. Many poor old women ended their days here

THE HAUNTED LADY, OR "THE GHOST" IN THE LOOKING-GLASS.

MADAME LA MODISTE: 'WE WOULD NOT HAVE DISAPPOINTED YOUR LADYSHIP, AT ANY SACRIFICE, AND THE ROBE IS FINISHED *À MERVEILLI*

15. The high fashions of the fine lady were produced at the expense of the sempstresses who wore out their lives sewing dresses for starvation wages

16. A mother returns to the Thomas Coram Foundation for Children. She is well dressed and perhaps in better circumstances than most women who relied on the Foundation; it was not inevitable that a child would return home

17. According to the House of Lords Committee on 'sweating' in 1888–90, sweated labour led to 'earnings barely sufficient to sustain existence; hours of labour such as to make the lives of the workers periods of almost ceaseless toil'. Pictured above are men's coat makers

18. Child care was expensive for working mothers, and they had to take whatever help they could get, like this old woman photographed in the East End in 1876

19. Annie Besant (top, third from right) with the Strike Committee of the Matchmakers' Union, whom she helped in their action against Bryant & May in 1888. The strike resulted in improved wages and conditions

20. Differences in social class attitudes, a gentle late-Victorian satire on the 'lady bountiful'

Lady Visitor (at Work-girls' Club, giving some advice on manners):
'AND YOU KNOW LADIES NEVER SPEAK TO GENTLEMEN WITHOUT AN INTRODUCTION.'
'Liza: 'WE KNOWS YER DON'T, MISS, AN' WE OFFEN PITIES YER!'

21. The courtesan and the drab

22. Suffragettes released from Holloway Prison in October 1908. They are dressed in replica prison clothing

often undermined the legal sanctions. One magistrate advised a victim of beatings to 'abstain from irritating her husband'. Another refused to pass sentence in wife-beating cases until he knew 'whether she was a woman whose bad temper gave her husband no peace, or whether the fault was his.'

Women in groups were often perceived by men as potential trouble-makers. Husbands often explained that they had been forced to beat their wives 'to keep them from associating with other women, in particular their mothers and sisters.' One blamed all his domestic problems on women who said to each other, 'You come to my house to have a cup of tea and I'll come to yours.' Another told a magistrate he blacked his wife's eye because she was 'so thick with the woman next door'.

Women's lives were held cheap by some Victorian courts. In 1862 a wealthy Kent farmer, Major Murton, was accused of beating his wife to death when she objected to his bringing home two prostitutes for the evening. Murton was sentenced to three years' imprisonment, the judge saying, 'I know that it will be a severe punishment, for you have hitherto occupied a respectable position in life – you have filled the office of overseer, churchwarden and surveyor.' Murton was thunderstruck by the sentence: 'But I provided handsomely for her!' he said. A year later, James Palmer, a labourer, beat to death the woman he lived with and explained that she had angered him by saying she was going to work in a tap room (a public house). The judge sentenced him to just three months in prison, saying, 'it was a minor offense of manslaughter. The blows were a mere chastisement. She was not his wife, or sister, or legitimately a member of his household, but human nature is human nature and he was provoked because she was drunk.' In 1877 Thomas Harlow struck his wife Ellen and inadvertently killed her, when she refused to give him for beer the money she had earned that day by hawking (street selling). The judge found Harlow guilty, but recommended him to mercy on account of the provocation he had received.

In contrast to the above cases, violence by women against men was found reprehensible, even when it was a defensive reaction. In 1869 Susannah Palmer appeared in the Recorder's Court in London, charged with stabbing her husband. After years of brutal treatment at his hands she left him, determined to support herself and her children in a new home. But her husband found her, and seized and sold all her possessions, which legally belonged to him. Then she stabbed him. Susannah was convicted and sentenced to a long prison sentence. In her case there was no recommendation to mercy on account of the provocation she had received.

In 1878, Frances Power Cobbe wrote an article called 'Wife Torture in England', and she had this to say:

The assault on a wife by her husband seems to be surrounded by a certain halo of jocularity which invites people to smile whenever they hear of a case of it (terminating anywhere short of actual murder), and causes the mention of the subject to conduce rather than otherwise the hilarity of a dinner party . . . In view of the state of things revealed by our criminal statistics there is something ominous in the circumstance that 'Punch' should have been our national street-drama for more than two centuries [&] that so much of the enjoyment should concentrate about the thwacking of poor Judy, and the flinging of the baby out of the window. The notion that a man's wife is his PROPERTY . . . is the fatal root of incalculable evil and misery . . . It is sometimes pleaded on behalf of poor men, that they possess nothing else but their wives, and that, consequently, it seems doubly hard to meddle with the exercise of their power in that narrow sphere.

Not only is an offence against a wife condoned as of inferior guilt, but any offence of the wife against her husband is regarded as a sort of Petty Treason . . . should she be guilty of 'nagging' or 'scolding', or of being a slattern, or of getting intoxicated, she gets short shrift and no favour – even humane persons talk of her offence as constituting if not a justification for her murder, yet an explanation of it.

This article was part of a successful campaign for the passing of the Matrimonial Causes Act of 1878, which enabled an abused wife to obtain a separation order and maintenance payments, if the husband was convicted of an aggravated assault upon her.

For most people in England marriage was an indissoluble union which ended only when one or other partner died. The Church Courts could grant a valid separation, but wanted evidence of severe cruelty or misconduct before they would accept a wife's right to leave her husband's home. This did not prevent people making amicable arrangements to live separately. For instance, early in the century the Earl Bishop of Derry and his wife were living separately, and each of their two daughters was separated from her husband. As late as 1906, the Duchess of Marlborough said that '[upper-class] husbands and wives who could not get on together went their separate ways.' But before 1857 people who wanted to divorce and remarry had to have passed a Private Act of Parliament for the purpose. It was an expensive and time-consuming business, since before the Bill could be laid there had to be a separation by the Church Court. A husband had to get damages for 'criminal conversation' (adultery) against his wife's seducer in the Common Law Courts. A Divorce Bill could be obtained as a matter of right by an innocent husband against a wife found guilty of adultery which he had not condoned. A wife who wanted a divorce had to prove not only adultery but further offences such as physical cruelty, bigamy or incest. This reflected the male view that the difference between the adultery of a husband and of a wife was 'boundless'. Lord Chancellor Cranforth said in the House of Lords in 1857 that

A wife might, without any loss of caste, and possibly with reference to the interests of her children, or even of her husband, condone an act of adultery on the part of the husband but a husband could not condone a similar act on the part of a wife. No one would venture to suggest that a husband could possibly do so, and for this, among other reasons . . . that the adultery of the wife might be the means of palming spurious offspring upon the husband, while the adultery of the husband could have no such effect with regard to the wife.

Not surprisingly, few Acts for divorce were passed for men, and even fewer for women. Between 1803 and the 1850s the upper classes got about half the divorces passed, the rest being middle class, with a few lowly petitioners such as salesmen, clerks and commercial travellers. The *Commons Journal* of 1837–52, shows that of the seventy-six Divorce Bills, five were brought by clergymen, five by army officers, two by titled women, and four against titled women.

In general, the aristocracy disapproved of divorce because the material repercussions were very inconvenient. Their concern to secure their property overrode all other considerations. So although high society was riddled with adultery and marriages were rarely romantically happy, broken marriages were few, though they did occur. Lady Holland said in her *Journal* that she was able to buy herself out of a marriage in 1797. Her first husband (Sir Godfrey Webster) agreed to a divorce on condition that she handed over to him all her fortune of £7,000 a year less £800 a year for her own use. She then married the fabulously wealthy Lord Holland. In 1801 Lady Augusta Fane divorced Lord Boringdon, 'whom she had married early in life and always detested', and afterwards married the Hon. Sir Arthur Paget, third son of the 1st Earl of Uxbridge, with whom she was apparently content. In 1810 the 1st Marquess of Anglesey (then Lord Paget), after being divorced by his first wife, married Lady Charlotte Wellesley, divorced wife of the Hon. Henry Wellesley (brother of the Duke of Wellington). Henry Wellesley was awarded £34,000 damages against Paget for 'criminal conversation'.

Divorce did not always make women happy ever after: the divorced wife of Bernard Howard, later Duke of Norfolk, married Lord Lucan, but they separated ten years later after squabbling endlessly about money. Lady Aldborough's granddaughter, Elizabeth Johnstone, left her husband in 1823 because she could not bear to be a poor man's wife. She fell in love with Lord Brudenell, heir to the 6th Earl of Cardigan, and her husband divorced her, but her subsequent marriage to Brudenell was a disaster. A dramatic divorcée was Jane Elizabeth, known as 'Iolanthe', and described by Lady Holland in 1824 as 'a poor girl who has not seen anything of the world.' She married Lord Ellenborough, was divorced in 1830 for adultery with Prince Schwarzenbergh, and later that year became the mistress of Ludwig I, King of Bavaria. She later married Baron de Venningen, Prime Minister of Bavaria, who committed suicide when she left him. Her third husband, Sheik Medjwas el Mizrab, was an Arab general in the Greek army. Iolanthe was making up for her earlier boring life.

The position of divorced aristocratic women who wanted to remain in respectable society was not easy. Punishment was often social exclusion, as in the case of Anne Wellesley (1788–1875), first the wife of Sir William Abdy, who gave birth to four children in less than four years after her elopement, divorce and subsequent remarriage to Lord Charles Bentinck. Her parents, the Marquess and Marchioness Wellesley, never saw her again, and she complained of 'loneliness caused by the neglect of the world'. In 1880 Ellen Miller-Mundy (granddaughter of the 7th Lord Byron) had been married for seven years and had one small daughter. She fell in love with the 20-year-old Earl of Shrewsbury and they eloped to Paris. Her husband divorced her, and she and the Earl were married in 1882, their son being born shortly afterwards. They were banished from Court but lived on their country estate, and the Countess survived to the age of ninety. Social sanctions, however, did not operate against the most powerful. Despite her divorce, Lady Holland was the queen of Whig society for half a century. By the early twentieth century, the Duchess of Marlborough realized that 'although divorced couples were not received in Court circles, London Society would not be so governed.' She might have realized this sooner, since her own mother-in-law had divorced her husband (as Lord Blandford, before he inherited the ducal title) when in 1876 he ran off with Lady Aylesford, and Lady Blandford had not been socially ruined. Nor was the life of Jennie Churchill (mother of Winston), who divorced her second husband, George Cornwallis-West, in 1914.

Divorce in the Royal Family was almost unknown. King George IV tried and failed to divorce his wife, Caroline of Brunswick, in 1820. Queen Victoria's granddaughter, the Princess Victoria Melita, did divorce. She married the Grand Duke of Hesse but fell in love with a Russian first cousin, the Grand Duke Cyril. Her divorce was postponed until after Queen Victoria's death. The Tsar, whose permission was needed for a Grand Duke's marriage, was opposed to admitting a divorcée into the family, and the Tsarina, who was the Grand Duke of Hesse's sister, considered that her brother had been badly treated. However, in 1909 the Tsar relented, and Victoria Melita was accepted as a Russian Grand Duchess, and splendidly established in St Petersburg until the Bolshevik Revolution of 1917 caused the family to flee to France.

Divorce in the upper classes was not common, but it was not unknown, and the consequences were not as dire as sometimes claimed. The Countess of Fingall reported that she sat at a dinner party in the 1880s beside Sir Francis Jeune, the famous divorce judge. She said, 'Sir Francis, you must see a lot of the seamy side of life.' 'Oh, yes, my dear Lady,' he replied, 'but not half as much as they see in the Probate Court! People don't break their hearts nearly as much for love as they do for money.'

By mid-century, attitudes towards divorce had changed, along with a weakening of belief in orthodox religion. There was mounting evidence that although the majority of husbands did not treat their wives badly, there were many more cruel husbands than was generally believed. The 1857 Divorce and Matrimonial Causes Act did not, as many people seemed to think, introduce any new principle of divorce. Its purpose was only to make the civil system of divorce more widely available. The main feature of the Act was the creation of a new Divorce Court, which also took over the duties of the Church Courts and could grant annulments and decree separations. The court sat in London only, thus putting it out of the reach of most people. The procedure for getting a divorce was cheapened, but even then was too expensive for working people. A husband could still get a divorce for simple adultery, whereas a woman had to prove adultery compounded by some other marital offence such as cruelty or desertion, so divorce was no easier for women than it had been before. But the Act did give the divorced woman complete control over her own property. These new procedures remained the basis of divorce in England up to 1923, when an Act of Parliament made wives and husbands equal before the law regarding grounds for divorce. Changes in 1914, 1920 and 1926 made divorce easier for the poor by providing courts outside London and giving financial aid for legal costs. In 1937 divorce was allowed to either partner on the grounds of adultery or desertion or cruelty or insanity, and a wife could claim on the grounds that her husband had been guilty of rape, sodomy or bestiality. Yet divorce remained a comparatively unusual solution to marital problems until after the First World War. The numbers did not exceed 1000 a year until 1918. Everyone blamed the increase in divorce on hasty war time marriages, but the numbers never returned to the pre-war level and indeed increased yearly.

It is often forgotten that although divorce was frowned upon in Victorian England, some famous middle-class women were divorced but remained prominent in public life. The actresses Fanny Kemble and Ellen Terry were divorced, as was the campaigner for contraception, Annie Besant, and (more surprisingly) the conservative writer Eliza Lynn Linton. And some famous men married divorced women: for example, novelist Robert Louis Stevenson married a divorcée ten years older then himself in 1882, and novelist John Galsworthy married the divorced wife of his cousin in 1904.

For the working classes, divorce was not the usual solution to marital problems, being too expensive both before and after 1857. In any case, the respectable working class did not think it proper to seek divorce. As late as 1909, in evidence to the Royal Commission on Divorce, representatives of the Women's Co-operative Guild said decent working women wished marriage to be irrevocable and there was no reason to make divorce easier. They said only a minority suffered so acutely from marriage that they found it unendurable, and even they thought divorce shameful.

Yet throughout the century some working-class marriages broke up. It was not uncommon for discontented husbands simply to run away, leaving their deserted wives and children to live on poor relief. The Poor Law authorities could sue a husband whose wife became chargeable on the rates either as a workhouse inmate or by receiving money to enable her to live at home – if they could find him. Some men left the country for good; others went to other parts of England and changed their names. Poor women rarely ran away without their children, though some did. Some couples separated by merely living apart and taking another partner. This was an amicable form of 'divorce' without the assistance of the courts.

Sales of wives – sometimes called popular divorce – occurred throughout England from as early as 1073, with scattered cases as late as the twentieth century. It was never sanctioned by law, but was said to be common among the Sheffield knife-grinders, and Smithfield market in London was famous for such sales. An astonishing case was that of Henry Cook of Effingham, Surrey, who in 1814 was forced under the bastardy laws to marry a woman from Slinfold, Sussex. Six months after the marriage the woman and her child were put in the Effingham workhouse. The governor there complained of having to keep the new arrivals, so the parish officer to Effingham prevailed on Cook to sell his wife. The master of the workhouse, Chippen, was directed to take the woman to Croydon market and there, on 17 June 1815, she was sold to John Earl for the sum of one shilling, and to bind the bargain a receipt was made out. In their satisfaction of having got rid of the chargeability of the woman the parish officers of Effingham paid the expenses of the journey to Croydon, including refreshments there, and also allowed a leg of mutton for the wedding dinner which took place in Earl's parish of Dorking. That the expenses incurred by such a transaction could be entered up in the parish accounts and passed by the parish vestry suggests that the custom was not considered illegal. It also shows the humiliating straits to which poor women could be reduced, since there is no evidence that Mrs Cook had any say in the matter.

It is also fair to say that some of these wife sales seem to have been good-humoured affairs in markets or pubs, where a wife was supposed to give her consent to the sale. She was sold to her lover by pre-arrangement with her husband, who might spend what money he got for her on drinks for all to celebrate the occasion. It was a form of public exchange which the parties really seemed to believe was legal, since they advertised the sale in local newspapers. Wife-selling became a theme for comic songs and several operatic farces. Such sales were not very frequent, but there were cases in Bristol in 1823, in London and in Carlisle in 1832, and in Bolton and Birmingham in 1850. In 1856, R.W. Emerson reported in his book *English Traits*, 'The right of the husband to sell his wife has been retained down to our times.' The practice scandalized the middle classes, as could be seen from their reaction to the fictional case at the beginning of Thomas Hardy's novel, *The Mayor of Casterbridge*, published in 1886 – it was then considered unbelievable. But some clergymen closed their eyes to the practice, and magistrates and judges seem to have been reluctant to punish wife-sellers severely. Those cases brought to court were meant only as warnings of the illegality of the custom. It was the working classes themselves who eventually rebelled against the sale of wives. Organized groups of working women began to disrupt the sales, and a common form of popular justice was to pelt the seller and his wife with mud, rubbish, stones or dead dogs and cats.

Bigamy, that is marrying when a first wife or husband was still alive, was illegal but not uncommon, and prison sentences for men brought before the courts were light. For example, Thomas Hall, a labourer, was brought to Warwickshire Assizes on a charge of bigamy in 1845. His wife had deserted him, and he needed someone to look after his young children. Rather than live in sin, he 'married' a second wife. In his judgment on the case, Mr Justice Maule pointed out that divorce had been available to Hall, if he had had the money to get a private Act of Parliament passed, but said that since he was a poor man the remedy was not truly available. So he sentenced him to imprisonment for one day, which he had already served.

The treatment of women who committed bigamy was much more harsh. In January 1863, Jessie Cooper was indicted for bigamy. Her first husband had abused and abandoned her, and then spread false rumours of his death to escape his creditors. Believing these reports, Jessie remarried. When her first husband was arrested and convicted of embezzlement he suggested that the police should arrest Jessie for bigamy. Her new husband swore that he thought she was a widow when he married her. She was found guilty of bigamy and sent to prison for some months, though the Kentish jury did express their sympathy towards her.

Lower-class women seem to have been more combative in their relations with their husbands than middle-class wives. In the Central Criminal Court more women were indicted for assault on men in the 1870s than in the 1860s, and in 1880 newspapers reported a number of cases in Rochester, Kent, in which women were fined or imprisoned for assaulting their husbands. The men were often small and wiry, whereas wives tended to be stout, with strong shoulders and biceps developed by heavy domestic labour. However, the women were usually weaker fighters and often received severe injuries from their domestic fights, which tended to be over money or food or men's drinking habits. Hannah Mitchell, who grew up in the 1870s in Derbyshire, said that her mother, a respectable and God-fearing farmer's wife, controlled her husband by the use of her violent temper which he could not deal with, though 'he could handle a savage horse or face an infuriated bull'. He was always the first to leave the house and the last to return when his wife was in a rage. Kathleen Dayus described her mother, a matriarch in the roughest part of Birmingham around 1900, as a regular tyrant whose husband was terrified of her.

However, there were many over-strained, exhausted mothers with drunken, brutal husbands who blighted the lives of their wives and hungry, miserable children. In 1874 the coroners in the 'Kicking District' of Liverpool recorded 160 verdicts of 'Found Dead' on wives who had been been violently assaulted. At mid-century British consumption of alcohol was prodigious, and the adulteration of beer to make it more profitable had very serious implications for the health, behaviour and domestic relations of the working class, Around 1830, when the Beer Act allowed the spread of beer-shops, strychnine and other poisons were added to the beer to compensate for its being diluted with water, and it was not until the 1880s that such adulteration effectively stopped. This was after the enforcement of the Adulteration of Food, Drink and Drugs Act, 1872. The consumption of beer reached its peak in 1874, and excessively heavy drinking declined towards the end of the century.

Magistrates and the police were loath to interfere in cases of domestic violence, believing that most cases settled themselves, but that does not mean that ordinary people approved of men beating their wives mercilessly. In Leeds around 1870 there was a custom called 'Riding the Stang', when a procession of men beating trays and cans preceded a man carried high on two poles who recited a poem levelled at 'Nick Wilbur', a notorious local drunkard and wife-beater. The men promised vengeance on anyone who followed his example by beating his wife, neglecting his children or consorting with loose women.

As mentioned earlier, the 1878 Matrimonial Causes Act gave magistrates power to grant a separation order with maintenance to a wife whose husband had been convicted of aggravated assault upon her. In 1886 the Maintenance of Wives (Desertion) Act gave magistrates the power to grant maintenance orders, for a weekly amount not exceeding £2, to women whose husbands were guilty of desertion and neglect. Despite the difficulty of enforcing maintenance payments, of which women were well aware, between 1897 and 1906 the courts granted 87,000 separation and maintenance orders. Divorce may not have been respectable, but working-class women were less willing to endure violence for the sake of having a home, and more willing to pursue errant husbands through the courts.

By the end of the First World War, the legal rights of married, separated and divorced women had been altered considerably. A father's right to custody of his children was no longer taken for granted. A husband no longer had the right to confine his wife to his home by force. His right to chastise his wife was challenged, and the courts gave some protection against physical abuse. The problem of domestic violence was not solved – nor is it to this day – but the legislation was an improvement on what had gone before. Attitudes towards divorce changed very slowly, and up to 1923 it was easier for a man to get a divorce than it was for a woman, though divorced women could control their own property. In 1914 there were fewer than a thousand divorces a year, in a population of forty million. The floodgates did not open until the 1960s and 70s, when the concept of no-fault divorce swept through the Western world. Up to then, most women sought a legal separation and maintenance order, if the husband had deserted her or been convicted of an aggravated assault on her. Yet it was difficult to enforce the maintenance order if the husband refused to pay or left the district. As a result, many women, then as now, could suffer severe financial consequences when they separated or divorced.

Although those who fought for change felt it took too long to achieve too little, England was less completely a man's world in 1914 than it had been a century earlier: wives were legally regarded as human beings with rights independent of their husbands. Caroline Norton and Frances Power Cobbe had been well rewarded.

7

Turning Their Industry to Best Account

WIDOWHOOD AND OLD AGE

It is a great trial for any woman after having enjoy'd every comfort and a happy Home for two and thirty years to find it all gone at the time of life when she naturally feels the most want of it.

Emily, Lady Cowper, after the death of her husband in 1837

My mother she was only forty [when she was widowed] and there was nothing then, you know, in them days, no pensions or nothing. She had to go out to work to keep us four children – washing and cleaning.

Lizzie J., b. 1896 in Liverpool;
mother widowed soon after Lizzie's birth

Marriage was not necessarily a lifelong provision for nineteenth-century Englishwomen. Death, rather than desertion or divorce, ended most marriages, and this was often when the partners were relatively young. About one in five marriages in the 1850s would not have lasted ten years. For the period up to 1850 there are no official statistics, but in the second half of the century one in twelve women aged 35–44 were widows, as were one in three women aged 55–64. The wife of a manual labourer could expect to be a widow longer than a middle-class wife, since there was a greater likelihood of her husband dying as a result of his job. Many young children lived in families headed by a widow. There were always a lot of older widows, and even more later in the century, when people lived longer. The number of widows aged over sixty-five doubled between 1871 and 1921. They outnumbered widowers by three to one, and they generally had a harder time surviving. What choices were open to women when their husbands died, and how they subsequently lived their lives, depended on their social class, whether they had private incomes, or whether their husbands had left them well provided for. Other major considerations were their ability to earn a living for themselves (women's wages were generally much lower than those of men), and whether they could rely on their children to help support them.

For some women, the death of the husband was a blow from which they never recovered. Queen Victoria is a prime example of a woman so devastated that she made widowhood her vocation. This, of course, was a choice available only to widows with ample means. When Albert died in 1861 the Queen was only forty-two years old. The struggle between her emotions and her sense of duty to her subjects is evident in her journals, but she went into virtual seclusion. She became more timid and prudish, and selfishly possessive of the members of her household. She slept with Albert's night-shirt in her arms and a cast of his hand within reach. Over his empty pillow she hung his portrait crowned with a wreath of evergreens. She wore her widow's cap – poor Ma's sad cap, as Princess Beatrice called it – for the wedding seven months after Albert's death of her daughter Princess Alice, and Victoria herself said the occasion was more like a funeral than a wedding. Henceforth, every action of her life was guided by the commands of her 'Angel'. She covered the landscape with Albert memorials. It was not uncommon for some of the ladies-in-waiting to the Queen to be widows, one reason being that they were free and glad of an occupation. But when Albert died the Queen built up around herself an entourage of widows for whom remarriage was blasphemy.

The Queen failed for forty years truly to reconcile the claims of public life and private grief. She continued to have the Prince Consort's clothes laid out each evening, with hot water and a clean towel, for what Bishop Davidson called 'the ghost of the dear departed'. Many other Victorians behaved in similar fashion when they were bereaved, and had she fulfilled her state functions adequately, few would have criticized her; but the general public did not think she needed to hide away from public life for longer than three years. As the years rolled on the Queen withdrew into even greater seclusion. The Prince of Wales told her that her people could not bear to see Buckingham Palace perpetually unoccupied, and that 'we live in radical times, and the more

the People see the Sovereign the better it is for the People and the
Country'. There were a succession of 'Brown rows' concerning John
Brown, the Queen's personal Highland servant, on whom she was so
dependent that it was whispered she had married him, or that he was
her lover. Victoria refused to send him away, despite appeals from her
children, and eventually the rumours died away, as did republican
sentiment.

For her Golden Jubilee of 1887 the Queen obstinately refused to wear
the crown and robes of state. All the women at the Thanksgiving Service in Westminster Abbey wore 'long High Dress without Mantel and
a bonnet', as instructed; the Queen wore a special bonnet with white
lace and diamonds. After the ceremony she wrote, 'I sat (oh! without
my beloved husband, for whom this would have been such a proud
day!)'. The congregation gave thanks to the music of Albert's Te Deum,
and the choir sang his anthem, *Gotha*. For the Diamond Jubilee of
1897, Albert's music was sung at the family Thanksgiving at St George's
Chapel, Windsor, and afterwards the Queen went to his mausoleum
for further devotions. The former Prime Minister, Mr Gladstone,
whom she loathed, hoped that she would abdicate after this Jubilee,
but she did not. 'The Widow of Windsor' reigned until her death in
1901, and was then buried alongside Albert.

The Queen was not alone in deciding that no other man could or
should replace her husband, but not all widows were so morbid.
Some were like the famous bluestocking, Elizabeth Montague, who,
having as a young woman enquired, 'Is it not a sad thing to be brought
up in the Patriot din of liberty and property and to be allow'd neither?'
said she got 'money and liberty' with widowhood and had no intention
of marrying again (though she had not been unhappily married). A
wealthy widow could do as she liked with her money, and follow her
inclinations. For example, Bedford College in London, offering
courses for governesses from 1848 and later to become a fully-fledged
college of London University, was founded through the initiative and
generosity of a wealthy widow, the Unitarian Elizabeth Reid, who was
passionately in favour of education for women. She hoped that the
organization of the college would be entrusted primarily to women, and
although this proved to be legally impossible at that time, women
retained a large share of control. This made Bedford College different
from most of the other schools and colleges for women, which
remained firmly under masculine control. Pleasing herself as a widow

in a different way from Elizabeth Reid was Isabella Bird, who resumed her life of travel when her husband died in the 1870s. She had been the most daring explorer of her time, the first woman to be elected a Fellow of the Royal Geographical Society, but at fifty she had married a doctor ten years her junior and settled down to domesticity. After his death, five years later, she went off exploring again, and apparently her health improved dramatically. In a somewhat different category was Priscilla, Countess Annesley, who married in the 1890s the 4th Earl, a much older man who was an ogre towards her, though always sexually faithful. They lived in Ireland, and when her husband became too odious Priscilla took the train to Castle Leslie and stayed with Leonie Leslie and her husband. When her husband died, Priscilla was immediately surrounded by new suitors, but she said she had had enough of husbands and that widowhood suited her.

Some women came to public prominence after the death of their husbands. One such was Millicent Garrett (1847–1929) who married when she was twenty years old Henry Fawcett, Professor of Political Economy at Cambridge and Radical MP for Brighton. He was blind as a result of a shooting accident, and Millicent eagerly helped him with his political work, which involved continuous support for the emancipation of women, by becoming his secretary and guide. Theirs was a happy partnership, but it was after Henry Fawcett died in 1884 that Millicent emerged as a leader of the suffragists – those who believed in rational argument by speeches and pamphlets, and pressure on politicians by petitions, to get women the vote. Yet she had no faith in the intentions of Gladstone or the Liberal Party on this issue, and in 1888 she led a faction out of the Women's Liberal Federation to form a separate suffrage society. She was an admirable speaker, tirelessly energetic, and with a rock-like determination to press the cause, which she did until it was won in 1918. But because she neither ranted nor raved, chained herself to railings, nor went to prison for her beliefs, the importance of her work for women's suffrage is often forgotten.

The militant suffrage movement is inextricably bound up with the name of Emmeline Pankhurst (1858–1928), happily married for many years to lawyer Richard Pankhurst, who stood twice for Parliament in the Liberal interest and once as a candidate for the Independent Labour Party, but was beaten on each occasion. Husband and wife were both active in politics and women's suffrage affairs. After the death of her husband in 1898 Emmeline took a salaried job as a Registrar of Births and Deaths in a poor district of Manchester. Here she talked to young women with illegitimate babies, and to women with large families who had been deserted by their husbands. Her reforming zeal turned to hatred of the men who were responsible for so much misery, and she came to believe that only when women had the vote would anything be changed to help poor women. She despaired of Millicent Fawcett's patient campaign to convert public opinion, and so she and her daughter Christabel triggered off the militant movement called the Women's Social and Political Union, whose members were known as suffragettes. This movement had immediate appeal to those who wanted to draw vivid and immediate attention to their cause. Its slogan, 'Votes for Women!' was far more compelling than the suffragist formula, 'To extend the parliamentary franchise to women on the same terms as it is or may be granted to men'. Its tactics were far more dynamic, and they were greeted by hysterical opposition from the press and politicians, instead of the withering silence that usually greeted Millicent Fawcett's activities. This is not the place to discuss in detail which tactics in the end proved most productive, but most people probably feel that both wings of the movement were necessary, and that Emmeline Pankhurst and Millicent Fawcett deserve equal praise for their efforts. Neither woman seems to have had any intention of marrying again and standing once more in the shadow of a man.

A more pragmatic reason why some wealthy widows did not remarry was that they stood to lose their incomes from jointure property if they did so. According to common law, a widow was customarily entitled to inherit a life interest in a third of her late husband's real estate (land). This was called her dower. In her capacity as widowed mother of the heir to a landed estate (as dowager) a wealthy woman could sometimes wield considerable power behind the scenes, but with her unmarried daughters she usually moved into the dower house, giving precedence to the heir's young wife. The Dower Act which was passed in 1833 was a minor piece of legislation, but nonetheless it registered a significant shift in attitudes and expectations. Although the right to dower was not officially abolished until 1925, from 1834 onwards a husband could bar his wife's right to dower by so making a will or legal declaration. If a man died without making a will, leaving a child or descendant of that child, the latter took two-thirds and his widow one-third of his personal property (money, stocks etc.). If there were no children, his widow took half and the rest was divided among the deceased's relatives. As regards real estate, the widow of a man who did not leave a will was entitled to a life interest in one-third of the lands, but had to pay any debts for which the husband's lands were liable.

In practice, dower had largely disappeared before 1833, and the reformers regarded the practice as archaic. With the passage of time, new forms of wealth had appeared, and many women came from families whose money was derived not from land but from industry and trade. What had gradually taken the place of dower was called 'equitable jointure', a widow's lifetime use of an amount of property specified in the marriage settlement. While dower represented a fixed share of the husband's real estate, a wife's jointure was often measured in cash or an annual pension rather than in landed property, and how much she got depended on the bargaining at the time of the marriage. In theory, a woman exchanged dower for jointure and should have continued to inherit close to a third of her husband's property. In theory, the bargaining power of her father and trustees should have ensured that a woman who brought a large amount of money to the marriage (her portion) received an ample jointure in return. But dower rights were increasingly whittled away by complex conveyancing techniques devised by lawyers, and the fact that a father's financial interests could differ from those of his daughter (for example, when his own indebtedness meant that he agreed to a smaller jointure in exchange for delayed payment of her portion). Some husbands evaded dower altogether, by placing their lands in trust.

The laws concerning widows were complicated and (as was the case with most laws) often misunderstood. For example, Charles Dickens, who began his working life as a law clerk in the 1820s, was inaccurate in his novel, *The Old Curiosity Shop*, on this subject. The character Daniel Quilp commits suicide, leaving no will, and his widow succeeds to his property. Yet at that time a suicide was considered a felon and a felon's property was forfeited to the crown; and even if he had not committed suicide his widow would have received only part of his property.

Sometimes lack of forethought rather than malice was responsible for a widow finding herself in reduced circumstances. The *Westminster Review* reported in 1856 that a Mrs X inherited from her father a comfortable property before she was married, and had never known any need to economize. She married, had great confidence in her husband, never thought about money matters and did not have her own property settled on herself, so it became her husband's. He died shortly after the marriage, without having made a will, and half of his money (originally his wife's) went to his nephew – a man who was almost a stranger to her. This left her in considerably reduced circumstances, but she had no legal redress.

To many widows, the most desirable option for the future was to find another husband, and this was true at all levels of society. The major need was not always to find a man to maintain her. Emotional needs and a secure social status were just as important. Mary Somerville, a widow with two young children, married for a second time in 1812 a man who (unlike her first husband) supported her scientific pursuits. Queen Victoria's mother was a poor but high-born German widow with two young children when she married the Duke of Kent in 1818 and gave birth to the heir to the throne, so establishing herself at the top of British society for life. Harriot Coutts, widow of the banker Thomas Coutts, inherited the whole of his fortune and his partnership in the bank in 1820, becoming one of the wealthiest women in Britain. She longed above all for a place in high society, and some years later married the Duke of St Albans, who was half her age. Despite the widespread sneers about her 'buying a coronet', they lived happily together until her death in 1837. Emily, Lady Cowper, belonged by birth in the highest circles in the land, but made it clear, two years after the death of her husband in 1837, that her worldly position would be improved by remarriage. She had for many years during her husband's lifetime been the mistress of Lord Palmerston, and it was a matter of much speculation whether they would now marry. The Queen knew of their past liaison, but was in favour of the marriage, writing to Prince Albert, 'I think they are quite right so to act, because Palmerston, since the death of his sisters, is quite alone in the world, and Lady C. is a very clever woman, and much attached to him.' They did marry and lived happily together until Lord Palmerston's death a quarter of a century later. We cannot be sure how many widows remarried in the early nineteenth century, but in 1851 one in ten of the women who got married were in fact widows. In 1870–2, two widows married for every spinster married in the age group over thirty.

Widowhood was never easy, except for the rich, but many widows showed an amazing capacity for hard work in supporting their families – not only their own children but often their own widowed mothers, and possibly brothers and sisters. Even among the rich, there

were some examples of widows who chose to work. For example, early
in the century, Elizabeth Montague was famous as a bluestocking, a
term applied to literary or learned ladies who frequented Montague
House in London, where a shining light of the assemblies was Benjamin
Stillingfleet, a near-poet who wore blue worsted stockings. In consequence, Admiral Boscawen dubbed the group the Blue Stocking
Society. Elizabeth also ran her own London salon, to which came the
writers, artists and politicians of the day, and she married a wealthy
northern colliery- and land-owner. She always took an active interest
in his business, and after his death she worked harder than ever, visiting
her agricultural tenants, rejoicing in the improvement of her land by
cultivation, and attending to the well-being of her colliery workers.
Lady Charlotte Guest, too, was interested in industrial affairs
throughout her adult life. A daughter of the ninth Earl of Lindsey, she
married in 1833 Sir Josiah John Guest, the Welsh ironmaster who
pioneered many of the advances in the production of steel. At the time
of their marriage she was twenty-one and he was forty-eight, and they
came from very different worlds. She was of the best blood in England.
He was a Dissenter and 'in trade'. Within the space of thirteen years
she gave birth to ten children, but also took a close interest in the ironworks, eventually working alongside her husband in the running of the
firm. Negotiations for the renewal of the lease of the Dowlais site from
Lord Bute were completed when Sir John was on his deathbed. When
he died, in November 1852, his widow became executrix and trustee
and was put in charge of the largest ironworks in the world. She later
defied convention by marrying a younger man who was private tutor
to her children.

Middle-class widows could find themselves in dire straits if they suddenly lost their incomes. For example, Harriet Martineau's father, a
Norwich manufacturer, died in 1826 and the family business collapsed
a few years later, leaving his widow penniless. Harriet became the
family breadwinner through her writing. As she pointed out in *A
History of the Thirty Years Peace (AD 1816-46)*, in the 1820s many
people invested their money in risky speculative ventures, and when
profits failed to materialize, 'The widow lady and her daughters, who
had paid ready money all their lives, now found themselves without
income for a year together, and could not enjoy a meal because the
butcher's and baker's bill was running on.' In 1859 Margaret Oliphant
found herself the widow of a glass painter, with three small children

to keep and £1,000 in debt. From then on, until her death in 1897, she wrote almost one hundred successful novels, to support her children and also her brothers, nephew and nieces. The father of Sarah Marks (better known as the scientist Hertha Ayrton) was a jeweller and clockmaker. When he died in 1859 there was no further income and his widow had a very hard time raising their eight children. She eked out a living by needlework and by considerable help from relatives. Young Sarah looked after her smaller siblings until, at the age of nine, she went to her aunt's private school as a boarder. Later she became a self-supporting governess, passed the Cambridge Higher Examination and went on to Girton College, becoming a physicist and an authority on the electric arc.

The novelist E.M. Forster said that his grandmother, Louisa Whichelo, whose husband had been an artist and teacher, was widowed in 1867 and had ten children to keep. To survive she took in lodgers and sent the older children to earn their own livings as clerks and governesses. Daughter Alice married in 1877, but her husband died three years later, leaving her to keep herself and her one son, Morgan, who was to become so acclaimed. Jane Coombs of Cornwall was widowed in 1876 and left penniless with two children to keep. Though her husband had been a successful building contractor, when he died suddenly she was reduced overnight to a pauper, widow of a bankrupt. She could not find work in Cornwall, so moved up to Lancashire to live with relatives, set up as a tailoress and sent her daughter Selina, aged ten, to work as a half-timer in a cotton mill. Jane's widowed mother-in-law, Catherine, came from Cornwall in 1881, at age seventy-eight, to live with Jane and her children. Strong family links, and acceptance of responsibility for older relatives, was not uncommon at the time, though not everyone felt such an obligation.

Middle-class widows who had no income and no support from friends faced a very grim life. The widow of an Army officer, left penniless five years earlier and with three children, told Henry Mayhew in 1849:

Needlework is what I have done ever since I have been a widow. But it is shocking payment for such hard work. I cry over it, but I am ill and we want food so badly . . . during this last month my daughter (aged eighteen) and I have earned only 2s 4d a week, and had to pawn our blankets and bedstead, so now we sleep on the floor. I don't consider that we have any merit or claim upon the Government, still I cannot but think it hard that the children of those who served their country so many years should be as destitute as we.

Middle- and working-class widows without skills competed with each other to earn a living by the needle, frequently as exploited outworkers, and their position became worse when they also had to compete with the sewing machine, which was invented earlier but much more widely used after 1850.

At the beginning of the nineteenth century England was still largely a country of small-scale businesses. In many trades the skilled worker was both craftsman and merchant, producing goods at home and selling direct to the consumer. Some tradesmen's wives with social ambitions had begun to aspire to a life of idleness, that they might be considered gentlewomen, and they did not want to dirty their hands with craft or shop work. Writer Daniel Defoe had complained as early as 1738 that 'they act as if they were ashamed of being tradesmen's wives, and scorn to be seen in the counting-house, much less behind a counter.' But there was also social pressure on such women not to do jobs that were needed by unemployed men. In many cases, however, the wife still worked in the business and was 'mistress of the managing part of it'. For instance, in the early nineteenth century two of the most noted occultists in London were Mr & Mrs Williams, who were honoured by royal patronage. During the husband's frequent absences in the country, Mrs Williams remained in town and received all their London patients. She could carry on in her husband's absence or after his death. There were innumerable examples of widows in business as printers, engravers, tailors, watchmakers, saddlers and chimney sweepers, and at Wrexham in 1794 the overseers paid yearly accounts to a Widow Evans for coffins. There is only limited information about the business interests of widows up to 1840, in contemporary newspapers and family accounts, but the first occupational census showed just how numerous were the jobs these women did. By custom, widows had the right to continue in their husbands' trades without having served any apprenticeship themselves, though some of the men in the craft regarded them with jealousy and hostility. Many widows found honest journeymen to assist them, and themselves kept the books, did the business abroad and conducted affairs until the eldest son had completed his apprenticeship with his mother and was ready to be taken into partnership. Of staymaking (corset making) it was said that 'the work is too hard for Women, it requires more strength than they are capable of, to raise Walls of Defence about a Lady's Shape, which is liable to be spoiled by so many Accidents.' Yet it can be seen from newspaper advertisements that early in the nineteenth century women began to start such businesses, and in 1811 Mrs Lloyd Gibbon of Sackville Street, London, was staymaker to members of the royal family, Letters Patent having been granted to her for her 'highly distinguished Anatomical stays'.

Widows also worked in trades which were almost entirely in the hands of women – as milliners, mantua makers, embroiderers and seamstresses. They worked in factories and mills. In Lancashire the skill of women operatives in the textile mills was frequently an insurance against family disaster. If they were left as widows with young children, they were able to provide for them out of their wages, which were higher than those earned by unskilled men in other parts of the country. Widows living in the countryside sometimes joined the gangs that did agricultural work. This was the most notorious and arduous form of farm work, and its worst abuses were not curtailed until the 1870s. Elizabeth Dickson of Norfolk told a parliamentary commission in the 1860s that when she was widowed she had nine children under sixteen years old, including three under three, two being twins. The parish allowed her 3s 4d a week in money and bread, and expected her children to work as early as possible. Elizabeth said, 'My Henry wasn't eight years old, and when I asked, "What, will you turn him out?" they said, "Well, he's big enough, he must help as well as the others." Jemima was not more than two months, I think, over six years old when she went out. She said, "Mother, I want some boots to go to school", so I sent her out and saved up what she earned till it was enough to get them.'

For some widows who had no special skills or technical training and yet needed to earn a living, retail shopkeeping was a popular occupation, as newspaper advertisements and early directories suggest. In Manchester it was poor law policy in the early part of the century to assist widows with families with a small stock in trade, by means of which 'they might turn their industry to best account'. Keeping an inn or an alehouse was generally regarded as a suitable occupation for a widow. It was less genteel to be a street trader or a pedlar, but many widows made their livings that way.

Widows found many casual ways to earn money, though like other women workers they were never well rewarded for their work. Many took in lodgers, some cleaned other people's houses, washed other people's clothes, took care of neighbours' children or their elderly dependants, or nursed the sick. In her autobiography *Jipping Street*, Kathleen Woodward recalled her widowed mother's bitter complaints about earning a living by washing clothes: 'Wash wash wash; it's like washing your guts away. Stand stand stand. I want six pairs of feet and then I'd have to stand on my head to give them a rest.' Kate Taylor said her Grannie Miller, living at Pakenham in Suffolk, was widowed in 1850 when she was still young but had nine children to support: 'She took in washing and needlework for the families of big houses in the parish, particularly the Vicarage where there was a large brood of daughters. These young ladies wore many petticoats, chemises, drawers and nightgowns, all made of fine linen and calico much betrimmed with tucking and fine lace. Grannie excelled at her work, though she had only a small oil lamp for night work and her hands were roughened by so much washing and ironing and no washing aids but yellow soap and soda.' Kate's other grandmother was Grannie Boyle, and she was widowed much later in life, in the 1890s. Her children were all married and she was by then bedridden, so she became chargeable to the parish.

Some working women survived widowhood quite well by living with their children. In 1851 Elizabeth Arscott of Devonshire was sixty years old, widowed and described as a grocer. She was the head of the household and lived with her unmarried son Philip (a woolstapler employing three men) and two unmarried daughters, Eliza and Elizabeth, who were woolsorters. Ten years later, the widow had obviously prospered and was described as a 'landed proprietor'. Only one of her children had married, and she and her husband continued to live with her mother and her siblings. Presumably the family had a better standard of living by remaining in one household, but there must also have been strong emotional reasons for choosing to live together in this way.

Some widows depended on the help of relatives for a time and then remarried. Take for example Elizabeth Furneaux, a serge weaver in Devonshire, who at the age of twenty-four in 1856 married Richard Routley, a carrier. In the next five years she had three children and also looked after two lodgers who were an important source of income. Her widowed mother, Mary, worked as a schoolmistress and lived nearby with a son who was a farm labourer. Elizabeth's husband died in 1865, and she inherited his carrier business and his capital. She continued to run the business, with the aid of one of her brothers, but four years later she married James Vile, and he took over the business. Several of Elizabeth's children by her first marriage were still living with her, but her inheritance of a small business had obviously put her in a strong position to find a second husband.

Compare the experience of Elizabeth Furneaux with that of Elizabeth Knowling, living in the same area of Devonshire, who at nineteen years old in 1853 married a farm labourer. When her father died a few years later, her mother Mary went to work as a charwoman and continued to live near to Elizabeth, with her three unmarried daughters who worked as spinners and weavers. Mary died in 1869, and so did Elizabeth's husband, William. Elizabeth had two dependent daughters still at school, no capital, no kin to help her, no skills to offer, so she was forced to go to work as a labourer in a wool mill, where her two older daughters were employed. Even with three adult women working full-time, their standard of living was very low because their earnings were so small. Elizabeth did not marry again.

Poor widows left on their own to bring up children were sometimes dependent on community support. John Castle, born in 1813 at Great Coggeshall, Essex, said that when his father (a silkworker) died in 1824, at the age of twenty-seven, he left a pregnant widow and four young children quite destitute. The parish allowed the widow seven shillings a week, and to survive she went out to work as a wet nurse. Throughout the nineteenth century widows with children formed the largest group of paupers receiving poor relief or entering the workhouse, where they were deliberately separated from their children. One child described being in a harsh and punitive workhouse in Stoke-on-Trent, known as the Bastille, in 1842. Sunday afternoon brought an hour of unspeakable joy, when children who had mothers were allowed to go to the women's room for an hour:

Bedlam was let loose for an hour. Wild joy, frantic exclamations, every conceivable form of speech possible to such people under such circumstances were employed. Love went mad in many cases. But all did not give way to the wild revelry of passion. Some mothers and children hung together in quiet, intense endearments . . . This was the one sweet merciful relief in the harsh discipline of the workhouse.

The Poor Law Amendment Act of 1834 intended that those physically capable of work should have no option but to support themselves. Public aid was given only to those – the aged, disabled, etc. – who could be supported neither by their own labour nor that of their families. Between the 1830s and the 1860s the Poor Law guardians in practice operated with considerably varying degrees of harshness or generosity. Some, contrary to the spirit of the 1834 Act, supplemented wages and gave outdoor relief which enabled families to exist in their own homes. Others offered only the workhouse. The situation was highly anarchic. Expenditure rose by forty per cent between 1850 and 1870, faster than the rate of population growth, and the response was a tightening of Poor Law policy from 1871. Wherever possible, outdoor relief was cut back, 'deserving' cases (those who were thought not to be personally responsible for their misfortunes) were referred to private charities for help, and the 'undeserving' (those whose lifestyles were not approved) were placed in workhouses. In 1871 the Poor Law Board was replaced by the Local Government Board, which laid down that widows should send their children into the workhouse and earn their own livings outside it, rather than receive the out-relief that enabled them to keep a family together. Small wonder that in 1870, and still in 1900, support from poor relief was the least sought and the last resort of the poor.

The numbers of women with children receiving outdoor relief decreased steadily from 1871 to 1892. The amount of money they received varied from 1s 6d to 2s 6d for the mother herself, with 1s 6d usually added for each child. Some relief was often given in kind, though many women resented the ignominy of 'fetching the parish' and the fatigue of a journey to claim the usually stale and monotonous food. Deductions were sometimes made if it was considered that mothers were not keeping their houses sufficiently clean. If the widow had an illegitimate child, outdoor relief was likely to be stopped altogether, so many pregnant widows sought to avoid scandal, poverty, or an unwanted marriage by procuring an illegal abortion. This was costly, dangerous and sometimes fatal, but desperate women continued to do it.

Society's ambivalence about whether poor women should be workers or full-time mothers was epitomized by the attitude to widows, who were at times objects of charity and at others punitively forced to work for the lowest wages or risk having their children taken away by poor law authorities or even private organizations. Widows with school-age children who did not go out to work were often called 'inferior types' or 'professional widows', yet they were blamed if any harm came to the children while they were out at work. The rules regarding outdoor relief for widows were significantly relaxed in 1911. Nevertheless, a 1914 government report cited the case of a widow found guilty of cruelty for locking her children up in one room while she went out to work for 10 shillings a week. She had feared that if she made a claim for poor relief it would have meant the break-up of her family. The original proposals for the National Insurance Act of 1911 had included a weekly allowance of 5 shillings to be paid to every widow having a child or children under sixteen years of age, but the government struck the widow out of the Bill altogether. According to Emmeline Pethwick Lawrence, 'It was done because Mr Lloyd George had to make his bill as attractive as possible to the working man . . . and he thought it would be a better bribe . . . if he increased the insurance of the man and withdrew the insurance of the widow.' Acute hardship persisted until widows' pensions – granted in 1925 – ameliorated the problem.

To be old, widowed, and poor was probably the worst possible situation for a woman. When poet Robert Browning wrote 'Grow old along with me/ The best is yet to be,' his optimism was not in tune with the reality for most old men, and it was ludicrous when applied to the lives of older widows. In fact, most men and women were not likely to survive what we have come to call middle age, but for those who did, growing old was very frightening. It represented failing strength, more and more serious illnesses, and approaching death. It was less threatening for men who could go on working and earning decent wages, and it was not uncommon for older widowers to remarry and start new families in their fifties or sixties. Alice Chase of Portsmouth told how her mother in the 1870s cheerfully married a man whose first wife had died, leaving him with four surviving children out of thirteen, and proceeded to give him nine more. And in the 1880s at Sutton Courtney, Berkshire, a labourer had twenty-five children from two marriages, and was able to field a family cricket eleven against the rest of the village.

By comparison with a man, an older widow was unlikely to have the skills to earn a good wage. If she went in search of a spouse she was not treated at all kindly by public opinion, for it was assumed that a man would marry her only for her property, despite the evidence that some widows had enough personal appeal to attract a husband. Generally speaking, however, a widower was three times as likely to remarry as his female counterpart in the period 1870 to 1914.

Women themselves often viewed growing old as a calamity. Since they were so valued in early womanhood when they were 'young and beautiful' and capable of bearing children, upper- and middle-class women had ample reason to be anxious about the time when they would be 'old and ugly' and barren. Women were generally considered old by the age of forty, though many still bore children when they were older than that. The author Fanny Burney had her first child when she was forty; Lady Caroline Capel gave birth to her thirteenth baby when she was forty-two (in 1815); Henrietta, wife of Lord Alderley, found herself pregnant again at forty (in 1847) and took steps to abort herself. After the age of forty, a woman was expected to 'act her age'. The puzzle is to know what she was supposed to have been doing before that, since it is unlikely that most women had been kicking up their heels. Moral tracts and beauty manuals counselled her to behave and dress in a manner deemed suitable for the 'decline of life'. The adventuress Lola Montez wrote in her book *The Art of Beauty* (1858) that paint and powder should not be used by 'ladies who have passed the age of life when roses are natural to the cheek. A rouged old woman is a horrible sight – a distortion of nature's harmony.' The best compliment a woman could hope to hear was that she was 'well preserved'. Male novelists and poets were generally unkind in their comments on older women, and women authors added to this negative image. Journalist Eliza Lynn Linton, for example, mercilessly ridiculed the English woman past her prime, in a series of unsigned articles in the *Saturday Review* in 1868, chiding her for acting and dressing inappropriately and for not attempting to find an interest outside herself. The most interesting thing to note from all this criticism is, however, that so many middle-aged women seem not to have been willing to stay put in the asexual, self-effacing, all-nurturing role that society had mandated for them.

The onset of the menopause was a perilous time for a woman. She was warned by medical books of the host of major or minor physical ills that could occur – hot flushes, severe vaginitis, life-threatening diseases of the uterus, breast cancer. Even if they survived all these, older Englishwomen could not expect to move into a position of power in the family and society as, for example, Chinese or Japanese women did when they assumed the role of mother-in-law. In general, women viewed the menopause with ambivalence. Liberation from menstruation and childbirth was welcome, but 'the change of life' signalled the end of a woman's importance as a reproductive creature. Some took this to mean the end of their sexual attraction for men (though this was not always so). Doctors emphasised the changes in character that they said came with the menopause – a predisposition towards depression, melancholia, and hysteria, as well as the querulousness and peevishness that had long been associated with old age. In a widely read study on the change of life, Dr Edward Tilt advised women to adjust to it by developing their moral qualities, through the pursuit of charitable endeavours. Whether following his advice or doing as they pleased, many older widows of the upper and middle classes had the time, energy and money to devote themselves to good works. Philanthropy and religion offered a respectable arena outside the home, and some widows, as we have seen, ventured into social and political causes. At the age of eighty-four (in 1909), Mary Haldane wrote a letter to *The Times* protesting that she had paid rates and taxes during thirty years of widowhood, but could not vote, whereas her male servants who paid no rates and taxes could vote.

The most popular and prescribed model for the older woman was, of course, the transformation into a grandmother. It was indeed a fulfilling role for many women, which overcame what we now call the 'empty-nest syndrome' – the confused sense of identity and loss of self-worth which so many older women feel. But it was not a completely happy role, for in the nineteenth century women were frequently called on to nurse and sometimes bury infant grandchildren, and, what was perhaps worse, their daughters and daughters-in-law who died in childbirth.

An older widow in the working class was usually worse off than other older widows. If she went out to work, she tended to earn low wages, finding that employers valued younger workers more than older ones. But even badly paid work provided her with a chance to support herself, rather than enduring abuse from unwelcoming kinsfolk or entering the workhouse. In the 1830s and 40s parliamentary investigators recorded the testimonies of some older widows who, despite illness and infirmity, worked gruelling hours in unspeakable conditions. Many, remarkably, kept both health and spirits, no matter how hard they worked. Mrs Fortescue, a forty-nine year old Nottingham cotton spinner, had worked in a factory since she was six and had borne seven children. She said, 'I don't think I look amiss for forty-nine; many people have said that. I keep pretty well as sharp as the young ones.' Sarah Siddons, a Leicester woollen worker aged fifty-eight, said she could still work twelve hours a day, but didn't want to work more. Elizabeth Hodges, a Burton silk worker of seventy-three, said the only thing she suffered from was 'swelled legs' from standing so long.

Old people understandably feared dependence on children, relatives, servants, public and private institutions or charity – whatever they were forced to accept. In England it was the custom in more affluent homes for one child, often the youngest daughter, to live at home, unmarried, caring for the parents when they could no longer care for themselves. It was also common for less affluent older widows to move in with their children, and some found loving and caring homes, where many made themselves useful as babysitters and housekeepers, but if they were unable to work or take care of themselves they were sometimes treated with varying degrees of indifference, resentment and even hatred. A lot depended on how much space there was in the house, how high the household income was, and how well the different generations got on with each other.

Perhaps the most unfortunate group of old women were the inmates of workhouses and asylums, who were virtually ignored by the outside world. Under the old Poor Law, each parish either provided them with money to live on in their own homes or a house where they could live with other paupers. The New Poor Law of 1834, and its workhouses, were not designed to provide mainly for aged paupers, but became effectively barracks for the infirm and closets for the dying. The exclusion of able-bodied women and dependent children became stricter through the middle years of the century, as separate boarding-out establishments were built for children and the women were forced onto outdoor relief.

In 1865 a group of doctors caused a flurry of interest when the *Lancet* exposed conditions in London workhouses, pointing out that over eighty-five per cent of the inmates were 'infirm'. Nearly all of them were 'permanents' leading a 'vegetable' existence. A parliamentary return of 1861 had shown that the largest single group of adult 'permanents' suffered from senility and that the majority had been incarcerated for at least ten years. There were attempts by Florence Nightingale and others to introduce trained professional nurses into the workhouses, but the guardians begrudged the money to pay them. The religious sisterhoods showed no interest in workhouse nursing, and the middle-class women in Louisa Twining's Workhouse Visiting Society concentrated on helping mothers and children rather than the elderly.

After 1871 the proportion of old and infirm inmates in workhouses increased to about seventy per cent. A civil servant named Geoffrey Drage said, in his book *The Problem of the Aged Poor* (1895), that the majority of paupers were widows whose main occupation earlier in life had been to keep house for their husbands. The women had had no opportunity to save anything for their old age, and when their husbands died, they usually lost their sole means of financial support. In a book called *Pauperism and the Endowment of Old Age* (1892), social investigator Charles Booth described some poor old widows in the Stepney district of London, who were forced to seek public relief at the parish workhouse at Bromley. They are heart-rending accounts of their struggles and family relationships:

Eliza English is a widow, now 83, whose husband (a stone mason) died 16 years before her application for relief. He was in no club, and had made no provision for her. She supported herself by charing until she was struck by paralysis. She stated that since then for 4 years she had lived with a daughter, and helped her at tailoring. She had no furniture of her own. It had been disposed of when she and her husband had both been in hospital 16 years before. No order [for relief] appears to have been made. After an interval of 7 years she again applied, stating that her son had helped her, but insufficiently, and could do so no longer. Her daughter was unkind, a terrible drunkard, pawning her children's clothes for drink. The daughter said her mother was troublesome and drank. The relieving officer found the house very dirty. The woman was admitted to Bromley.

Old Mrs Stimson has been asking for assistance ever since 1877. It has been usually refused . . . [but] she has struggled on and is now 75. She obtains some food from her daughters, and does needlework to pay the rent. Admitted to Bromley.

Mrs Bennett is a widow and blind and 73 years old. While her husband lived she and he hawked bathbricks and hearthstone, and earned about 6s a week. In December 1884 she asked for medicine for her husband, and the doctor's order was renewed in January 1885. In February he grew worse, and when visited was found very ill in a small and dirty ill-smelling room with bed on floor. He died before he could be moved to the sick asylum. In May the widow asked for admission to the house. She looked ill, dirty, and miserable, and was admitted.

In workhouses were the incurable masses the hospital authorities refused to treat. The London ones provided nearly three times as many beds as the hospitals. The conditions are vividly illustrated by the Bethnal Green workhouse infirmary in the 1890s. Among 335 women inmates, there were sixty-five over 80 years old, ten totally blind and twenty-six crippled. Another one hundred were infirm. Yet there was only one nurse, who found it utterly impossible to keep the women clean and wholesome. There appears to have been little intentional ill-treatment, but workhouse life was pervaded by a painful austerity and a lack of clothes, food, warmth and affection. The pervasive smell was of sour potato and stale urine, the prevailing noise a mingling of intermittent groans, oaths and screams.

By the end of the century the plight of the aged poor had become a public issue in England. In 1892 approximately one in four persons over sixty-five was classified as a 'pauper'. The term applied to 'indoor paupers' living at public expense in workhouses, and 'outdoor paupers' living in their homes and receiving medical and financial aid. In the 1890s a Royal Commission investigated pauperism among the aged, and Charles Booth publicly advocated the introduction of old age pensions. His help in converting public opinion to this cause was invaluable in securing the passage of the Old Age Pensions Act in 1908. This was a payment of 5 shillings a week (10 shillings for a couple) to men and women over seventy years old whose income from all sources did not exceed £26 a year. It was supposed to be withheld from 'those who had habitually failed to work according to ability and need and those who had failed to save money regularly'. It was welcomed wholeheartedly by the people themselves because it was at first non-contributory and it gave the old some sense of dignity.

The minority report of the Royal Commission on the Poor Law in

1909 provided the groundwork for future social legislation. It was a bleak picture of the old and insane living in workhouses, yet British paupers did better than their counterparts in Europe, and to keep the situation in perspective it is well to remember that the majority of old people lived out their lives in their own homes, or lived with relatives who looked after them.

8

Making Their Own Way

THE LIVES OF
UNMARRIED MIDDLE-CLASS WOMEN

> I believe we are touching on better days, when women will have a genuine normal life of their own to lead. There perhaps will not be so many marriages, and women will be taught not to feel their destiny *manqué* if they remain single. They will be able to be friends and companions in a way that they cannot be now . . . I regard myself as a mere faint indication, a rudiment of the idea, of certain higher qualities and possibilities that lie in women . . .
>
> Letter from Geraldine Jewsbury to Jane Carlyle, 1849

Despite Geraldine Jewsbury's hopes, throughout the nineteenth century unmarried women were generally regarded as social failures, and treated with alternating pity and contempt. Most of all they were regarded as anomalies who challenged the notion that being a wife and mother was the natural expectation of women. The social ideal was that all women would marry and be kept by a husband, yet the 1851 Census showed there were half a million more women than men in Britain. It also revealed that a million women remained unmarried (by 1911 this number rose to nearly one and a half million). To some observers it seemed there had been a breakdown in the social system. About twenty per cent of men had never married, many of them pleading they could not afford to, and this was accepted as an understandable if regrettable reason. But people found it hard to believe that a woman remained single from choice.

No one knows how many spinsters would have married if they had received acceptable proposals. No one knows how many women were like Jane Austen, who had no aversion to marriage but remained unmarried because she felt it was dishonourable to marry 'without Affection'. But Jane was fortunate, as were many unmarried women of her social level throughout the century, in having a family that could maintain her in comfort; she could not have supported herself on the meagre earnings from her novels. Unusual contemporaries of Jane Austen were the unmarried sisters Sarah and Mary Spencer, daughters of a gentleman in Sussex, who found themselves with a very limited income when their father died early in the century. To earn a living, they bravely rented a farm, which they worked for many years in the village of Rottingdean. The local yeomen and peasants resented them, calling them Captain Sally and Man Mary, but the local gentry respected their work and continued to visit them as social equals.

Figures are unobtainable on how many middle-class women lived with men as their wives, without going through a marriage ceremony; it was an unusual and daring thing to admit. There were some famous such liaisons: for example, the novelist George Eliot lived with George Henry Lewes for twenty-five years from 1854 (though the reason they remained unmarried was that he could not get a divorce from his wife, having condoned her adultery). Mary Braddon (1837–1915) wrote sensational novels and had a rather sensational life, for she lived with a married man whose wife was in a mental asylum. She bore five children before his wife died and they were finally able to marry. And Karl Marx's daughter, Eleanor, lived openly for many years from 1880 with a man to whom she was not married.

As far as the law of England was concerned, for most of the nineteenth century an unmarried woman was more independent than a married woman. As Barbara Leigh Smith pointed out in her 1854 *Summary*, a spinster had the same rights to property and protection from the laws, and the same obligation to pay taxes to the state, as a man. If duly qualified she could vote on parish questions and for parish officers, though not for her Member of Parliament. Unlike a married woman, she was free to act as agent for another person, as a trustee, as an executrix under a will, or an administratrix of the personal property of a deceased next of kin. Legitimate children belonged to their father; illegitimate children belonged to their mother, and the father could not take possession of them, even if he avowed he was their father.

Despite the ferment of popular discussion about the legal subordination of married women, and the novels and conduct books which laid bare 'the trials of married life', it was still generally assumed that being married was preferable to being single. As Charlotte Williams-Wynn (who never married) wrote ironically in 1845:

Keep your daughter's intellect back. Let her draw, sing, study botany, languages etc. etc. but do not urge her to think . . . [or she may] desire to find a husband to whom, in strict justice, she can look up, instead of doing so as her duty . . . whether he deserves it or not.

In the nineteenth century it was *not* the aim of of all English women to marry. Some believed that marriage was incompatible with a higher life of the spirit; the religious revolt was an old one, usually practised by nuns and sisters in religious orders. But many other women simply did not want to marry. As Elizabeth Sandford (herself married) said in *Female Improvement* (1836), 'The fact of remaining single may presuppose the not being easily won, as well as the not being sought . . . in the majority of cases, the former is the cause.' Writer Mary Russell Mitford declared in a letter to a friend in 1810, when she was twenty-three years old:

I shall not marry Sir William Elford, for which there is good reason; the aforesaid Sir William having no sort of desire to marry me; neither shall I marry anybody. I know myself well enough to be sure that if any man were so foolish as to wish such a thing, and I were foolish enough to answer 'yes', yet a timely wish of wisdom (caprice some might call it) would come upon me, and I should run away from the church door.

Mary happily devoted herself to looking after her adored but irresponsible father, who was recklessly extravagant, addicted to gambling, and had lost the family fortune. She took on the responsibility for earning the family income by writing. Many other women preferred, as an alternative to marriage, to live with a father or a brother. Writer Mary Berry, the elder of the two accomplished ladies whom Horace Walpole once called his 'twin wives', took complete charge of her father's affairs when she was sixteen years old. She described her father as a gentleman of independent means and a 'yielding indolent character'. Her mother had died when she was still an infant. Mary never married and early took to authorship, but her books were published under her father's name for propriety's sake, and her work was not publicly acknowledged until 1844. Dorothy Wordsworth, sister of the poet William, was his 'Perfect companion' who inspired him in success, and without whom he could not have been a poet, he said, because of the contribution she made to his poetic imagination. She never married, because 'her passion for her brother was so intense as to preclude her feeling for any man an emotion which would have satisfied the physical as well as the spiritual side of her nature.' The Journal she commenced in 1798 recorded everyday impressions and seemingly trivial events with a wonderful vividness. It also recorded the agony she felt when William married in 1802; but she and Mary had been friends from infancy, and they lived together with William in harmony, sharing the upbringing of the five children and the copying out of William's poetry. Charles and Mary Lamb lived so closely together that when the latter had a mental illness and went into an asylum, her lonely devoted poet brother wrote, 'I am a widow's thing, now thou art gone!' Elizabeth Sewell, an educationist who never married, said of her brother William, 'I never loved anyone else in the same intense way, and to him I owe all that is precious for Time and Eternity. I was so engrossed in my feelings for my brother that I had no thought to give to anyone else.' Passionate devoted love for a member of one's close family was considered by the Victorians pure, safe, untainted by sex.

Although young women were expected to remain emotionally tied to their families until marriage, they often developed when young (possibly at boarding or finishing school) close friendships with women of the same age and class. Such relationships might last a lifetime, even if the friends lived far apart and met infrequently. 'Romantic friendship' with another woman was encouraged by conservative writers of conduct books, and it was an outlet for women to confide their most intimate fears and plans, as Charlotte Brontë did to Ellen Nussey, or Florence Nightingale to her friend, Clarkey, in Paris. There was often tension between family claims and those of friendship, and as writer Dinah Mulock Craik pointed out in 1858, the ideal romantic friendship was supportive, loyal, but limited:

For two women, past earliest girlhood, to be completely absorbed in one another, and make public demonstration of the fact, by caresses and quarrels, is so repugnant to common sense, that where it ceases to be silly it becomes actually wrong. But to see two women, whom Providence has denied nearer ties, by a wise substitution making the best of fate, loving, sustaining, and comforting one another, with a tenderness often closer than those of sisters, because it has all the novelty of election which belongs to the conjugal tie itself – this, I say, is an honourable and lovely sight.

Many women agreed with Craik that excessive displays of emotion between romantic friends were unwise, but they did not think of their friendships as 'second best' to marriage. They preferred relationships with their own sex. Constance Maynard, for example, did not marry, but while at Girton formed a passionate attachment to Louisa Lumsden, who called Constance 'her wife'. There are famous and well-documented lesbian relationships between aristocratic women, such as 'The Ladies of Llangollen', in the diaries of Anne Lister (1791–1840), and between various members of the Bloomsbury set such as Vita Sackville West, Violet Trefusis and Virginia Woolf. Such friendships between women were not regarded as being in any way sinister or 'deviant' until the 1920s. Parliament attempted to bring lesbianism within the scope of the criminal law for the first time in 1921, and in 1928 Radclyff Hall's new novel, *The Well of Loneliness*, which defended female emotional and sexual relationships, was judged obscene by the courts. By the 1930s the intense female networks and support systems taken for granted by nineteenth-century women were no longer openly possible.

Some women toyed with the idea of getting married, but then went off the idea. Harriet Martineau, who got engaged in the 1840s but whose fiancé died before the marriage could take place, wrote later that she wondered if she would have had the strength to go through with a marriage that would have distracted her from her path of duty (her writing). Charlotte Brontë remained from choice a spinster most of her life; she had three proposals of marriage which she refused, on the grounds that she did not wish to make marriage the principal object of her actions, and anyway she did not find her suitors attractive enough! She decided that there was 'no more respectable character on this earth than an unmarried woman who makes her own way through life quietly, perseveringly – without support of husband or brother.' Later Charlotte did marry, but within months died of consumption aggravated by pregnancy. Florence Nightingale turned down an offer of marriage from the rising young journalist Richard Monckton Milnes, because of her own sense of destiny. She was often 'agonizingly lonely' afterwards, but said she could not have borne to share his life. Constance Maynard, later Principal of Westfield College, refused when young to marry a highly eligible Scots minister, writing in her diary that he never mentioned giving her a fine, full, rounded life, and only saw her in relation to himself. She never married. The *Englishwoman's Review* insisted that 'the higher a woman's nature is, the more likely it is that she will prefer rather to forego marriage altogether, than surrender herself to a union that would sink her below her own ideal.'

Ann Richelieu Lamb wrote in 1844 this spirited defence of remaining single:

> The unmarried woman is *somebody*; the married, nobody! The former shines in her own light; the latter is only the faint reflection of her husband's, in whom both law and public opinion suppose her 'to be lost' . . . Surely the state of the much-ridiculed spinster is better than this very equivocal position, in which there is a great risk of losing our very identity . . .

Why, she asked, since there was no disgrace in being a bachelor, was it considered disgraceful to be a spinster? She thought the unmarried women amongst her friends were the most kind-hearted, happy and intelligent women she knew, and that many married women would have been happier remaining spinsters.

Frances Power Cobbe, too, painted a buoyant picture of spinsterhood:

> The 'old maid' of 1861 is an exceedingly cheery personage, running about untrammeled by husband or children; now visiting her relatives' country houses, now taking her month in town, now off to a favourite pension on Lake Geneva, now scaling Vesuvius or the Pyramids. And what is better, she has found not only freedom of locomotion, but a sphere of action peculiarly congenial to her nature.

She later wrote her autobiography 'to show how pleasant and interesting and useful a life was open to an unmarried woman'. Elizabeth Haldane (1862–1937) wrote of her long unmarried life:

> This book shows how a woman passed from the restrictions of one century to the interest of another. It may also show how she may have a perfectly happy and full life, though devoid of some of the ameliorations that novelists and psychologists tell us make life worth living.

It was not difficult for upper- and middle-class women of independent means, or with the ability to earn a decent living for themselves, to stand by their determination not to marry, and to have fulfilling lives. Most of the intrepid Victorian Englishwomen who travelled abroad to 'wild' places were unmarried and financially independent. Many of them travelled for reasons of frail health, and found themselves, once abroad, miraculously cured of their dyspepsia, depression and ennui. Isabella Bird Bishop (1831–1904) had been a sickly girl, and was operated on for a spinal tumour when she was eighteen. When she was forty, and both parents were dead, she commenced her life as a serious adventurer and writer of travel books. She was the most daring solitary woman explorer of her time, travelling in Australia, New Zealand, Hawaii, North America, Japan, Korea, China, Malaya, Egypt, India, Tibet, Persia, Kurdistan and Turkey. From the paddle-steamer *Nevada*, on the Pacific, Isabella wrote to her sister in 1872, 'I am often in tempestuous spirits. It seems a sort of brief resurrection of a girl of twenty-one.'

Mary Kingsley had a tiny annuity which left her free at the age of thirty, after her parents' death, to travel to Africa and embark on anthropological studies and collect fish for the British Museum. In 1893 she published one of the most brilliant and entertaining books ever written about Africa. From SS Lagos, off the West African coast, Mary wrote to a friend later that year, 'I am fit and young again.' She thought the correct dress for a woman traveller was that of a lady, and wrote of taking depth-soundings in Africa with her umbrella, and of fending off crocodiles in a mangrove swamp while dressed in a high-necked white blouse and long black skirt. Back in England, she enjoyed dressing like a maiden aunt and then relating *risqué* stories of her life among naked cannibals. Marianne North travelled extensively to many parts of the world, between 1870 and 1884, to paint flora, and Constance Gordon Cumming travelled in Fiji, Hawaii, California, the Himalayas, India, Ceylon, China and Egypt. Alexandra David Neel disguised herself as a Tibetan peasant woman and trekked through the deserts and mountains to Lhasa. She was the first white woman to see the fabled city. Always ill in Europe, she achieved astounding feats of endurance in the Himalayas, even at the age of sixty.

These women found their liberation in travel, in testing themselves against hardship and danger. Intensely individualistic, happiest in solitude, they felt oppressed by the demands and restrictions of their own culture. Obedience to Victorian home life often led them to make endless excuses and self-abasements in the pages of their books. And when they returned to England they found it hard to get the male world to take them seriously as professionals. In 1892 the Council of the Royal Geographical Society resolved to admit women to Fellowship (membership) on the same terms as men, and soon afterwards elected twenty-two women, including Isabella Bird. The Council's action was opposed tooth and nail by members who thought 'the genus of professional female globetrotters . . . is one of the horrors of the latter end of the nineteenth century', and no more women were admitted for twenty years. Then in 1912, faced with the expense of finding new premises, the Society decided to admit women again. Constance Gordon Cumming was made a Life FRGS in 1914.

Unmarried women without independent means often became the mainstay of aged parents or other relatives, being expected to remain utterly self-sacrificing for all who needed them. Harriet Martineau was recalled from her journalistic work in London to act as companion to her widowed mother in Norwich in the 1830s. Charlotte Brontë nursed her sick father in the 1840s. Rachel McMillan, socialist activist and educational reformer, was called from school when she was eighteen years old, to take care of her sick grandmother. She loved the old lady, but the nursing lasted for eleven long years until the grandmother died in 1888.

Some women enjoyed their family responsibilities and felt their lives were useful and worthwhile, but others felt completely exploited and imprisoned. Mrs Maria Grey (1818–1906), a reformer of girls' education, who worked in close partnership with her unmarried sister, Emily Shirreff, was full of praise for spinsters, saying she knew of no class of the community whose service was so valuable as that of unmarried daughters in whom fathers and mothers found comfort in their declining years, elder sisters who took a lost mother's place, and maiden aunts who stepped into every gap in the household. However, she quoted a maiden aunt of hers who had told her in childhood (around 1830): 'My dear, if you don't marry, you will find that you have on your shoulders half a dozen husbands, and as many families of children.' It was not a prospect that enthralled most young women.

The relationship of a man with his deceased wife's sister became a focus of controversy in Victorian England because the pattern of family living made it especially sensitive. It was common for unmarried women to live with a married sister, and to take care of the children if the mother died. It followed that the possibility of a widower wanting to marry the sister was high. Before 1835 it was possible to do this, but then an Act of Parliament prevented unions viewed as incestuous (though marriages made before that date remained valid). Attempts to go back to the old ways began in 1842, and the 'Wife's Sister's Bill' became a hardy annual for sixty-five years, until passed in 1907. By that time, supporters of the Bill were arguing that the prohibition of such marriages actually encouraged sin, since widowers often lived as man and wife with their deceased wife's sister.

The consequences of remaining unmarried, for those who had no money and could not live with family members, were often economic hardship and social marginality. Ann Richelieu Lamb pinpointed the heart of the matter when she wrote in 1844 that the reason many unmarried women were unhappy was not that they were old maids, but that they had insufficient income. As Jane Austen had said, ironically, spinsters had 'an unhappy propensity to be poor'.

The plight of single women, rudely called 'redundant women' by some social commentators, was discussed by a well-known journalist, W.R. Greg, in 1862. He lamented the 'unnatural' number of spinsters living in industrial England:

There is an enormous and increasing number of single women in the nation . . . a number which, positively and relatively, is indicative of an unwholesome social state, and is both productive and prognostic of much wretchedness and wrong. There are hundreds of thousands of women . . . scattered through all ranks, but proportionately most numerous in the middle and upper ranks – who have to earn their own living, instead of spending and husbanding the earnings of men . . . who are compelled to lead an independent and incomplete existence of their own.

In his calculations, Greg omitted unmarried domestic servants, because 'they fulfil both essentials of women's being; they are supported by and they minister to, men.' His solution to the problem of the others was twofold: first, he advised single women to adopt the pleasing manners of expensive prostitutes in order to marry their way out of their 'economic redundancy' (at the same time he advised men to marry earlier and settle for a modest style of life); secondly, he said single women over thirty years of age should be sent to Canada, Australia or the United States, where there was a surplus of men and they would find husbands. These ideas enraged the strong-minded women who were fighting for women's rights, but remained popular with the general public throughout the century.

Going to one of the British colonies had been an avenue of escape for women long before Greg advocated it in the 1860s. For example, Charlotte Brontë's friend, Mary Taylor, went to New Zealand in 1835, seeking activity and independence. As the daughter of a well-to-do Yorkshire businessman she was not poor. She quickly adjusted to the new life, taught for a time and then dealt in cattle, bought land, built a house and later opened a successful shop. Although powerful factors operated to discourage poorer middle-class women than Mary from risking the hardships of emigration, many took advantage of the meagre facilities which enabled them to do so. Once abroad they proved to be remarkably adaptable, willing to risk their gentility by undertaking work which would have been unthinkable for them in England. Two societies aided them in the 1840s: Caroline Chisholm's Family Colonization Loan Society and Sidney Herbert's Fund for Promoting Female Emigration.

Caroline Chisholm, wife of an Indian Army officer, is best known for her rescue work in Sydney, Australia, where she lived from 1838. Without official help, she gathered abandoned and friendless female immigrants, set up a home for them, established an employment register and conveyed the women to their employers. When she returned to live in London she besieged the Colonial Office with proposals for more humane and efficient methods of female and family emigration and then set up her own emigration society as a moral and matrimonial crusade. She believed in the female civilizing mission, and stressed that Australia needed good and virtuous women to become wives and mothers who would stabilize society. The prospect of boatloads of brides for bushmen was not universally welcomed, some people being 'shocked to think that women should be exported like so many bales of printed cotton', as the magazine *Household Words* put it. But 409 women were sent to Australia in 1850, most taking work as domestic servants.

Sidney Herbert's society was originally aimed at 'distressed gentle-women', but interest soon shifted to the lower middle class and educated women of some gentility. By 1853, emigration had become a more respectable proposition, and lower middle-class women paid £22 each to take ship to Australia, 'solely with a view to marriage'. The two emigration societies were successful in their aims for about four years, but they gradually dwindled due to lack of funds, and the outbreak of the Crimean War hampered shipping arrangements.

The Female Middle-Class Emigration Society, formed in 1862 to send women out to Canada, Australia and New Zealand, had only modest success because it found itself in conflict with the settlement colonies over whether there was really a demand for working gentle-women, such as governesses. Only 302 women emigrated between 1862 and 1886. From 1880 to 1914 a variety of female emigration organizations came into being, and they had no difficulty in finding lower middle-class women, as well as respectable working-class women, willing to go out as domestic servants, with the hope of marriage. They established hostels where women could live before leaving England, sent matrons to supervise each party of women on the voyage, set up welcoming hostels in the colonies, and arranged for the women to get respectable employment.

Poor but genteel spinsters who did not emigrate often needed to earn a living not only for themselves but for dependants – some daughters had to support a father or mother (or both), some sisters had to support their siblings. Middle-class women had little choice of work in the first half of the century: in the 1850s the Church and nearly all offices of government were closed to women; the Post Office afforded some employment, but there was no important office (other than being the sovereign) which a woman could hold. The professions of law and medicine, whether or not legally closed, were closed to women in fact. A small number of women made a living by writing, some very successfully indeed. But most middle-class women had to choose between three underpaid and overcrowded occupations: governess (or teacher in a small private school), paid companion (usually overworked and underpaid) or seamstress (making or altering or mending clothes for the well-to-do). The most fortunate teachers were those who had capital to start a school of their own, and were successful in the venture. For example, Anne Jemima Clough (later Principal of Newnham College, Cambridge) was born into an affluent family in Liverpool in 1820, but in 1841 her father's cotton business failed. Self-taught Anne opened a small school in the family home, and on the proceeds she kept the family. Women of lesser gentility and a little capital could gain a lower middle-class income by keeping a shop (as did Miss Matty in Elizabeth Gaskell's novel, *Cranford*), or a superior lodging house, or a tea-room. Harriet Martineau was appalled at the low wages distressed gentlewomen received, saying, 'Their condition is such that if their sufferings were but made known, emotions of horror and shame would tremble through the whole of society.' But those who employed them had no such feelings, even when their plight became widely known.

In 1850 there were estimated to be 21,000 governesses and many more would-be governesses. For lack of an alternative job, many women took the work without any interest in teaching and even with a dislike of children. No one envied the life of a governess, caught between classes in a rigidly class-structured society. Too low for the family, too high for the servants, she was isolated, yet had no privacy, and was almost universally despised. She worked all day, often sharing a bedroom with the children and taking care of their baths and meals as well as their lessons, yet was discouraged from being affectionate to them; in odd moments she did family mending. Wages ranged from £10 to £30 a year plus room and board. Although that was well above what women earned as factory workers, it was less than men made as tutors, teachers or clerks. When her services were no longer needed, she was out of work and home without a pension. Florence Nightingale noticed that many governesses ended their days in hospitals or insane asylums. The Governesses' Benevolent Institution was founded in 1843, to help the unemployed find work, and provide a place for them to live in old age. Charlotte Brontë was deeply unhappy as a teacher and as a governess, and wrote about it in *Jane Eyre*. Lady Eastlake felt Brontë's novel showed ingratitude to employers, but her 1848 essay in the *Quarterly Review* supported Charlotte's views:

A governess has no equals, and therefore can have no sympathy . . . The servants invariably detest her, for she is a dependant like themselves, and yet, for all that, as much their superior in other respects as the family they both serve. Her pupils may love her . . . but they cannot be her friends. She must, to all intents and purposes, live alone, or she transgresses that invisible but rigid line which alone establishes the distance between herself and her employers.

The growth of elementary and secondary education in the second half of the century (described in Chapter 2) made most governesses obsolete. The new secondary schools required a teacher with formal training, and Queen's and Bedford Colleges, originally set up in the early 1850s for the purpose of better educating governesses, provided such training. Elementary schools provided opportunities for better-off working-class girls to progress from an apprenticeship at age thirteen to training school and finally a salaried teaching post. By the end of the century, teaching was professional work with clear standards of certification and pay. The average starting salary of a woman elementary teacher was about £90 a year in 1909, that of a High School teacher £90 to £100. When Sara Burstall began her career as assistant mistress at her old school, the North London Collegiate, in the 1880s, 'at what was for those times an exceedingly good salary, £120 per annum', she reflected that 'economic independence is, after all, one of the requisites of a full and happy life . . . The joy and satisfaction of the modern woman's independence is sometimes not stressed as it should be in the many discussions of feminism.' As an example, she said, 'The first time I cashed a cheque, I thought the shining sovereigns passed across the counter were magical.'

Women encountered strong resistance to their entering traditionally male professions, as seen in the case of women becoming doctors (see Chapter 2). But they were widely accepted into nursing, subject to the supervision and authority of male doctors, after Florence Nightingale (1820–1910), born into a wealthy upper-class family, made it respectable. Hospitals in the early nineteenth century were generally places of abominable filth and stench. Nursing duties were minimal, and the low-paid, untrained nurses were reputed to sustain themselves by drinking alcohol. They were also accused of loose sexual behaviour with male patients. In 1853 Florence undertook the administration of the

Hospital for Invalid Gentlewomen and proved herself a forceful manager. The Crimean War broke out in January 1854, and by the autumn *The Times* was printing accounts of the terrible neglect of the English wounded. In October, at the request of the government, Florence Nightingale set out with thirty-eight women to tend the sick soldiers. Conditions in the Crimea were nightmarish: war wounds accounted for only one sixth of soldiers' deaths – typhus, cholera, dysentery and other diseases accounted for the rest. The doctors and military personnel did not welcome her, but since Florence had money, and friends in the War Office such as Sydney Herbert, they were forced to work with her. Under her direction, sanitary conditions improved and lives were saved. She returned to England in 1856 a national heroine, and by 1860 money had been raised to found the Nightingale School and Home for Nurses associated with St Thomas's Hospital. She succeeded, through courageous and stubborn self-assertion, in establishing the nursing profession. The *Victoria Magazine* said in 1876 that the wages of a trainee nurse were £12 for the first year and £20 for the remaining two, with board, lodging and uniform. Trainees had to be aged between twenty-five and thirty-five. The magazine asked whether it was likely that 'a woman of culture' would accept such wages – less than a nursemaid or a plain-cook would demand. But some middle-class women did accept the job. The traditionally female occupation of midwifery, from which men had tried to exclude them, was reclaimed when the Midwives Act of 1902 re-established the profession by setting up clear, modern standards and licensing procedures.

Women benefited from the growth of commercial and government office work, related to England's burgeoning role as an imperial and industrial nation. The Society for Promoting the Employment of Women was founded by Barbara Leigh Smith, Jessie Boucherett and others of the Langham Place Circle in 1859, 'to help those who have been born and bred ladies to preserve the habits, the dress, and the countless moral and material associations of the rank to which they were born.' The Society lasted into the twentieth century as a source of referrals, training, and short-term educational loans for women seeking employment in skilled lower middle-class jobs, such as book-keeping, law copying, typewriting and telegraphy. The Post Office and particularly the telegraph system were among the first to employ women – although at lower pay and in lower-status jobs than those of men. More than half of all male clerks were earning over £100 a year by 1901, while almost all female clerks earned less than that and had a hard time making ends meet (it should be remembered, however, that an entire working-class family was expected to get by on £1 a week at that time). By the end of the century, the number of women clerical workers had grown from a handful to an 'army' of typists, clerks, telegraphers and bookkeepers. 'Typewriting machines' came into wide use in the 1880s, and shorthand, a male skill acquired by parliamentary reporters such as Charles Dickens, was increasingly learned by women. Although clerical work was considered 'genteel', requiring a degree of literacy and a formality of dress associated with professional life, working conditions were often unpleasant. Women worked as long as twelve hours a day in poorly ventilated, dirty rooms with inadequate toilet facilities.

Women eventually benefited too from the expansion of the retail trade. However, the work of a shop assistant, considered the province of a man until the 1870s, although higher in status was no less arduous than that of a factory worker, and no better paid. A shop assistant worked perhaps seventy-five hours a week, standing on her feet all that time, with only forty-five minutes away from the counter for two daily meals. The pay was about 10 shillings (half of one pound) a week, out of which she had to find 'decent' clothing, and a woman was often forced to take part of her salary as room and board. Near the shop employers provided barrack-style housing, which was usually overcrowded, poorly ventilated, dirty, and inadequately supplied with water and toilets. Meals were served in damp, insect-infested basements and consisted largely of bread and tea. The supposed gentility of the job did not exempt the women from humiliating and costly supervision, which included an extensive system of fines for such offenses as giving the wrong change, lateness, incivility to customers or floor managers, or even failure to make their own beds. All this was vividly described by Margaret Bondfield, who started work in 1887, when she was fourteen, as a draper's assistant in Brighton. She was an early and active member of the National Union of Shop Assistants, formed in 1891, and eventually she became a Labour Member of Parliament and, in 1929, the first woman cabinet minister in Britain. There were attempts to limit shop workers' hours by legislation from the 1880s onwards, but it was less well regulated than factory work until well into the twentieth century.

In 1889, reformer Maria Grey noted the result of the feminist re-evaluation of middle-class women's work:

> Within these few years a vast and sweeping change has taken place,
> of unprecedented rapidity, causing a reaction from this doctrine of
> idleness and dependence as essential to ladyhood toward the opposite
> extreme, of work and independence as essential to honourable
> womanhood; work, meaning paid work, and independence, meaning
> life apart from the home life, and free from the duties and constrain-
> ing order of the home.

The *Englishwoman's Review* said in October 1909 that the average
schoolgirl at the end of her course had a choice of between thirty and
forty vocations, for example, she could be a teacher, nurse, journalist,
chemist, doctor, bookkeeper, laundry manager, rent collector, hair-
dresser, commercial traveller, keeper of a teashop, sanitary inspector,
Post Office clerk, actress or asylum attendant. The magazine thought
teaching was the best prospect, 'considering the short hours and long
holidays, as well as the salaries paid.'

Whether or not they needed to earn their own livings, a passion for
meaningful paid work became the focus of many middle-class women's
lives as the century progressed. It was a way out of the confining
'garden' of home life into perceived freedom and adventure. But Bessie
Rayner Parkes believed it was the economic need of work that created
the mid-century women's movement; she wrote in *Essays on Woman's
Work* (1865):

> Except for the material need which exerted a constant pressure over
> a large and educated class, the women's movement could never have
> become in England a subject of popular comment, and to a certain
> extent of popular sympathy.

By the end of the century, fifty years of agitation, work and education
had radically changed working possibilities and conditions for women,
but it was still important to struggle for further changes, such as to
gain more public respect for their activities. Their efforts to gain a
foothold in male professions had everywhere been met with defeat or
very partial victory, and occupations regarded as 'women's work' were
generally undervalued and underpaid.

9

Cheap Labour

THE LIVES OF
UNMARRIED WORKING-CLASS WOMEN

In manufacturing towns, look at the value that is set on women's labour, whether it be skilful, whether it be laborious . . . Why, I ask, should women's labour be so undervalued?

Frances Morrison, a Radical, in 1834

A man thinks himself badly off if he cannot earn more than seventeen shillings a week. It is no exaggeration to say that there are thousands of girls in Manchester who think themselves lucky if they bring home seven shillings at the weekend, and more older and skilled women who can never hope to earn more than twelve shillings to the end of their lives.

Women's Committee of the Manchester and
Salford Trade Unions Council, 1903

Three-quarters of nineteenth-century English women were born into the working classes; theirs was a childhood that did not last long. The innocence of infancy was soon stripped away by the reality of their overcrowded, dirty, cold environment. For their parents, the struggle to keep alive obliterated most other considerations, and everyone in the family had to earn money as soon as they were able. In the early part of the century, girls as young as five or six were employed in mills, mines and workshops, often in degrading and dangerous conditions, though much depended on the location of the factory and the character of the individual employer. Elizabeth Bentley, then twenty-three years old, told a parliamentary committee in 1832 of starting her working life at six years old in a linen factory. She worked as a 'little doffer' (taking full bobbins off spinning frames and replacing them) from six in the morning until seven at night in the slow season, and from five in the morning until nine at night in the six months of the year when the mill was busy. If she fell behind, the foreman beat her with a strap. Her parents, working in the same factory, dared not complain for fear of losing their own jobs.

Bad as were the accounts of girls' work in textile mills, they were surpassed by stories of girls working in coal mines. Sarah Gooder, aged eight, a 'trapper' in a Yorkshire mine (she opened the air-door to allow waggons to pass through) said, 'It does not tire me, but I have a trap without a light, and I'm scared. Sometimes I sing when I have a light, but not in the dark; I dare not sing then. I don't like being in the pit.' Eleven-year-old Eliza Coats said, 'I hurry [push carts loaded with coal] with my brother. It tires my back and arms.' The 1830s was perhaps the first time in English history when the upper class decided that working long hours, in certain jobs, was unsuitable for children. An early Factory Act of 1833 provided that no child under thirteen should work more than eight hours a day, young persons aged between thirteen and eighteen might work twelve hours, and night work for children and young persons was forbidden. The 1842 Mines Act forbade the employment underground of girls and boys under the age of ten.

However, the great majority of girl child workers were in agriculture, small workshops and 'domestic industry' (producing goods in their own homes, for employers who provided the raw materials and paid them according to results). Many of these industries were not controlled by protective laws until late in the century, and only in 1876 were children under the age of ten forbidden to work for employers at all. Agricultural gang work, mainly in the eastern counties of England, consisted of bands of men, women and children under the direction of an overseer, moving from farm to farm to work as required. It was indescribably hard work for young children, and their wages were pitifully low. The father of a girl of eleven who had been a gang worker for two years said in 1843, 'I'm forced to let my daughter go, else I'm very much against it . . . She has complained of pain in her side very often; they drive them along – force them along . . . she is sometimes so tired, she can't eat no victuals when she comes home.' On the day she was eight years old, around 1858, the future Mrs Burrows left school in Lincolnshire and started work for fourteen hours a day; she was the eldest of about fifty child workers, some of whom were only five: 'We were followed all day long by an old man carrying a long whip in his hand which he did not forget to use,' she wrote later. 'For four years, summer and winter, I worked in these gangs – no holiday of any sort, with the exception of very wet days and Sundays – and at the end of that time it felt like Heaven to me when I was taken to the town of Leeds and put to work in a factory.' The gang system was widely condemned, but continued and increased because it was so profitable to the farmer and the gang master. The first check on the system came in 1867, when the Gangs Act prevented the employment of children under eight, and the death blow came with the Education Act of 1876.

Girls working at home in the domestic industries (also called outwork) were just as exploited as those in factories. The majority were trained in cottage schools owned either by the mistress herself (a dame school) or by a dealer who provided materials and employed a teacher. In some areas, where there were well-established local crafts at which children worked from an early age, 'academic' study was combined with instruction in these, such as lace-making, straw-plaiting, glove-stitching or knitting. But Mrs Watts, mistress of a straw-plaiting school at Hemel Hempstead in Hertfordshire, said, 'The mothers task the children too much; the mistress is obliged to make them perform it, otherwise they would put them in other schools . . . I have offered to teach sewing and reading as well as plaiting to my scholars, but the parents care nothing for it – plaiting alone is everything to them.' Jane Keynes, aged eleven in 1843, said, 'Been at lace-making ever since I was five; the work ain't so hard; some days I feel poorly, have sick headaches; don't know, but think it is from sitting so long and confinement.' Eva Paine, also a lace-maker, said, 'Work is hard and very tiring; my hands and arms ache.' Betty Yewsdale said of her Yorkshire knitting school, 'We knit as hard as we can [because] the one who knits the slowest gets well thumped.' Yet workers doing outwork regarded the discipline of factory work with horror, one girl telling the Factory Commission in 1833, 'I like it better than the factory, though we can't earn so much. We have our liberty at home, and get our meals comfortable, such as they are.' Down the century, there was continuing exploitation of young girls in what became known as the 'sweated trades' – such as the making of clothes and furniture – particularly in London. And all over England children continued to help their parents with outwork done in their homes, since there was no way to control this. In 1905, Robert Sherrard found late one evening in Birmingham 'three little children, busy at work at a table on which were heaped up piles of cards and a vast mass of tangled hooks and eyes. The eldest girl was eleven, the next nine, and a little boy of five completed the companionship. They were all working as fast as their little fingers could work. The girls sewed and the baby hooked.' The problem was poverty, endemic as it had been a century earlier.

Most girls preferred almost any work to being domestic servants, but when nothing else was available that is what they had to do. There were more women and girls in domestic service than in any other trade: in 1851 there were more than a million; in 1891 there were 1.4 million. It was a life of unremitting toil, though their labours made life easier for their employers. Hannah Cullwick (1833–1909) entered service at the age of eight in 1841, and wrote pathetically, 'Mrs Phillips was so very kind to me and taught me how to do everything properly – to wait at table, to wash up, to clean silver, and indeed everything . . . She always praised me after I'd cleaned the red brick floor on my hands and knees, and scoured the big white tables in the kitchen.' It is tempting to think that Hannah was being ironical when she wrote that, but the rest of her autobiography shows that she genuinely enjoyed housework, unlike the majority of servants. At the age of nine in 1867, the future Mrs Wrigley left home in Wales to become servant to a family in Stockport, Cheshire; she had no wages, but her parents were relieved of the need to board and lodge her. Unable at that time to read and write, she said she could not let them know how unhappy she was and how she 'fretted very much for my home'. Eventually a kindly neighbour wrote to her parents, and they came and took her to an employer closer to her home where she was happier.

Rose Ashton was thirteen when in 1905 she was sent to the local hiring fair at Ulverston, Lancashire, and became a farm servant. For six months she was virtually a slave, working even on Christmas Day: 'We had a nice Christmas dinner and I washed all up and she come out to me and said, "Have you finished, Rose?" And I said, "Yes, madam." She said, "Well, there's a bowl of string there and there's a big needle, and there's a heap of papers. I want you to go down the paddock." Now the paddock was their toilet . . . and I had to sit there and tear those pieces of paper into pieces like you have on a toilet roll and then I used to thread them and hang them on the back of the toilet door.

Well, I think I shed a bucket full of tears. That was my Christmas Day.' Such working conditions for servants changed only when other jobs became available and many women voted with their feet.

The girls who tended to have the bleakest lives of all were those who did not belong to any family, either because they were abandoned by their parents, or they were orphans. In the 1840s and 50s crusading journalist Henry Mayhew discovered and wrote about the bands of tiny children surviving by their wits on the streets of London, and he was appalled to find them so worldly-wise, earning their own livings and sometimes sexually experienced at the age of eight or nine. He talked to an eight-year-old girl selling watercress, who was proud of her independence and business ability: 'I'm a capital hand at bargaining . . . They can't take me in,' she bragged, 'I ain't a child and I shan't be a woman till I'm twenty, but I'm past eight, I am.' The problem was not new, but the number of destitute children grew alarmingly. Early in the century, attempts were made to provide them with relief and training for a job, in the hope that they would not become criminals, but since, as Mayhew said, they had been 'either untaught, mistaught, neglected, maltreated, regularly trained in vice, or fairly turned into the streets to shift for themselves', many found themselves before the courts for offences against property. Such children, said Charles Dickens in *Household Words*, 'hop about like wild birds, pilfering the crumbs which fall from the table of the country's wealthy.'

From 1834 large numbers of children were admitted to the workhouse because their parents were refused 'outdoor relief' and could not keep them. Lucy Luck recalled the heartbreaking day in 1852 when her mother, deserted by her husband, had to put her children into the Union workhouse in Tring, Hertfordshire: 'There my mother sat down on the steps with one of us on each side of her, and one in her arms, crying bitterly over us before she took us to the Union.' These pathetic pauper children had no holidays and no home to return to. Later in the century more and more children were cared for by national and local agencies under the scrutiny of the law, and some private charity orphanages were opened, such as Dr Barnardo's. Nora Adams lived in one from 1904 to 1911, and said her feelings were of hate, fear and rejection. Although she and her sisters stayed together, she said, 'We were as isolated from the world as if we were on a desert island.' She described punishments such as having to sit still for two hours, denial of food, being forced to eat all the nauseous food provided (it was cooked by the older girls, and often consisted of burnt porridge), being locked in a cupboard, and ritualized whippings. Most girls disliked living in such institutions, yet these orphanages rescued thousands of children from the streets and transformed them into young adults able to maintain themselves.

The nineteenth century was a harsh period in which to be a working-class spinster. As Ethel Snowden said in 1913, 'The plain unvarnished truth is that work open to women is not sufficient in amount or sufficiently well paid to enable them to live in a condition of ordinary comfort and decency.' Unable to earn enough to keep a home of her own, a spinster had to rely on a male relative for a roof over her head. As the dependent old maid, she was expected to attend to everyone's needs. Reasonably fortunate were the female pupil-teachers who provided the majority of recruits in elementary schools from the 1830s up to 1914. Maud Clarke told how, at the end of the century in West Bromwich, she was first appointed a monitress at age thirteen, earning 3 shillings a week until she took Candidates' Exams two years later. She then attended a day pupil-teacher centre for three years of full-time secondary education, taught by specialists who were graduates. Aged eighteen she won a government 'scholarship' by examination, and was then qualified to teach a class of fifty children and be paid fifteen shillings a week, or go on to a training college for two years at her own expense. But she said, 'there were no grants for further study, and very few girls went to college.' Like many others, Maud took a correspondence course, paying for her own fees and books, and when she had passed a further examination she became a certificated teacher on a salary rising to £90 a year.

Most working-class spinsters, however, were much worse off than elementary school teachers. There were four chief ways an unmarried woman could earn money: domestic service, factory work, street-selling and manual labour, and prostitution (this will be discussed later). Between one third and one half of all women who earned money outside the home did so as domestic servants. As wealth grew, more families could afford to hire a servant. As new industrial jobs opened up for men, they left domestic service to women, though men who remained as servants commanded better wages and conditions than females; *Punch* magazine featured a cartoon in 1863 showing a haughty butler carrying a letter upstairs on a silver tray, preceded by a female drudge hauling a heavy scuttle of coal. One woman recalled her service as 'a continuation of slavery, except that you were able to hand in your notice and leave instead of staying for life . . . maids had no liberty, status, or privileges.' They worked long hours and usually lived in squalid attics or basements. Worst off was the maid-of-all-work, sometimes called a skivvy, who was often the only servant in the home. Those who worked in larger houses with a retinue of servants might be kitchenmaids, housemaids or parlourmaids. Some, like Rosina Harrison, born 1899 in rural Yorkshire, were told by their mothers to smarten themselves up a bit, learn French and dressmaking, and get a job as a lady's maid. Rosina got her first job as lady's maid to the two daughters of Lady Irene Tufton, when she was nineteen, and later worked for Viscountess [Nancy] Astor. She never married. The advantages of a 'good' position in domestic service were the food and the wages, which were competitive with or better than other jobs available. Most women tended to work as servants for about ten years, saving up their wages to make it possible for them to marry.

In industrial areas, young women chose to work in the factories and mills, rather than become servants. It was unskilled, exhausting, monotonous and unhealthy. Conditions in pottery factories caused lead poisoning, workers in match factories got phosphorous poisoning, and work in cotton mills affected the lungs. Textiles employed the largest number of women in industry. Seventy-six per cent of all fourteen-year-old girls in Manchester in 1852 worked in cotton mills. 'It was a vast unexplored region, stifling, deafening and incredibly dirty,' said Alice Foley, who worked in a mill in the 1890s, and she also said, 'At first I was highly terrified by the noise and the proximity of clashing machinery.' Some factory women prided themselves on being 'ladylike'; others enjoyed rough play. Harry Pollitt said, of his entry as a lad into a Lancashire mill in the 1890s, that the female weavers played only polite tricks on him, but 'It was left to the buxom girls and women in the cardroom to break me in by taking my trousers down and daubing my unmentionable parts with oil and packing me up with cotton waste.' Factory women prided themselves on their ability to find a good husband, as the following folk song shows:

You'd easy know a weaver/When she goes to town
With her long yellow hair/And her apron hanging down.
With her scissors tied before her/Or her scissors in her hand.
You'll easy know a weaver/For she'll always get her man!

In factories women often earned more than they could in other jobs, but their wages were only between two thirds and one half of men's wages, even for identical work. Most women accepted the notion that their labour was less valuable than that of a man, and accepted unskilled, inferior, underpaid jobs of any kind available, because they desperately needed to earn money and did not have the power to demand anything better. As early as 1804, a Ladies Committee, formed with the object of 'promoting the education and employment of working women', stated that women were being 'grievously and unjustly intruded upon by the other sex', who were even pushing them out of occupations previously regarded as 'women's work'. Jobs for women were not available all over the country, and local attitudes varied. For example, women did not usually work outside the home in the coal-mining areas of Northumberland and Durham, whereas this was normal in textile mills in Lancashire and the potteries in Staffordshire, which were also coal-mining areas. Similarly, while many women worked in the hosiery works in Leicester in the late nine-teenth century, the same was not true of the lace and hosiery factories of Nottingham, where women were employed only as outworkers. Legal intervention in women's employment increased significantly from the 1840s, when their working conditions *in certain industries* came to be seen as a matter of public importance. The Mines and Collieries Act of 1842 excluded all women from underground mining; the Factories Act of 1847 limited the hours of women's work to twelve a day; another Act of 1853 established a normal working day of ten and a half hours for everyone except adult men. Most people probably thought these were excellent measures, but the women miners were not pleased because they found themselves excluded from better-paid work that they could otherwise get. In view of the widespread practice of women undertaking heavy work, the 'natural' physical weakness of women was not cited to justify these protective laws. As the report of the Commissioner on Mines, and the parliamen-tary debates on both the Mines and the Factory Acts show, it was not the gruelling hard work that outraged Victorian society, but the possible immorality of women engaged in such work. Horror was expressed at the close proximity of men and women in both mines and factories, their near nakedness and the perceived consequent high rate of illegitimacy. Protection was only slowly extended to other trades, such as living-in shop workers, who appear to have been equally overworked and at risk of sexual harassment.

Trade unions for women came later than those for men. Until the end of the century male trade unionists opposed both women's factory work and women's unions. The match workers' strike of 1888 was a key victory that encouraged the work of union organizers in other fields. The work of Emma Paterson, who had founded the Women's Provident and Protective League in 1874, of trade unionists like Clementina Black, and of female factory inspectors and investigators like Clara Collet, began to make a difference by the end of the century, although equitable rates of pay still remained largely unavailable to women.

Some women took badly-paid jobs which they considered 'genteel', such as working in a small shop or dressmaking, in preference to better-paid factory work. Dressmaking and millinery offered girls both skill and respectability, though they were always overworked. Some tended to be daughters of clergymen and half-pay officers and professionals in the fashionable London 'Houses'. No working-class household could afford the £30 to £50 premium for a two to five year apprenticeship in such a House, though some served an apprenticeship in the country and came to London to be improved (a process which took nine months to two years and cost £10 to £15). But most dressmakers and milliners were daughters of tradesmen or of the poor, either 'out-door' apprentices paying no premium and receiving no wages, or day workers employed for the season (February to July; October to Christmas) and paid perhaps £12 to £20 for the year. Like upper servants and shop assistants, milliners and dressmakers had to dress well as part of their job.

In her analysis of the 1851 Census data, Harriet Martineau destroyed the popular fiction that most women were entirely supported by men, reporting that 'three out of six million adult Englishwomen work for subsistence.' Yet even a small wage gave them a feeling of independence. Lord Ashley said, in a debate in the House of Commons in 1844, that working women were forming female clubs: 'Fifty or sixty females, married and single, form themselves into clubs, ostensibly for protection; but in fact they meet together to drink, sing, and smoke; they use, it is stated, the lowest, most brutal, and most disgusting language imaginable.' Behaviour that would have been acceptable in working men was beyond the pale in working women, as far as Lord Ashley was concerned. Similarly, a country doctor warned in the 1860s that 'all gregarious employment gives a slang appearance to girls' habits. That which seems most to lower the moral or decent tones of peasant girls is the sensation of independence of society which they acquire when they have remunerative labour in their hands.' And author Elizabeth Gaskell, who was very sympathetic to working women, said the loud voices and strident behaviour of Lancashire mill girls made the middle class afraid of them.

Pre-marital sex was common among some sections of the working class throughout the nineteenth century. Even among the respectable it was often considered unthrifty and unnecessary to marry a girl who had not given evidence of fertility. The mildly censorious, but also indulgent, attitudes of the early twentieth century can be seen from the following exchange between an aunt and a young woman who has recently arrived in the town of Barrow-in-Furness in Cumberland, finds herself pregnant and is having to get married: 'Ah, Anna, thou has been tasting the soup before it was ready.' To which Anna replies, 'Yes, and I found a carrot in it.' It was taken for granted in rural areas that marriage would follow when the woman got pregnant, though Eliza Lynn Linton said of the village of Cladbeck in Cumberland, where her father was vicar from 1814 to 1855, that many marriages only occurred when the pregnant condition of the woman was 'too manifest to be concealed'. A contemporary wrote of rural Norfolk in the 1850s, 'Young people come to a distinct understanding with each other to cohabit illicitly . . . They meet occasionally and are thus relieved of the responsibilities and duties of housekeeping.'

Early in the century, any man charged by a woman as the father of her illegitimate child had either to contribute towards its maintenance, marry the woman, or submit to imprisonment. Samuel Bamford, the Radical weaver/poet, did not marry the Yorkshire woman by whom he had a child in 1807, but she was apparently happy with her weekly allowance from him, as long as he paid regularly. He also had a child out of wedlock in 1810, by Jemima whom he married a few months later. If a man did not keep up his payments, the parish officials intervened: as a Poor Law Commissioner said, 'The officer of the parish upon default of payment under the order of maintenance sometimes takes the woman in one hand and the warrant in the other, and gives the man the option of going to church or to gaol.' If the father disappeared, the parish could give the mother an allowance, but, up to mid-century, if a woman considered able to maintain her bastard child did not do so, and it became chargeable on the parish, she could be punished as a rogue and a vagabond. Up to 1865, if a pregnant woman ran away from home and applied for poor relief elsewhere, she could be sent back to her parish by overseers who did not want responsibility for her.

The New Poor Law of 1834, in an attempt to promote female chastity, deprived a mother of the right to bring the putative father of her child to court to induce him to marry her or provide weekly payments. In 1844 this law was reversed, but women had a hard time tracking down a man in an increasingly urban and mobile population, so the situation of a pregnant single woman could be very precarious. If a woman was 'let down' by the man she expected to marry, the results could be tragic; for example, the Reverend Francis Kilvert described in his *Diary* a West Country inquest in the 1870s on a pregnant barmaid in Hay-on-Wye who committed suicide by drowning herself when the man responsible refused to marry her. But farmer and journalist Richard Jeffries, also writing in the 1870s, said he thought a lot of women in Wiltshire produced babies and then applied for paternity orders, but preferred to remain unmarried, get money from the fathers, and continue working in the fields. He thought these women wanted independence, and in rural society there was no social stigma in their situation. In the North and West of England, too, many unwed mothers supported themselves with the help of their families and by working in the factories or mills. Many were lucky and found relatives or friends to care for their offspring, though they sometimes paid for the service. Some parents preferred their daughters to stay unmarried and live at home with the babies, contributing their wages to the family income. Shotgun weddings were far less common in the North, where women seemed more independent, than in the South and East. Stella Davies's grandmother, living in Rossendale, Lancashire, and working in a local mill, was an extreme and unusual case. She had three illegitimate children before she was twenty, by different fathers, and did not want to marry any of them. She disappeared shortly after giving birth to the third child in 1857, leaving her parents to look after all the children. She reappeared in 1902, dripping with diamond rings and necklaces, having married a wealthy mill-owner and gone to live in Russia. She seemed surprised that her children were not enthusiastic about her return!

Harriet Kidd was a very different sort of woman from Stella's grandmother. She was raped by her employer when she was a worker in a silk mill in Leek, Staffordshire, and thereafter felt deeply guilty:

> When I was a girl of seventeen [in 1884] my employer, a gentleman of good position and high standing in the town, sent me to his home one night, ostensibly to take a parcel of books, but really with a very different object. When I arrived at the house all the family was away, and before he would allow me to leave he forced me to yield to him. At eighteen I was a mother. During the first years of my boy's life my employer compelled me by threats to keep the knowledge of his part in the affair secret, and I had to bear the whole of the burden myself. My people, who were also in his employ, suspected him but did not dare to charge him, consequently the real truth never transpired.

Harriet's parents stood by her, and she took no action against her employer, but continued to work, brought up her son, and went on to start and become president of a trade union among the mill girls, as well as secretary of the Leek and Macclesfield branches of the Women's Co-operative Guild, a mutual aid movement with wide working-class appeal. Later she became a clerk in the head office of the Guild, first in Westmorland and then in London. Being an unmarried mother did not ruin Harriet, though she felt it had undoubtedly 'cast a shadow' over her life.

There were wide differences in the number of illegitimate children born in different regions of England. Virginia Woolf wrote in 1912 that the proportion of illegitimate children in rural Sussex was 'quite amazing'. Yet by then the number of bastards had dropped from fifteen per thousand births (to married/unmarried women aged 15–44) in 1871, to eight per thousand in 1911.

The most unfortunate unmarried pregnant women were those seduced and then abandoned in the towns, far from family and community support. In nineteenth-century England there were several ways to rid oneself of unwanted children. Abortion was available, although it was illegal, highly dangerous and often costly. Many women therefore went to full term and then decided what to do with the child. If a woman could not have her child at home, she had to go to a lying-in hospital or enter the workhouse, where the labour wards were wretched places until they were cleaned up in the 1860s. Afterwards, a woman alone had a hard time trying to keep herself and her baby alive, and desperate new mothers often resorted to infanticide. The percentage of illegitimate children who died in the first year of life was twice as high as that of legitimate children. No one is sure to what extent infanticide was active or passive – did mothers set out to kill their babies or did they die because they were not fed properly, or were not given sufficient care during sickness? In 1844, Thomas Wakley, surgeon and coroner for Central Middlesex, declared that child murder was going on 'at a perfectly incredible extent'. For much of the century, London alone accounted for about half of all reported homicides involving children. Reports of 150 dead infants found in the streets during 1862 led *The Times* to lament that 'infancy in London has to creep into life in the midst of foes'. Some unmarried mothers were tried and sentenced for the murder of their babies. A pitiful example in literature is Hetty Sorel in George Eliot's *Adam Bede*. Hetty, seduced and abandoned by her upper-class lover, left her baby in a field where it died. She was first sentenced to be hanged, but then instead she was transported to Australia. Yet in real life, juries were generally reluctant to convict, or find a case against, a woman whose baby had died in suspicious circumstances. Proof of infanticide was difficult. Doctors were less than expert in pronouncing on the cause of infant death, and sometimes colluded with midwives in concealing the violent death of a newborn infant. Coroners were often complacent in the face of infant death. The police were either lethargic, or prone to cut legal corners. The Registrar General's Annual Reports are of a dubious nature on the subject; if children murdered at or soon after birth were not baptized, they would not have been recorded.

For an unmarried mother who could not contemplate the murder of her baby, and had no family to help her, the problem was how to earn a living and have the child cared for. Some new mothers were recruited from the workhouse as wet-nurses for the children of the 'better classes', whose own mothers could not, or would not, breast-feed them. Doctors examined the women for VD, smallpox etc., before recommending them as wet-nurses, and the mothers had to wean their own babies after fourteen days, leaving them in the workhouse where they often died from lack of nourishment. Mr Gladstone, the Prime Minister, worried in 1842 about the rights and wrongs of getting a wet-nurse for his infant son, when his wife Catherine was unable to feed him, but he swiftly decided in favour of the survival of his own child.

Some fortunate women got their babies into the Thomas Coram Foundling Hospital in London (an orphanage), which was founded in 1801 as a benevolent institution for the care of illegitimate children. Only the children of mothers who had 'previously borne a good character for Virtue, Sobriety and Honesty' were accepted, which meant the mother had to prove she had no previous illegitimate children, little experience of intercourse, and had conceived the child either through belief in a promise of marriage, through rape, or (not infrequently) both. Far from being feckless and promiscuous, these unmarried mothers had for the most part led lives of respectability until they were betrayed by men who had promised to marry them. The rituals of courtship had been observed, and the father had in many cases been welcomed by the woman's family, who remained supportive during the pregnancy. Most of the women had been domestic servants. Their dreams of escape from the hardships below stairs encouraged some of them to submit to the sexual demands of employers or sons of the household. The Victorian middle-class home, with its attics, basements and backstairs, was an ideal location for rape and seduction. In fact, however, only a minority of those who brought their babies to the Foundling Hospital had been seduced by someone from the middle class. The majority of their lovers were artisans, skilled workers, junior clerks, policemen – the sort of men whom an ambitious cook or chambermaid could hope to attract as a husband. The men gave pitiful excuses for refusing marriage, and went to extreme lengths to avoid it, such as emigration. The children admitted to the Foundling Hospital were well treated, and presumably the mothers were able to resume their respectable lives and work. A typical case history was that of Ann Thain, twenty-four years old, a dressmaker, who in 1845 became pregnant by Isaac Parting, a chronometer maker, who disappeared immediately he heard the news. Ann's very respectable mother supported her through the pregnancy and birth, keeping the information secret from the rest of the family. Afterwards, Ann wanted to go into domestic service if she could be relieved of the child. The child was taken into the orphanage.

Another option available to the unmarried mother was to pay someone else to house and care for the child, under a system which became known as 'baby farming'. In the absence of legal adoption the baby farm often seemed, to a mother desperate to work, the most humane alternative. But whatever the mother's intentions, the farmed-out child frequently met with a gruesome fate, as the testimony of various people showed concerning Mary Hall, living at Cold Harbour Lane, Camberwell, whose house served as a lying-in hospital. Mrs Warren, living next door, said that having seen a great number of pregnant women go there, she never heard a baby cry or saw one leave the house, and once or more a week she 'experienced a most sickening odour of something being burnt or boiled of a fleshy kind'. Another neighbour, Mrs Tennant, said, 'A little hunchback woman used to come after each confinement, and take away parcels.' A servant who worked for Mrs Hall said she saw infants thrown down a hole in the garden. The mothers said Mrs Hall had told them she had found good homes for their babies, and they had paid her substantial sums of money for this service. However, some months after the births the mothers were usually told their babies had died. Mary Hall was never properly punished for her crimes against children, though she was sentenced to two years' hard labour and fined £100 for fraudulently claiming that a baby was the child of a woman who was not the mother. However, another notorious baby-farmer, Margaret Waters, was exposed, tried and executed in 1870.

The outrages of the 'baby farms' had been known for decades. For example, Disraeli's novel *Sybil* made effective use of such scandals. But public indignation over the scandalous revelations in 1870 led to the passing of the Infant Life Protection Act of 1872, which made local authority registration and inspection of child minders compulsory. Enforcing the legislation was a very difficult matter, however. At the heart of the problem lay the mother's inability to support her child, although the Bastardy Laws Amendment Act of 1871 strengthened the mother's claim for maintenance from the putative father. This Act governed the maintenance of illegitimate children until 1957.

A large number of illegitimate children born in England were in fact the offspring of common-law unions, that is, couples who lived together as man and wife, but without bothering to go through a marriage ceremony. What is striking is that these people were by no means just the vagabonds and the disinherited. Common-law practices were embedded in whole communities, often places where small-scale farming mixed with new manufacturing pursuits. At Culcheth in South

Lancashire, for example, the illegitimacy rate rose to 30 per cent in the early nineteenth century. In the same period, at Ash-next-Sandwich, a rural area in East Kent, at least fifteen per cent of couples omitted marriage. In the 1840s Henry Mayhew found the London coster-mongers, chimney sweeps and dust collectors positively hostile to church marriage, which they said 'only served to put money in the par-son's pocket'. He reckoned only about 10 per cent of them were mar-ried. Charles Booth concluded in the 1890s that although legal marriage was 'the general rule, even among the roughest class, at least at the outset of life non-legalised cohabitation was far from uncommon'. Interestingly, though, he also said that 'rough labourers . . . behave best if not married to the woman with whom they live'. Apparently they did not feel they 'owned' the woman, as they would have done if she had been a wife, and so concluded they had no right to beat her. Lady Bell thought this was true of working women in Middlesbrough, whom she surveyed in 1907, saying they feared that getting married would alter the balance of power in their relations with men. And Margaret Loane, a nursing visitor, quoted in 1911 a London woman living with a man who would gladly have married her, who steadfastly refused because 'she didn't choose to be knocked about, or see her children treated bad'. Loane also said 'living tally' often caused gossip or quar-rels, but rarely resulted in permanent ostracism in rough working-class communities. In evidence to the Divorce Commission in 1910, representatives of several Poor Man's Lawyer organizations confirmed that very little importance was attached to the marriage tie by the peo-ple they advised. But in many cases marriage was not possible for couples living together, because one or other was married to someone else. The Majority Report of the Royal Commission on Divorce (1912) used this as an argument in favour of relaxing the divorce law and thus permitting remarriage.

In fact, spinsterhood became more rare in the working class as the century progressed; at the end, 88 per cent of women got married. Their sexual and economic vulnerability, their desire for respectability and security, and their longing (in many cases) for children, combined with the growing ideal of romantic love to place great pressure on them to marry. The consequences of remaining single varied greatly, of course, according to the amount of emotional and other support a woman found in living with her family or friends. Many spinsters were dearly loved for the devotion they showed to elderly parents, for helping to bring up nephews and nieces, and for nursing sick family members. Yet most of them were also despised as 'unable to get a man', and none was well off financially, despite having earned wages from an early age. All had to continue to earn money for as long as their health and strength held out.

However, marriage seldom relieved a working-class woman of the need to earn money, as the next chapter will show.

10

Obliged to be Breadwinners

THE LIVES OF
MARRIED WOMEN WORKERS

In a kind of despondency she sits down, unable to contribute anything to the general fund of the family, and conscious of rendering no other service to her husband except the mere care of his family.

Society for Bettering the Condition of the Poor, discussing in the early nineteenth century the plight of village wives

The wives and daughters of men of small producing and earning power have at all times been obliged to be breadwinners.

Report of the Lady Commissioners, 1895

Up to, and in the early stages of the Industrial Revolution, society was not rich enough, and the methods of work were not sufficiently productive, to allow anyone to escape work – except the tiny minority who exploited the labour of others. Marriage was not looked on as a liability for a man and a favour for a woman, but as a necessity for their joint personal survival. There was hardly any job that men did which was not also done by women. They laboured in the fields and mines, in factories and shops, in markets and on the roads, as well as in workshops in their homes. They worked with their menfolk or replaced them in their absence. Yet however skilled the women were, their work was always considered subsidiary to men's, and was paid at lower rates. This custom of considering women's work as less valuable than men's continues to this day in many occupations.

At the beginning of the nineteenth century, most of the population of England lived in the countryside; only a quarter lived in towns. The rural poor were isolated, hidden, inarticulate. A cottage in Bedfordshire was described in 1800 as 'almost tumbling down, the wind blowing through it on every side . . . My heart sank within me at the sight of so much misery, and so dark and cold, tattered and wretched a room'. In it was a desperately ill woman who had just given birth, but the baby was dead in a cradle. There were four other children. One third of all families in England at this time were dependent on agriculture for work, but the wages of labourers were so inadequate that wives who were no longer able to supplement their husband's wages by work at home (knitting, spinning, lace-making, weaving) were forced themselves to work on farms as day labourers. In some districts such as Lincolnshire and Pembroke there was little farm work available for women, though in thinly-populated areas like Durham things were better. In areas where men's labour was subsidized out of the poor rates, it was not until after the new Poor Law of 1834 that there were large numbers of women working on farms as day labourers. They were badly paid, and when other work was available, such as shirt button-making or lace-making, they preferred to stay at home, but a report in 1836 said, 'The custom of the mother of a family carrying her infant with her in its cradle into the field, rather than lose the opportunity of adding her earnings to the general stock . . . is becoming very much more general now.' The child was kept quiet by being given some form of opiate as a pacifier. Medical opinion held that agricultural work was healthy apart from the rheumatism many labourers developed, and many women themselves said they preferred it to being at home, and felt healthier when working outdoors. But the health of agricultural workers was adversely affected by lack of food, poor and inadequate clothing, damp and ill-ventilated cottages and the fatigue caused by having to walk so far to work (sometimes fifty or sixty miles a week).

Things were worse in the South of England than in the North, where real wages were higher due to the competition of mines and manufacturing industry. Farm labourers in the North still possessed a little land where they could grow food or keep chickens. Furze, heath and brushwood could be found or bought inexpensively, for heating and cooking. In the South, free fuel had disappeared with the commons, and fuel prices were high, so labourers' wives were prevented from doing any cooking at home and had to use the village bakehouse. Since they could not afford to lay in stores of provisions from cheaper shops in nearby towns, they had to buy in village shops which charged exorbitant prices for poor goods. Rising prices and stagnant wages during the Napoleonic Wars overwhelmed the labourers' families in the South and East of England. Conditions did not improve much by mid-century. Charles Kingsley described a labouring family's diet in 1847 as potatoes, bread and tea. Writer Richard Jeffries said that in rural Wiltshire in the 1870s people ate vegetables, potatoes, bread, occasionally a piece of bacon or mutton, and had weak tea to drink. Up to then, milk had been used for making butter and cheese on local farms, leaving buttermilk which labourers could buy, but by the 1870s most milk was sent to London for sale to the urban population, leaving the farm labourers with none.

In 1843 a government inquiry found women working at 'all the chief tasks in agriculture' in all counties, though the kind of work depended on the season of the year and the custom of the particular area. A Commissioner reported, 'Their earnings are a benefit to their families which cannot be dispensed with without creating a great deal of suffering.' Another inquiry in 1867 found a considerable decline in the number of women day labourers, the women themselves apparently having 'made up their minds that it did not answer, and that they would not encourage their children to take it'. Presumably other work was available to women by this time. The number of people living and working in the countryside had been falling throughout the century, and in the mid-1870s it fell still more when increased imports of cheap food from abroad caused unemployment among farm workers. By the end of the century women's employment as day labourers on farms had almost ceased, though social investigator Maud Davies found in 1909 that in Worcestershire wives 'working under a farmer' took as much share of farm work as had their grandmothers; many families lived in 'tied cottages', rent free on condition that the wife worked for the farmer as well as the husband. In rural Wiltshire, Maud Davies found married women homeworkers making gloves and earning only 2 shillings a week, but they needed that money to eke out their labouring husbands' low wages of around 12 shillings a week. In rural Essex she found wives working for the tailoring industry, with cloth sent from Manchester, East London and Leicester to be made up. Their pay of around 7 shillings a week was a significant addition to the husband's earnings of 12 to 15 shillings.

Growing industrialization transferred many activities from the home to the factory, but this process was gradual and well into the nineteenth century numerous trades were still carried on in small workshops, often on a family basis. Dorset was noted for its trade in string, pack-thread, netting, ropes, sailcloth and sacking; some midland counties for lace-making and straw-plaiting, others for framework knitting and machine lace-making. Essex was noted for basket-making; Stafford and Worcester for mail- and chain-making. In all these industries married women were employed, but it was no 'golden age' for them, even though they could control the pace at which they worked and were able to take care of their children at the same time. Trades performed in the home were done in appalling conditions that allowed no ease, peace or comfort for the family. Francis Place, a tailor, said, 'Nothing conduces so much to the degradation of . . . the woman, than her having to eat and drink and cook and wash and iron and transact all her domestic concerns in the room in which [the family] work, and in which they sleep.' Elizabeth Smith, living in Nottingham with her unemployed husband in 1843, said that as a lace runner working twelve to fourteen hours a day in her home she earned only 5 shillings a week in summer and 2s 6d a week in winter, and she had ruined her eyesight. Little of value seems to have been destroyed when domestic work was transferred from insanitary, overcrowded cottages where the air was full of fluff or dirt, to factories.

Some domestic industries that were respectable at the beginning of the nineteenth century later became 'sweated industries', some of which survive to this day. This work was defined by a Select Committee of the House of Commons in 1890 as 'work carried on for inadequate wages and for excessive hours in insanitary conditions', and it was mostly done by women. It included work in unregulated workrooms and also in homes, in a wide variety of jobs from matchbox-making to furpulling. Life was bleak and hard for women workers, wherever they worked and at whatever occupation. For married women it was often a case of domestic industry or nothing, and the necessity of contributing something to the family income made them ready and anxious to work for wages on which a single woman would have found it impossible to live. In 1906 the wretched working conditions of cardboard-box makers, needlewomen, artificial flower makers and brushmakers who earned about a penny an hour were revealed. Homeworkers had to supply their own heat, light and some materials such as glue, paste or thread. Needleworking was the single largest paid occupation for women who worked in their own homes. A needleworker earned as little

as half as much as a female factory worker and worked at least as long.
The work was considered more respectable than work in a mill, but was
arduous and solitary. Dressmakers often had to hire a sewing machine
at 1s 6d to 2s 6d a week. Piecework done at home on inexpensive goods
was the resort of the least skilled, and it was subject to seasonal booms
and busts. Because of the large number of women looking for work,
employers could keep lowering the rate for the job. Indeed, there is
evidence that homeworkers' earnings were declining during the early
twentieth century. Some observers thought the only women who would
do such work were those working for 'pin-money' or pocket money, but
an investigation of Birmingham outworkers in 1906 found more than
half the women were married to men earning inadequate wages, almost
half were widows, and only 0.4 per cent worked for pocket money.

Women's organizations continually raised these issues, and the
Fabian Women's Group took them up actively in 1905, putting on the
famous 'Sweated Exhibition' in London in 1906, backed by the *Daily
News*. This, combined with pressure from the Anti-Sweating League
which was backed by trade unions, forced action by the Liberal government. Winston Churchill introduced the Trades Boards Act in 1909 to
deal with some of the worst areas. Trades Boards were set up,
empowered to regulate pay and conditions in four of the most notorious
trades, the largest being tailoring and the others cardboard-box making,
lace-making and chain-making. This was the first time that representatives of government, employers and workers got together to fix
minimum wages in the largely non-unionized 'sweated' industries. How
effective the Boards were is uncertain, because the civil service did not
have the capacity to inspect and supervise all the small workshops, still
less how women working in their homes were treated. However, there
were some initial improvements, and during the First World War the
Trades Boards were extended to a wider range of non-unionized
industries until by 1921 they covered sixty-three occupations and three
million workers. Trades Boards were later re-named Wages Councils,
and they continued to ensure that some powerless and non-unionized
workers (mainly women) got an agreed minimum wage. The abolition
of the Wages Councils, proposed by the Conservative government in
1992, would take away that guaranteed, though low, level of wages.

Simultaneously with the decline of domestic industry in the textile
trades came the development of the factory system. The number of adult
women employed was very small at first, but increased when steam

power resulted in more complicated machinery, and when the Factory Act of 1833 limited child labour. Yet in 1841 female factory operatives numbered only 8,879, so this was not the typical form of employment for women. Wives of distressed handloom weavers (who often themselves had experience of weaving) left their homes to work on power looms, and weaving became a woman's occupation because employers preferred them to men. This was because women were 'easier to manage and cost less'. A factory inspector testified before Parliament in 1844 that 'a vast majority of the persons employed at night and for long periods during the day are females; their labour is cheaper and they are more easily induced to undergo severe bodily fatigue than men'. The married woman with children was even cheaper and more tractable. A manufacturer testified at the same hearings that he employed only women at his power looms and gave a 'decided preference to married females, especially those who have families at home dependent on them for support; they are attentive, docile, more so than unmarried females, and are compelled to use their utmost exertions to procure the necessities of life.' This put the average married woman worker among the poorest and most exploited. It also created antagonism with male workers, who viewed women as harbingers of unemployment and underpayment. In 1906, official statistics showed that the average earnings of an adult woman in a full working week ranged from 18s 8d in the cotton industry (where women earned the highest wages) down to 11s 3d in food and tobacco. About one-third of all working women earned less than 12 shillings a week. By comparison the average earnings for an adult man were 25s 9d a week. These conditions followed thirty years of continuous effort to organize women into trade unions. Women were often afraid to join unions, or thought of them as a male province, or could not afford to pay the 'dues'. Yet the full measure of trade union achievement can be seen from a comparison between organized Lancashire, where wages for an adult woman cotton worker in a full working week were 18s 8d in 1906, and the unorganized Bristol district where female weavers still belonged to the class of sweated workers. In 1914, weavers' earnings in Bristol were as low as 10 shillings a week (that is, below the minimum rate at that time for sweated workers, as fixed by the Trades Boards Acts).

Although only a minority of married women were employed in factories, the system raised questions in middle-class minds about the quality and nature of working-class home life. It was claimed that when a married woman went out to work in a factory her efficiency as a wife and mother was greatly reduced, since she did not have time to do the housework, sewing, and cooking except in the evenings, when she was tired, and on Sundays (when she should have been in church). Clearly these observers had exaggerated ideas of how much housekeeping a woman had been able to do when her home was also a workshop. In fact, married women factory workers tended to be well organized and good managers. From the earliest days, for instance, Lancashire women cotton workers arranged their own networks of support, using friends, relatives, old people and young girls aged between seven and eleven to help with housework, washing, child-minding. They even paid an old man to go round in the early morning, knocking on cottage windows to rouse workers and make sure they got to work on time. Neighbouring bakeries and shops provided ready-cooked food to lessen the burden of providing meals. Lancashire was the first home of fish and chip shops, which also sold cooked offal such as tripe and cow-heels.

In the cotton districts in 1851, about thirty per cent of all married women were employed, and of these almost two-thirds were textile operatives. In North Staffordshire the proportion of married women working in the potteries was nearly the same. Babies of working mothers often had to be weaned early, but some women had their babies taken to the factory by the childminder, so that the mother could feed the child during breaks from work. Infants whose mothers worked for pay, either in the factory or the home, did not get much attention by modern standards, and in many cases 'pacifiers' were liberally administered. A chemist testified that large quantities of opium preparations were sold in the poorer parts of Nottingham in the 1840s, and many mothers confirmed that it was common to give Godfrey's cordial (an opium preparation) to infants to keep them quiet whilst their mothers worked at lace-making. There is no evidence that relatives and neighbours acting as childminders did not do their job well, according to the standards of the day (though baby farmers were another matter entirely). They were often genuinely fond of their young charges, and in close communities people got 'a bad name' if they treated children badly. Childminding was a job for which a mother paid a reasonable amount of money, so a minder in charge of several children had a fair income.

In 1894 a Mrs Ashworth from Burnley, Lancashire, herself a weaver for over twenty years, conducted a survey of the conditions under which children were left when their mothers went to the mill each day. She found that what seemed 'unnatural' to some observers had been normalized and absorbed into community life. Out of 160 cases she investigated, half the children were left with relatives, nearly half with neighbours; only in nine cases were children left with no one to take care of them. Nonetheless, Lancashire factory women figured prominently in the heated debate on the causes and prevention of infant deaths. Their work required them to stand for a considerable period of the day, and many women worked right up to the birth of the child. A law was passed in 1891, requiring women to stay away from factory work for at least four weeks after giving birth, but it was unenforceable. It was leave without pay, and many women could not afford to take the time off. Some women actually gave birth at their looms. After the birth, those babies who could not be taken to the mill to be fed by the mother during work breaks were often fed by unhygienic methods which led to their deaths. Fewer babies died in Lancashire when mothers were not at work (for example, in periods when they were laid off work because of bad trade conditions), and breast-feeding was probably the major reason. Yet greater numbers of babies died in the Staffordshire Potteries, where fewer married women worked than in Lancashire (a low state of health among the entire population was caused by industrial poisoning), and also in Durham and Northumberland where very few married women worked at all. So there was no simple correlation between working mothers and large numbers of babies dying. Infant mortality was frequently due to unhealthy conditions both inside the home and in the towns themselves.

Many kinds of industrial work were dangerous to women's health. Women fork-grinders in the Sheffield cutlery trade developed grinder's asthma; in the needle-making trade in Alcaster women workers were damaged more than were men. Females doing lace-making in their homes in Newport Pagnell, Bedford and Towcester, those in cotton manufacturing, and those in straw-plaiting, all had twice as many chest diseases as the male workers. Female weavers in the cotton trade suffered from lung complaints because they sucked the weft from the bobbin through the hole in the shuttle whenever they changed it. Female miners (who still numbered 11,000 in the 1850s) had a very high sickness rate. Many domestic servants were ill fed and commonly suffered from anaemia. The one piece of good news that emerged in the 1860s was that sempstresses using sewing machines suffered less from contracted chests, pallid colour and weakened eyes than their predecessors, who had sewn by hand.

For wives who had no special skill and yet had to earn a living, retail shopkeeping or street trading was a possibility. In London, for centuries before the Married Women's Property Act in 1870, a Saxon custom permitted a wife to trade on her own account, *if her husband agreed*; she then had all the powers of a single woman, including control of her earnings. In other areas wives ran businesses with the backing of their husbands. They were drapers, grocers, haberdashers, bakers, butchers, wine merchants, to name but a few of the shops they ran throughout the century. The keeping of inns and alehouses was regarded as suitable business for women. There were also many wives engaged in peddling, hawking and street selling of all kinds. Milk selling was mainly a woman's business, according to the Census of 1841; the majority were wives of labourers and drawn from the lowest classes, though some money was needed in the first instance to purchase the milk round. Similarly, the distribution of fruit, vegetables and fish in London was largely in the hands of women who were the wives of labourers. The importance for a wife of being able to start a business can be seen from the case of Francie Nicol, who in the early twentieth century in South Shields exhibited seemingly unlimited vitality and resourcefulness. She was poor, had little education and was married to a drunken husband who gave her little support. But she opened a fish and chip shop to support herself and her children, and when her husband drank away the profits, she started over again.

National income in Britain doubled between 1867 and 1908, despite the depression of the 1870s, growing competition from other countries, and the erosion of Britain's dominant position in the world. Yet most working men did not earn enough, even when working full-time, and *could* not earn enough in every week of the year, to support their families unaided. Most men were on low wages, work was not always available because of slumps in the economy, and ill-health affected everyone from time to time. (There was until 1911 no state insurance scheme to provide unemployment or sickness benefits.) Throughout the century most men in the unskilled, unorganized sections of the working class remained dependent on the earnings of their wife and children to keep the family from starvation or to enable them to raise their standard of living slightly. It was not that all wives worked full-time or permanently, but most worked from time to time, at whatever work they could get, of any kind and however badly paid. Mrs Burrows said that in the 1850s her father had a tumour in the head and could not work for sixteen years until his death. She said her mother 'worked like a slave to keep a home over our heads'. Mrs Layton said when her railway worker husband was out of work in 1882 she helped by going out to work and then by doing washing for others in her home: 'I turned my hand to anything that would honestly bring in money,' she wrote. When pregnant, Mrs Wrigley 'worked night and day to save a little, working the [sewing] machine and washing, anything to bring in a shilling or two'. Stella Davies said when her mill-worker uncle was unemployed around 1900, her Aunt Lizzie 'slaved away at her sewing machine making infinitesimal sums for a long day's work' to buy food.

No one knows how many married women earned money by taking in lodgers, or by casual work such as taking in washing and ironing, nursing the sick, dressmaking, looking after children, doing housework for others, though it is rare to find a nineteenth-century woman's autobiography which does not mention the mother or the writer doing such work. The census figures consistently under-recorded the numbers. One reason was that, asked her occupation, a woman who was primarily a housewife categorized herself as such, without mentioning other work she did. Also, the working class never gave information to 'authority' that might penalize them in times when they needed to claim poor relief. As far as lodgers were concerned, only those who ran 'Common Lodging Houses' were counted in a census as lodging-house keepers.

Those who made money by washing clothes had to work very hard for their money. As was explained in Chapter 4, it was a major operation before the availability of water on tap and the invention of the washing machine. The clothes had first to be fetched from the person who was going to pay for the work. Water had often to be carried indoors from a communal tap, then heated on the fire or in a boiler. Clothes were put in to soak the evening prior to washday, and next morning put in hot water in a tub, then rotated by hand with a dolly. The clothes were rubbed where necessary, boiled for half an hour, rinsed, blued and starched. This process was repeated for different kinds of clothes and household linens, 'whites' coming first, 'coloureds' next and heavily soiled clothes last of all. On fine days the clothes could be dried outside, but on wet days they decorated the living room which had the only fire. Ironing began as the clothes dried, and this was another major operation when irons had to be heated by the fire. When the job was finished, the clothes had to be taken back to the owner. For all this work a woman was paid perhaps one shilling.

Changes in women's employment over time can be seen from census evidence. In 1851 almost one in four married women worked regularly outside the home; by 1861 the proportion was one in three. However, by 1911 only ten per cent of married women were working full-time outside the home. Rising real wages after 1850 allowed the 'aristocrats' of labour – the tradesmen and skilled artisans who represented about ten per cent of working men and earned much more than the others – to emulate the middle class and withdraw their wives from the labour market. As four women investigators commented in 1894:

> The industrial position of women varies with the degree of material prosperity of the man in the class to which they belong . . . As men's earning power increases, it becomes possible for the family to be supported by the husband's earnings, and the greater comfort thus obtained in the house creates a general feeling that the wife at least should abandon breadwinning.

This was not a point of view that appealed to feminists who wanted women to be financially independent of their husbands, but many men came to feel their manliness would be at stake if their wives worked, and many wives accepted this idea gladly. Yet even at this level there were good times and bad. Henry Mayhew found wives of skilled workers in the 1860s taking in washing, needlework or other outwork to earn extra money, and the wives of less affluent lower middle-class men with large numbers of children were rarely free of the need to earn. Mrs Layton described her father as 'well-educated, employed in a government situation . . . always went to business in nice black clothes and a silk hat' but she also recalled the hardships of her childhood as one of fourteen children in Bethnal Green, East London, in the 1860s: 'As our family increased and my father's wages remained stationary, it was necessary for my mother to earn money to keep us in food and clothing.' Her mother did so by nursing women such as the clergyman's wife, when they were ill or had just had a baby.

The middle-class ideal for the working class was that all girls should marry, and that the husband should be the sole breadwinner, the wife staying at home to concentrate on her domestic duties and child rearing. To this end they disapproved of wives working outside the home, and supported higher wages for men than for women. They ignored the problem of wives who had to be the sole breadwinners, because their husbands were ill, disabled, unemployed or had disappeared. The models in the prescriptive literature were vastly different from the reality of most women's lives. Those passive, dependent 'angels in the house', so beloved by many middle-class men, bore no relation to Lancashire women mill workers, described by Elizabeth Gaskell as 'rushing along, with bold fearless faces and loud laughter and jest, particularly aimed at all those who appeared to be above them in rank and station', or to other working wives. The fact that most working-class married women had always worked out of necessity, did not convince middle-class observers that it was *really* necessary and desirable for them to do so. And even when it was agreed that some unfortunate wives needed to earn, only certain types of jobs for them were approved and encouraged – mainly those connected with domestic work, though these were notoriously badly paid. The moralists often blamed the poor themselves for their poverty, assuming that with more careful budgeting (and less drinking) they could avoid it. There was little understanding until late in the century that no amount of personal effort by the poor could overcome slumps in the economy which made work uncertain and caused wages to fluctuate. And it was rarely admitted that the poor had little or nothing over from their weekly income to put aside for times when they were sick, unemployed or working short time.

Members of the women's movement of the mid-nineteenth century, including such passionate defenders of women's rights as Barbara Leigh Smith, Bessie Rayner Parkes and Jessie Boucherett, thought that unmarried women deserved to get any jobs that were available, and that caring for a home and children was the most important work a married woman could do. They did not think married women needed work outside the home as an emancipating experience, and believed they should not look for it unless they *really* needed the money. Bessie Rayner Parkes wrote in 1862, ' . . . the fact remains clear to my mind, that we are passing through a stage of civilisation which is to be regretted, and that her house and not the factory is a woman's happy and healthful sphere.' Feminists later in the century believed that wives should be economically independent of their husbands, and had a perfect right to work outside the home if they wished to do so. In 1915 Clementina Black, President of the Women's Industrial Council, identified four separate groups of wives: those who worked to supplement the family income, because of their husbands' low pay, irregular work or sickness, thereby staying just above the poverty line; those with similar needs,

who could not or would not work, and so sank into abject poverty; those
who had no economic need to work, and stayed home as full-time
housekeepers; and those, although also without economic need, who
chose to work for independence and a sense of self-identity. The fourth
group was the one that feminists most admired. There was evidence that
many women preferred to be with friends at work, rather than stay at
home. They liked an evening out with their mates, for which they could
pay with their own earnings. Some were thrifty and put aside money
'for a rainy day'. Some had ambitions for their children and wanted
extra money to pay for schooling or an apprenticeship such as dressmaking for a daughter. One old woman said in 1906, after sixty years of
factory life, that 'a shilling you can earn yourself is worth two given you
by a man'. But however much women enjoyed work outside the home,
and the feeling of independence it gave them, they were not properly
rewarded for it. As Cicely Hamilton wrote in 1912:

> Because her work as a wife and mother was rewarded by a wage of
> subsistence, it was assumed that no other form of work she undertook
> was worthy of a higher reward; because the only trade that was at
> one time open to her was paid at the lowest possible rate, it was
> assumed that in every other trade into which she gradually forced her
> way she must also be paid at the lowest possible rate. The custom of
> considering her work as worthless (from an economic point of view)
> originated in the home, but it has followed her out into the world.

By 1913 nearly all the organized forces in society were against the
married woman worker, whatever her circumstances. Single women
regarded them as unfair competition (the theory being that a married
woman with a husband to keep her could afford to work for less money,
or even 'pin money', and would do so). There was also a widespread
belief that husbands became lazy when their wives worked. Most commentators felt it was a national evil for a woman to have to leave her
children in the care of others in order to earn a few shillings in a wretched
underpaid trade. A social survey in Birmingham in 1906 showed that
the majority of children of working mothers (62 per cent) were 'well or
fairly well' cared for; by comparison, 73 per cent of the children of
mothers who stayed at home were 'well or fairly well' cared for, so the
difference between the groups was very small. Yet the male investigator
still maintained that 'it is obvious that no woman can do all the home

work required by a growing family and at the same time spend the day at the factory. A great many try to lead this double existence, washing and cleaning on Saturdays, and paying parents and neighbours for a little care and supervision of the children during the week.' He put his finger on the very real problems working mothers faced, but did not see that poverty was their problem, and that with better wages they could have paid for more help in the house and more child care.

Certain it is that, throughout the century, married women of the working class carried the double burden of work both outside and inside the home, and they had little time for hobbies or enjoyment. State power and agencies increasingly affected their lives, and they were subjected to a host of advice from middle-class social workers on how to clean and cook and bring up their children. They often resented and resisted this, even when the intention was really to help them, regarding it as tantamount to surveillance in their own homes. Emancipation came to be seen as being free of the necessity to work without ceasing. As Clementina Black said in 1915, 'to lighten [women's] toil so as to leave them breathing space for a little personal life is, surely, a duty which organised society owes them.' She wanted to increase the rates of pay of working women, and to decrease their burden by providing them with improved household appliances and cheap washing, cooking and child-care services. This was an agenda that women would still be fighting for at the end of the twentieth century. It is perhaps not such a paradox, then, that just when middle-class women were agitating for the right to work and enter the male-dominated professions in the late nineteenth century, and bemoaning the legal subordination and economic dependence of wives, many working-class women wished to withdraw from the labour market and stay at home, if their husbands could provide for them. The two groups were talking about different kinds of work, of course. The middle class thought of well-paid and interesting professional careers; the working class knew they had little or no chance of getting into the better-paid skilled trades.

By the beginning of the nineteenth century most middle-class homes were separated from the family's business premises, and wives ceased to take an active share in their husband's affairs. The really affluent adopted the upper-class ideal of a woman being entirely supported by a man, and extended this to include the life of idleness which they thought was the mark of the gentlewoman. It was the ambition of the wealthier farmers' wives to achieve gentility by having nothing to do.

'I see sometimes, for instance,' wrote Arthur Young, 'a pianoforte in
a farmer's parlour, which I always wish was burnt . . . a post-chaise to
carry their daughters to assemblies . . . these ladies are sometimes
educated at expensive boarding schools . . . all these things imply a
departure from that line which separates the different orders of beings.'
Those less affluent clung to the ideal even when it was not adhered to
in practice. Margaretta Gray suggested in 1853 that changing ideals of
womanly behaviour in the form of 'a spurious refinement' had cramped
the usefulness of women in the upper middle classes and that 'a conventional barrier had sprung up which pronounced it ungenteel to be behind
a counter or serving the public in any mercantile capacity.' She also said,
'Men in want of employment have pressed their way into nearly all the
shopping and retail businesses that in my early years were managed, in
whole or in part, by women', (implying that up to the 1830s it was not
uncommon for a middle-class wife to work in that way). She blamed
the increasing pressure of population for this change, and accepted that
ladies must not 'invade the rights of the working classes, who live by
their labour'. From then on, it was generally accepted that upper- and
middle-class women should not work outside the home, the role of wife
and mother being considered all-important. Some wives made money
by writing, but even though they had servants to do their housework
and child care they felt their first obligation was to the home. According
to Elizabeth Gaskell in 1862, 'a wife and mother cannot drop the
domestic charges devolving on her as an individual, for the exercise of
the most splendid talents that were ever bestowed.' She bore six children
and carried the burdens of a minister's wife, and still managed to be a
prolific writer. Other successful married women writers early in the century were scientists Mary Somerville (mentioned earlier in the book) and
Jane Marcet (1769–1858), who wrote books on chemistry, political
economy, natural philosophy and vegetable physiology; 160,000 copies
of Marcet's books were sold in America, and they were to be found in
almost every classroom in Britain. Sydney Owenson (Lady Morgan) had
already made £5,000 from literary earnings when she married in 1812,
and afterwards made a lot more; Sarah Ellis, Elizabeth Sandford and
Sarah Lewis gave advice in the 30s and 40s on how women should live
their lives; Caroline Norton became one of the most popular literary
figures of the 1830s to 50s, as did novelist Frances Trollope in the 1840s
to 60s, and Mrs Henry Wood and Mary Ward (who called herself Mrs
Humphry Ward) in the 80s and 90s. Educationist Emily Davies (herself

unmarried) was one of the few to argue that housekeeping took up little time and that middle-class women could combine work and marriage; Doctor Elizabeth Garrett Anderson was one of the select group who actually did so in the 1860s. Even at the end of the century, influential feminists such as Cicely Hamilton completely failed to understand middle-class married women who wanted to work. They argued for 'a fair field and no favour' in job opportunities, and the repeal of all laws that gave special consideration to women (including those relating to childbearing). From the 1880s they found themselves in open conflict with the women's trade union movement on these issues, because powerless working-class women welcomed protective legislation. The feminists advocated the deliberate choice of spinsterhood for those who sought intellectual fulfilment and a successful career. In line with that thinking, Molly Thomas gave up her lectureship at Bedford College as soon as she married Arthur Hughes in 1897, never taught again, and said she never felt any sense of loss.

Yet a quarter of the women teachers in late Victorian and Edwardian London schools were married. They were recruited from the respectable working class and lower middle class. Some married socially upwards, some married unskilled or semi-skilled manual workers, but most married men from similar backgrounds with similar jobs. These wives worked to achieve a better standard of living, and certainly did not think working could not be combined with marriage, or lowered their social status. From the 1890s, however, some married women teachers were forced to give up work when they married (and in 1923 the marriage bar became universal, only being lifted after the Second World War).

For most Victorian middle-class married women, a paid job was out of the question, and nor did they have the talent to earn money by writing. For those with energy to spare, and a wish to know more of the world outside the home, philanthropy and voluntary work provided an opportunity to spread their wings, as will be seen in the next chapter.

11

Ladies Bountiful

PHILANTHROPIC,
VOLUNTARY AND POLITICAL WORK

Women, as well as men, have high and holy duties. They have much
to learn, to suffer, and to do.

Elizabeth Sandford, a clergyman's wife,
Female Improvement, 1836

For centuries prior to the Victorian era, upper-class English women were
engaged in charitable activities on behalf of the poor and sick. Philanthropy, usually performed under the auspices of religious bodies, was
long considered the proper work of privileged women. They also had
no hesitation in getting involved in politics. Although women did not
sit in Parliament, they expected to exert direct influence over their
friends who did, and gain patronage for their relatives, friends and pro-
tégés. The greatest families kept large town houses and used them as
centres of national politics. More important than any formal education,
perhaps, was the knowledge of politics that upper-class girls absorbed
from adolescence onwards.

In the first half of the nineteenth century Lady Holland, known as
the queen of Whig society, was as important as her husband in attracting
men of culture to their salon at Holland House, and there are many
tributes to her beauty, personality and brilliant conversation. Diarist
Mrs Arbuthnot, wife of a Member of Parliament and close friend of
the Duke of Wellington, said politics was her major interest in life, and

the Duke said he preferred to discuss politics with women and found their comments pertinent and useful. Disraeli said similar things in his novel *Coningsby*, and he corresponded vigorously about politics with Lady Londonderry, Lady Bradford and Lady Chesterfield, as well as with his sister.

Cambridge House, home of Lord Palmerston from 1850 to his death in 1865, and including the years of his premiership, was called 'the mansion, hallowed by a mighty shade,/Where the cards were cut and shuffled when the game of state was played.' The functions were said to owe much to the grace and suavity of Lady Palmerston, who knew well the value of asking to their Saturday soirées the wives of MPs likely to give her husband trouble in the House. After years of enmity, Lady Palmerston and Caroline Norton became friends, and when Lord Palmerston died Caroline wrote to her:

> It was my dream when I thought to marry and live among men who influenced their time, to be what I think you were, in this, the only reasonable ambition of women . . . to have so far added to the happiness and security of a career in public usefulness and public elevation.

Caroline envisaged women's power and influence to operate through men, but nonetheless saw it as real and effective.

Louisa, Duchess of Manchester, was more politically ambitious for her lover, Lord Hartington, than he was for himself, though she was an ardent Tory and he a Liberal; she prodded and drove him, and warned him of Gladstone's ambitions. Margot Asquith described her as 'the last great political lady in London society as I have known it. The secret of her power lay not only in her position . . . but in her elasticity, her careful criticisms, her sense of justice, her discretion.'

The Countess of Warwick, known as Daisy Brooke, who had been the mistress of the Prince of Wales for nine years, later became unusually sympathetic (for her class) to the vast world of suffering around her, and in 1895 got herself elected a trustee of a workhouse. She financed out of her own purse a number of philanthropic schemes to help the poor and unemployed (cripples' schools, women's hostels, agricultural training centres), to the point where in 1898 her annual income of over £30,000 (inherited from her grandfather) slid down to £6,000. She played an important part in the propaganda campaign for free school meals, accompanying Sir John Gorst and a famous children's doctor on a surprise visit to a Lambeth school and then writing a vigorous and influential article on the subject in the *Fortnightly Review*.

Some of the earliest attempts at united political action by women in the nineteenth century came not from ladies, however, but from working women. According to Samuel Bamford, women 'voted with the men at the Radical meetings' in 1818, when distress following the Napoleonic Wars was severe. Bamford's wife Mima left an impressive written account of what she saw and experienced when she went on the march to St Peter's Field in Manchester in 1819, which resulted in the Peterloo massacre. It is a moving testament to her support for her husband and the political cause he led. She said, 'I was determined to go to the meeting, and should have followed, even if my husband had refused his consent to my going with the procession.' Previously, women's share of working-class agitation had been almost entirely confined to food riots, in which they took a leading part. Now they joined in the movements for parliamentary reform and against the new Poor Law of 1834. They supported the Chartist movement in the 1830s and 40s, selling the unstamped popular press and organizing the Victim Fund for those imprisoned. And it was to women that factory reformers Richard Oastler and J.R. Stephens denounced the evils of the industrial system from 1837 onwards, developing a Tory radical vocabulary which was used by novelist Charlotte Tonna in her fictionalized biographies of working girls. Although women were marginalized in the early socialist movement of Robert Owen in the 1820s and 30s, many were attracted to its meetings which stressed moral improvement, family participation, music, temperance and education. Working women took a major role in building up a national network of 'rational' Chartist activities in the 1830s and 40s. Besides organizing the Chartist Sunday schools, social teas and dances, women attended and sometimes addressed meetings, formed their own political associations, signed petitions and engaged in boycotts of shopkeepers who disapproved of Chartism.

From the beginning of the nineteenth century there was a great outburst of philanthropic voluntary work by middle-class women, not just in local charities but in great humanitarian and reforming 'moral' campaigns. This was partly a reaction to the French Revolution. Any sympathy the English might have felt with French cries for liberty, equality and fraternity, was quenched by the bloodshed that ensued after the Revolution. Quite different ideals gathered strength around 1800 and were powerful throughout the following century: a vision of Britain as the greatest of nations, upholding truth and justice and teaching other races what freedom and a sense of duty meant; and a new conception of God's interest in human affairs, including the belief that the middle class should impose its Christian morality on the rest of society and attempt to solve some of its social problems. Middle-class women had an important role to play in both these visions. First, they despised the 'levity and licentiousness of French manners' prevalent in the English upper classes and the fashionable circles who mimicked them, and saw themselves as the bearers and rearers of the future upright rulers of the world. The hand that rocked the cradle (or controlled the nursemaid who performed that chore) would be supremely important, they believed. Secondly, they supported the Evangelical Christian movement in its reverence for religion, marriage and domesticity as the guarantors of social cohesion. In order to clean up society's manners and behaviour, women were encouraged to get involved in campaigns to deal with social evils. In the early decades of the nineteenth century, middle-class women such as the conservative writer Hannah More and her sister Martha ran schools for village children in remote areas, like Cheddar in the West Country. Other women offered remedies to the sick, ran soup kitchens for the poor, worked in lying-in charities (where some poor women had their babies) and in asylums for the deaf, blind, destitute, and insane. Quaker Ann Ecroyd provided relief in the village of Marsden, Lancashire, during times of hardship between 1824 and 1843. In acute periods of privation she distributed boiled rice, seasoned with allspice and salt, rationed at a pint a head daily. Religious bodies relied heavily on women volunteers for parish visiting, though they were told not to neglect duties to their own homes in their zeal for visiting the homes of the poor.

Religious belief gave many middle-class women the courage to tackle social evils, and they gained wide experience and leadership skills in charitable organizations. Some spent their entire lives promoting important social reforms under the aegis of philanthropy. Although men usually controlled the governing boards and finances of such organizations, they did not have the same amount of time to spare, or devotion to the cause, as women. Middle-class women, after all, were constantly being told not to take paid work if they thereby took a job that was needed more by someone else. The charities often preferred to use women to visit the poor because they alone could advise other women on housewifery, nursing, and child care. Women rarely analysed the significance of their activities, or worried about the limited usefulness of unorganized charity. Nor did it occur to most of them that they might be intruding on the privacy of the poor when they exhorted them to give up drinking; or that it was meddlesome and condescending to assign religious texts for memorization by people who were in no position to refuse their visits. An extraordinarily patronizing example was Blanche Montgomery, who published a letter in *The Monthly Packet* in the 1860s. A daughter of the manor, she was newly married to the vicar of a church on the outskirts of a large town, and wrote, 'My husband wished me to get acquainted with everybody and to use my influence with the young women of the middle class to raise their tone a little. I am very fond of poor people, and whenever we were at home we used to go and see them a great deal; but then it was a nice, quiet little village all belonging to Papa and none but poor people.' In her new parish the young women did not wish to have their tone raised and were not interested in literature or conversation other than gossip: 'If I try to be very kind and friendly with the tradespeople's wives and daughters they put themselves quite on an equality with me', she wrote. And the poor of the parish were even less amenable. One child refused to take a tawdry artificial flower out of her hat at Blanche's bidding, and none of the children would call her 'Ma'am'. This letter provoked a flood of replies about 'the undisguised contempt often entertained for us by the wives of our clergymen' and one pointed out that these women had ample means, leisure and the opportunity to interfere in other people's lives. Yet some do-gooders were much more perceptive than Mrs Montgomery. They began to see the point of view of those she criticized, and to realize that the standard lady bountiful amalgam of soup and religious instruction was not enough to solve deep problems. By the end of the century the more involved women formed the largely unpaid foundation of the social service system. They had been successful in carving out for themselves a special sphere that filled a growing social need.

This type of work began with Elizabeth Fry (1780–1845), a Quaker who married at twenty and had ten children, but also did local charitable work and became a preacher when she was twenty-nine. In 1813 she found there were three hundred women and their children in Newgate Prison in London, the convicted and untried all kept together, all of them lacking clothing, unsupplied with beds or bedding, but given access to alcohol. The conditions were notoriously dangerous and unruly. Elizabeth brought clothes to the prisoners, set up a school, and instituted a system comprising matrons, monitors, severe clothing, moral supervision, mandatory needlework and chapel, which brought order and routine to the prisoners' lives (and also made the prison easier to run). Many other women joined her in her work, and Ladies' Associations for the Improvement of Female Prisoners were formed throughout the country. Elizabeth's journal shows that even with many children and family claims, as well as her preaching, she felt she had 'a second family' in the desolate and oppressed. Until her death, she worked without ceasing for penal reform. To accomplish her objects she formed a widespread organization of committees and correspondents such as had hardly been attempted before in philanthropic work. Elizabeth was totally opposed to capital punishment for any offence, but in this was far ahead of her time. However, she and her friends did persuade Parliament to abolish the death penalty for minor offences such as picking pockets and petty theft.

Sarah Martin (1791–1843) showed that a poor woman could also do philanthropic work for prisoners. The daughter of a small shopkeeper at Caister, near Yarmouth, Sarah was apprenticed to a dressmaker at fourteen, and became a Christian at nineteen. She often heard of the misery in the local gaol, whose inhabitants were uncared for in filthy underground cells, and longed to help, but was driven away by the doorkeeper. Then in 1820, she heard with horror of a woman who had been imprisoned for cruelty to her own child. Sarah was determined to visit this woman and persuade her to a better way of life. This she managed to do, and then she began to visit the prison regularly, teaching the inmates to read and write and conducting religious services. When she inherited from her grandmother an income of £12 a year she devoted herself full-time to prison work. The local borough offered her a small salary for her work, but she refused because she felt it might injure her relations with the prisoners.

Among other pioneers of charitable work were Mary Carpenter (1807–77) and Louisa Twining (1820–1912). Mary was the daughter of a Unitarian headmaster in Bristol. In 1846 she realized that nothing was being done for the so-called 'gutter' children and she started a 'ragged' school in the slums. Frances Power Cobbe said it was inspiring to see her 'teaching, singing, and praying with the wild street-boys, in spite of endless interruptions caused by shooting marbles into hats on the table behind her, whistling, stamping, fighting, shrieking out "Amen" in the middle of the prayer, and sometimes rising *en masse* and tearing, like a lot of bisons in hobnailed boots, down from the gallery, round the great schoolroom, and down the stairs out into the street'. Fortunately, Mary had infinite good humour and patience, as well as love for the children. She became famous for her reformatory work, opening separate schools for delinquent boys and girls. She worked on the principle that children who would otherwise be criminals could in healthy home surroundings become useful members of society. She loved her delinquents and trusted them. Her methods were amazingly successful, though there were lapses, of course. In one report she said of a boy who absconded from her school, 'He came back resembling the prodigal in everything except his repentance.' Mary had no legal power to deal with juvenile delinquents, but she had powerful friends and was largely responsible for the passage of the Youthful Offenders Act of 1854, which authorized the establishment of state reformatory schools. She also established industrial schools where poor children received vocational training, and the Industrial Schools Acts of 1857, 1861 and 1866 owed much to her ideas and example. Mary was also troubled about the condition of women and girls in India, and when she was over sixty she paid four visits to India, studied prison reform and opened a girls' school in Bombay.

Running parallel with Mary Carpenter's work was that of Louisa Twining, daughter of a prosperous tea merchant and the originator of workhouse reform. In 1857, in the course of district visiting, she was shocked by the state of the Strand Union Workhouse in London. The building was always full of steam from the laundry in the cellars. The food was disgusting and totally inadequate. There were no proper arrangements for nursing the sick, and the death rate among mothers and children was appallingly high. The only occupation of the inmates was coffin- and shroud-making. When Louisa first asked if she and some friends could visit the inmates she was refused, on the grounds that voluntary efforts would endanger discipline. It took her a year to get that ruling changed, and she then began to write articles on the conditions in workhouses. This led to the formation of a Workhouse Visiting Society. Gradually, some of the worst workhouse abuses were reduced or abolished, particularly after 1875 when for the first time some women became Poor Law Guardians. Less successful was her attempt to provide a home in London for adolescent girls who would otherwise have had to live in workhouses: Louisa expressed her 'grief and disappointment' that so little could be done to combat 'the inherited wickedness, vice, and drunkenness of generations'.

However devoted and hardworking these reformers were, they needed money to do their work, and for example, Louisa Twining's home for workhouse girls was supported by that most generous of all Victorian benefactors, Angela Burdett-Coutts (1814–1906), who for her philanthropy was created a Baroness in her own right. Angela inherited her vast fortune from her step-grandmother, Harriot Mellon, an actress of the frivolous Georgian stage who married banker Thomas Coutts when his wife died, and to whom Thomas left all his wealth, and a directorship of the bank, when he in turn died. Harriot later married the Duke of St Albans, but when she died she left him a modest fortune, the bulk going to Angela Burdett. Angela gave away immense sums of money to charities ranging from the endowment of colonial bishoprics to prizes for costermongers' donkeys; from the construction of model dwellings in the East End of London to the provision of drinking fountains for dogs. Her special concern with the welfare of women and girls was shown in the establishment and upkeep of schools and reformatories, and in the provision of improved facilities for the training of girls in the National Schools. Typical of less wealthy benefactors than Baroness Burdett-Coutts was Lady Byron (1792–1860), who despite her stormy private life opened in 1834 a number of schools for pauper children. Harriet Martineau wrote in 1854, '[Lady Byron] spent her income in fostering every sound educational scheme, and every germ of noble science and useful art . . .'

In July 1857, forty-three notables including several ladies attended a private meeting in Lord Brougham's house and passed a resolution 'affirming the necessity for a closer union among the supporters of the various efforts now being made for social advancement, and establishing THE NATIONAL ASSOCIATION FOR THE PROMOTION OF SOCIAL SCIENCE'. The list of members was a roll-call of the mid-Victorian intellectual and administrative establishment, with more than a sprinkling of leading politicians. Lord Brougham (the inventor of the carriage) welcomed women to membership of the Association, encouraging them to address the meetings. This innovation was greeted by howls of abuse and ridicule from the press, since women did not generally attend public meetings. Yet the shy and retiring Mary Carpenter, for example, became a regular speaker on the subject of delinquent children, and at the Association's annual congress in 1859, author Anna Jameson spoke on the need of middle-class women for employment.

Lord Brougham was in fact keenly aware of the significant role women could play in politics. He had enlisted their support in the anti-slavery campaigns and admired the way they formed abolition societies all over the country. The first person to put forward the doctrine of immediate, as opposed to gradual, emancipation, was Elizabeth Heyrick, a Quaker from Leicester, who published *Immediate Not Gradual Abolition* in 1824. Mary Dudley (1782–1847), the daughter of a famous Quaker preacher of the same name, was author of *Scripture Evidence of the Sinfulness of Injustice and Oppression* (1828), an anti-slavery tract. And it was, of course, the controversy in 1840, when the American delegation to the London conference against slavery was denied seats for their women members, that led to the founding of equal rights movements for women in the United States and in Britain.

The early temperance movement of the 1820s was supported publicly by many Quaker and Evangelical women, though the full-time temperance lecturers of the 1850s and 60s were all men. It was Anna Carlile who, when visiting a Leeds Sunday school in 1847, first applied the term 'Band of Hope' to groups of children organized for temperance work, and a Leeds Ladies' Committee launched a new movement under that title. From the 1850s there were two wings of the temperance movement, one devoted to moral suasion and the other to prohibition (on the grounds that the former method was achieving nothing). When the 1872 Licensing Act further restricted the opening hours of public houses they felt they had made some ground. From the 1860s the National Temperance League, working in the Army through Miss Robinson, and in the Navy through Agnes Weston, tried to provide an asylum for soldiers and sailors in every military town or seaport. But the task was formidable. Most drunkenness resulted from the social situation, and without wider social changes, attempts to solve drunkenness by forming associations of abstainers could never hope to succeed. During the first forty years of temperance agitation per capita consumption of alcohol showed an actual increase, and the movement was in decline when the most striking reduction in the level of drinking in England occurred (after the First World War).

Some female philanthropists in the Social Science Association used their organizational skills to set up woman-run institutions. One such was Jessie Boucherett (1825–1905), born into the landed gentry, who helped Barbara Leigh Smith and Bessie Rayner Parkes to found the Society for Promoting the Employment of Women. She was an ardent Tory and believed in pig-farming as a career for educated women. She also worked as editor, writer and proprietor of the *Englishwoman's Review*, which she founded in 1866 and carried on at her own expense (as the successor to the *English Woman's Journal*). The Review was *the* magazine for the feminist movement in England and abroad until 1910. Emily Faithfull (1835–94), novelist, essayist and public speaker, persuaded the Society for Promoting the Employment of Women to establish the Victoria Press, which employed only females, in order to get them into the printing trade. Compositing was considered appropriate work, because it required 'chiefly a quick eye, a ready hand, and steady application' and involved 'no exposure to weather, no hard labour'. Although printing did not become an important category of women's jobs, the number of female printers increased from 419 in 1861 to 741 in 1871, and the Victoria Press undertook publishing such as the *English Woman's Journal* (1858–64) and the *Victoria Magazine* (1863–70).

Upper-class women volunteers aided working-class women to speak publicly and work for change. Margaret Llewelyn Davies (1861–1944) was the niece of educationist Emily Davies. She went to Girton College and then became a sanitary inspector in London, where she saw the misery of social deprivation. From 1889 to 1921 she was General Secretary of the Women's Co-operative Guild, founded in 1883 with the modest aim of giving the wives of male co-operators an interest in the movement. Under her tutelage it became a vigorous body of some 67,000 working women in 1,400 branches, campaigning to improve the virtually non-existent maternal and infant care then available to poor women, as well as for a minimum wage for Co-operative employees, women's suffrage, better housing and divorce law reform. Margaret was always the investigator; in Sheffield in 1902, trying to spread the Co-operative idea into the poorest areas that had not been touched by the doctrine of organized mutual aid, she went tirelessly round the worst of the slums, noting wages, housing conditions, numbers of children, and the feelings of women about their lives. Constantly she emphasized the need to listen to what women said, and to get them to say it for themselves. There was a warmth and affection about her which never suggested condescension to those less privileged, but rather encouragement and new hope. Jenny Davie, aged seventeen, a tobacco worker, wrote to Margaret that if she were asked to do 'an exercise [essay] about an Ideal Friend, mine will be about you', followed by twenty-nine kisses. Virginia Woolf was Margaret's friend and supporter, and Leonard Woolf described her as 'one of the most eminent women I have known'. She was never paid for her work as General Secretary.

Volunteers also helped women to become trade unionists. From the 1860s onwards there were advocates of separate trade societies for women, and in 1874 a Women's Protective and Provident League was founded by Emma Paterson (1848–86). It was composed mainly of middle-class men and women who were willing to provide money to launch women's trade societies. The difficulty was not in getting a union started but keeping it going, in the face of low wages paid to women, their constant change of occupation, and the animosity of most men. Isabella Ford of the Leeds Tailoresses' Union wrote in 1897, 'It is a common excuse amongst the girls with whom we have to do that they do not join a union because their fathers do not urge them or care for them to do so.' Emma Paterson's main success was in the fight for the rights of women workers in existing unions – a fight against men determined to keep women out. In 1875 she was the first woman to attend the Trades Union Congress, and thereafter year by year she attended and strove to break down male prejudice. Women's determination to fight their own battles was shown in July 1888. Annie Besant of the Fabian Society published an indignant article in *The Link* on the harsh conditions of women making lucifer matches. To the surprise of everyone, including Mrs Besant, this resulted in nearly 700 match girls going on strike. Still more unexpectedly, their revolt won support from people of all classes; and although the match workers were entirely without funds, £400 was quickly subscribed, making it possible for them to strike long enough to win substantial increases from the employers. By the end of the century, small women's unions were dying off, but many women were admitted on reasonable terms to men's unions.

The growth of democratic institutions from which women were excluded paradoxically helped to politicize women. Egalitarian ideals were spreading to both men and women of all social classes, but women were left out of the political process and denied the vote. The granting of the vote to middle-class men in 1832 was not viewed with favour by upper-class women who considered themselves socially superior; the granting of the vote to some working-class men in 1867 was similarly irritating to middle-class women. Women responded by founding their own organizations, to protect their rights and promote their interests. The result was a women's movement of considerable power and effectiveness which emerged from the 1850s onwards to fight for married women's control of their own property and earnings, access to easier divorce, child custody rights, higher education, and entry to the male professions, as well as to fight for women's suffrage. The first manifesto on votes for women promulgated by a female organization was issued in 1851 by the Sheffield Female Political Association, which was founded by Anne Knight (1792–1862), editor of *Schoolroom Lyrics*.

In November 1865, Barbara Leigh Smith Bodichon read to a group of friends a paper on women's suffrage, and she determined to start a campaign, along with her friends who had been active in the Married Women's Property agitation ten years earlier. Among the signatures on the first petition of 1,500 names were those of Harriet Martineau and Mary Somerville. Florence Nightingale refused to sign, saying the vote was the least of women's problems. Despite its sponsorship in Parliament by John Stuart Mill, nothing came of the petition. Barbara Bodichon wrote to Emily Davies: 'You will go up and vote upon crutches, and I shall come out of my grave and vote in my winding-sheet.' Barbara was indeed dead when women first voted in 1918, but Emily Davies walked to the polling station unaided, at the age of eighty-eight.

The long fight to get votes for women was studded with hopes and disappointments. The important roles played by Millicent Garrett Fawcett and Emmeline Pankhurst, especially during their widowhoods, were outlined in Chapter 7. Millicent, who became the leader of the constitutional wing of the women's suffrage movement, known as the suffragists, made her first public speech on the subject in 1869, when she was twenty-two years old. An influential aristocratic woman supporter was Lady Amberley (mother of Bertrand Russell). She formed a small suffrage committee and thereby greatly annoyed Queen Victoria, who wrote, 'The Queen is anxious to enlist everyone who can speak or write to join in checking this mad, wicked folly of "Women's Rights" with all its attendant horrors, on which her poor feeble sex is bent, forgetting every sense of womanly feeling and propriety. Lady Amberley ought to get a good whipping.' As so often was the case, the Queen reflected the views of the majority of her subjects. For the rest of the century brave women did all they could to advance the cause, but to no avail.

However, in 1883 there occurred an event which was to make voluntary work by women essential to the political parties and thus involve them directly in the political process. This was the passage of the Corrupt Practices Act, which forbade payment for canvassing and the other subsidiary work of elections. Previously the work had been done by men specially engaged and paid for the job, and with the exception of a few of the candidate's relatives no woman had taken part. After the passing of the Act the work still needed to be done but men refused to do it voluntarily. So, not surprisingly, it was given to women. A whole new election machinery began to develop, based on women volunteers. So eager were women to do the work, and so successful, that the parties decided to give them formal recognition. The Conservative Party set up the Women's Council of the Primrose League in 1885; there was no pretence that women's help was wanted in other than practical matters (the body had no power to initiate or criticize party policy) but as a deeply conservative body of support for the *status quo*, in which they could hob-nob with women from other social classes, it was a great success. The Women's Liberal Federation was similarly called together by Mrs Gladstone, 'to help our husbands', and likewise it was intended that women would not criticize party policy. But when, in 1880, despite election promises, 104 Liberal members who were pledged supporters voted against the women's suffrage amendment, and it was later defeated in the 1884 Reform Bill, this betrayal led to widespread criticism. A women's group was formed which vowed only to work for those pledged to the suffrage cause, but little happened and the press and public got tired of hearing about votes for women. The mere existence of these political associations did a great deal for women, however. The old notion that the rough and tumble of elections was unfit for women could not survive their involvement as canvassers, and merely being there changed the participants. Many educated and intelligent women who had previously accepted that they should not have the vote were now coming face to face with uninformed men who *could* vote. Women began to realize there was much prejudice and lack of logic in political decision making. However, during the years between the passing of the 1864 Reform Bill and the close of the century the party leaders showed no sign of granting women the vote. The Conservatives disliked the principle; the Liberals were afraid that most taxpaying women would vote Conservative. In 1889 the *Nineteenth-Century Magazine* published a Solemn Protest against women's suffrage, which carried considerable public weight. It was signed by Mrs Humphry Ward, Mrs Creighton and Beatrice Webb, amongst others.

There was not total inaction on the other side, however. In the North of England in the 1890s there was a movement in favour of women's suffrage among the mill hands and textile workers. The political levy was being discussed, and the Labour Representation Committee was beginning its work. The Independent Labour Party, which included equal rights for men and women in its programme, was entering practical politics, and the formation of an effective Labour Party began to gain credence. Women who were members of trade unions expected to pay the political levy if it was called for, but they saw no reason why they should not have the right to vote for the candidates they were asked to support financially. A petition bearing the names of 67,000 textile workers was sent to Parliament, asking for votes for women. Labour leaders, afraid that support for women's suffrage would damage their wider claims, said like the Chartists of the 1840s that women would have to wait. But a Textile and other Workers' Representation Committee was formed in 1901, and in 1903 the Women's Co-operative Guild came out publicly in favour of votes for women, thus providing a wider backing than the middle-class support previously obtained.

The militant suffragette movement began in a simple and almost unpremeditated fashion in 1903. After a Private Member's Bill was talked out, Mrs Pankhurst, Mrs Elmy, Labour Member of Parliament Keir Hardie and others decided that the old methods had achieved nothing, and it was time for fresh enterprise. When the government collapsed in the autumn of 1905 there was a great meeting of the Liberal Party in Manchester. Annie Kenney and Christabel Pankhurst attended on behalf of the Women's Social and Political Union, asked questions to which they got no answers, unfurled their banners demanding votes for women, and were roughly attacked by the stewards. The outrageous behaviour of Sir Edward Grey and the stewards fired a new strain of bitterness and anger. The same evening, Annie and Christabel were arrested outside the Free Trade Hall for obstruction, taken to the police station, found guilty the next day, and sentenced to fines or imprisonment. They both chose imprisonment and thereby got all the publicity they wanted. The issue of women's suffrage was alive again.

Women actively and effectively participated in local government decades before they won the parliamentary vote. Thousands of women fought elections, often hotly contested, to enter a chosen life of service

to the community. The thought of these women engaging in – and win-
ning – electoral contests challenged the accepted view of the Victorian
woman; but they actually won elections not by denying the accepted
view of women's role, but by exploiting it. Women insisted that their
'special knowledge' of children and the weak, of home and family, gave
them the credentials they needed to serve a wider community. They
argued that women belonged in public life because they understood how
public issues affected the home and the family. In 1870 Dr Elizabeth
Garrett Anderson and Emily Davies were elected to the London School
Board; Emmeline Pankhurst was elected a Poor Law Guardian in 1894.
In 1895 three women were appointed to the Royal Commission on
Secondary Education; Octavia Hill had refused to serve on the Royal
Commission on Housing in 1889 but agreed to serve on the one on the
Poor Law in 1905. Other women served on various parliamentary com-
mittees and commissions of inquiry. Sadly, it was not always the case
that these women were sympathetic to the problems of less fortunate
women.

The two women whose work complemented but also exceeded that
of the others were the great social reformers Octavia Hill (1838–1912)
and Josephine Butler (1828–1906). Josephine's work for prostitutes will
be discussed in the next chapter. Octavia, the pioneer of housing reform,
was the daughter of reforming parents in Cambridgeshire. When her
father's banking business failed, she was first sent to work for the
Ladies' Guild in London, teaching toy-making to children from a ragged
school. Later she taught classes for working women. She always claimed
her fellow teachers looked down on her because she accepted a salary
of £25 a year instead of working as a volunteer. Octavia was exercised
about the problem of how to rehouse some of London's poorest people;
she interested John Ruskin in her ideas, and in 1865 he advanced the
money to buy three houses near Nottingham Place. Already occupied
by tenants, living conditions in these houses were squalid, but Octavia
provided wash-houses, replaced bannisters and reglazed the windows.
Within weeks the new windows were broken and the bannisters had been
burnt. In an effort to get to know the tenants, she decided to collect
the rents herself. At first she met with hostility but her courage and
friendliness gained the tenants' co-operation eventually. Her reforms
were sensible, her methods businesslike, and she put the project on such
a sound footing that she was able by 1866 to buy six additional houses.
The new property had an open space which Octavia converted into a

playground for the children and a place for the adults to sit. She attracted many helpers and trainees, and her system was adopted on the Continent and in America, but she lost the support of Ruskin when he heard she had expressed doubts on 'his ability to conduct any practical enterprise successfully'. She was freed of the need to earn a living when her friends raised a fund in 1874 which enabled her to give up teaching. Thereafter she devoted her life to housing reform.

Octavia Hill was never a supporter of women's suffrage, believing that 'political power would militate against women's usefulness in the large field of public work'. She was closely connected with the activities of the Charity Organization Society, which drew a distinction between the 'deserving' and the 'undeserving' poor (those who were believed to help themselves and those who did not). She never took part in organized political effort, but her appreciation of the need of town-dwellers for open spaces led her to help found the National Trust in 1895.

The notion of the Victorian middle-class woman as the 'angel in the house', totally dependent on her father or husband, helpless, brainless and concerned only with social life and family matters, never seems less apt than when women's great achievements in the area of philanthropy and voluntary work are considered. All the great moral and social changes of the nineteenth century were pioneered by private activity and benevolence. Both unmarried and married women gave their time and energies to a vast number of associations, societies, leagues, guilds and alliances. The ideology of the separate spheres – men for work and women for home – was used by women to advance rather than restrict their cause, bringing issues regarded as theirs into the political arena through voluntary work. Even the fiercest of suffragettes learned to use the separate spheres ideology to the advantage of the movement, just as local government women did. As well as the great and famous there were vast numbers of ordinary women doing grassroots voluntary work. Baroness Burdett-Coutts prepared in 1892 a report, *Women's Mission: A Series of Congress Papers on the Philanthropic work of women by eminent writers*, containing 322 pages and a summary of the work of over 220 philanthropic organizations and individuals in England, fifty-two in Ireland and forty-four overseas. It is a touching tribute to that much-mocked figure, the Victorian lady bountiful.

Early charitable societies had ties to organized religion, and although women's efforts to convert 'sinners' to repentance were largely unsuccessful this does not diminish the value of their relief work for the poor, or their part in suppressing brutality and cruelty to animals and children (in that order). Though they were always admonished to remain amateurs, women took the initiative and extended their 'maternal influence' to local and national affairs.

The decline of Christianity, due to the progress of physical science during the nineteenth century, meant that a passive acceptance of life, as ordained by God, was no longer tolerated by large numbers of educated people. Poverty, and to some extent the subjection of women, were no longer irremediable. As Beatrice Webb said:

It seems to me that two outstanding tenets . . . were united in this mid-Victorian trend of thought and feeling. There was the current belief in the scientific method, in that intellectual synthesis of observation and experiment, hypothesis and verification, by which alone all mundane problems were to be solved. And added to this belief was the consciousness of a new motive: the transference of the emotions of self-sacrificing service from God to man.

Philanthropic activities expanded, and in keeping with the scientific spirit of the time, systematic investigations were made which mark the beginning of social science. There was also an almost naïve belief in the power of science and expanding capitalism to solve all problems.

But as far as middle-class women were concerned, the greatest social evil was one which grew and flourished during the century, and for which they tended to blame in particular the women who practised it, not their male clients. Prostitution and prostitutes were regarded with shame and horror by the bourgeoisie, as we shall see in the next chapter.

12

A Separate Species of Womanhood

THE DEMI-MONDE

What do I think will become of me? What an absurd question. I could marry tomorrow if I liked.

A 'kept mistress' interviewed by Mayhew in the 1850s

To a most surprising, and year by year increasing extent, the better inclined class of prostitutes become the wedded wives of men in every grade of society, from the peerage to the stable.

Dr William Acton, *Prostitution*, 1857

Of all the women who did not fit the bourgeois ideal of a domestic angel, prostitutes were the most visible and the most upsetting to respectable Victorians. In London alone, at mid-century, it was estimated that 8,000 women were making a living at prostitution, and substantial numbers were doing so in the provincial cities, military and market towns. Many people felt threatened by the vulgar, sexually aggressive women of the streets. Charles Dickens, for example, once pursued a woman across London and had her arrested for using indecent language to him. Such raucous behaviour mocked men's notion that women were sexually passive. In Victorian drawings and illustrations a prostitute was immediately recognizable by her direct gaze or uncovered head. So different was her bold demeanour from that of respectable women, privileged or poor, that a prostitute was often considered a separate species of womanhood.

There was in fact a wide spectrum of women earning their living by

selling sex, ranging from the celebrated courtesan to the syphilitic outcast. Most typical was the underpaid working woman of around twenty,
who was using part-time prostitution to supplement her low wages.
Many of these women would have sex for money when an easy opportunity arose, but they did not walk the streets regularly. An 'occasional'
prostitute aged nineteen told Mayhew in 1862 that she worked in the
office of a London newspaper and had an understanding with one of
the men there that she would marry him, but she often went to the
Haymarket and picked up a man, to earn extra money. Her fiancé did
not suspect her, and she said, 'I shan't think anything of all this when
I'm married.' London costermongers told Mayhew that their women
were normally faithful to husbands or paramours, but 'in the worst
pinch of poverty, a departure from this fidelity – if it provided a few
meals or a fire – was not considered at all heinous.'

The high-class courtesan was in such demand that she could command
vast fees, and if she was a kept mistress she had a rich protector to pay
for a lavish house and lifestyle. These *poules de luxe* could pick and
choose whom to take as lovers, and change protectors when they wished.
The less favoured woman offered indiscriminate sexual intercourse, and
earned less than a top courtesan, but a smart West End prostitute could
earn more in a night than a working man could earn in a month. A drab
in Drury Lane could earn in ten minutes against a wall as much as a
dock labourer could earn in five hours of back-breaking work. In
working-class Whitechapel and Bethnal Green a prostitute could easily
earn as much as an unskilled man, and this was better pay than she could
earn from respectable employment. A young woman who had earned
about 4 pence a day by shirt-making, and then turned to prostitution,
told Mayhew in the 1850s, 'Sometimes I get 4 or 5 shillings a day, and
sometimes more.' So she was earning about fifteen times more than she
had as a shirtmaker.

Yet it was not always easy to be a prostitute. The work involved risk
of disease, humiliation, being exploited by a pimp, beaten up by a client,
and frequently not being paid at all for her services. Higher-priced
whores often had to cope with the eccentric demands of the kinky rich,
though there were special brothels for flagellation, known on the Continent as 'the English vice'. Mrs Theresa Berkley of Charlotte Street, London, made £10,000 in the eight years between 1828 and her death in
1836, by using her flogging machine which she called 'the Berkley horse'.
The medium-priced whores serviced less wealthy clients. The most

vulnerable group were those without protectors or pimps, who often lived in common lodging houses. During 1888 and 1889 they were the special prey of the Whitechapel murderer known as Jack the Ripper, who killed eight prostitutes after having sex with them, and then cut out their wombs. This became the most celebrated crime of the century because of its barbarity and rarity. Murder has never been common in Britain; in Victoria's reign it ran at around 200 a year, so a 'mass' murderer struck terror in the popular mind and caused a huge public outcry. Rumour and ingenuity proposed many celebrated names to identify him but 'Jack' was never caught.

For the majority of women life was harsh, and the dangers of prostitution seemed to many no worse than those they faced already. Some chose the life freely, but the majority resorted to it because they could not find respectable work that would pay them a living wage. The life was not necessarily one of irreversible sin and doom. As Dr Acton said in 1870: 'Most women who have resorted to prostitution for a livelihood, return sooner or later to a more or less regular course of life . . . Incumbrances rarely attend the prostitute who flies from the horror of her position. We must recollect that she has a healthy frame, an excellent constitution, and is in the vigour of life . . . Is it surprising, then, that she should . . . make a dash at respectability by a marriage?' It was easier for a working-class prostitute who had saved up some money to find a man to 'make an honest woman of her' by marrying her, than it was for a divorced duchess to meet Queen Victoria socially. And it was not always a question of money: in E.M. Forster's *Howards End*, published in 1910, the bank clerk Leonard Bast marries the ex-prostitute Jackie for love, and it is not his relationship with *her* that causes the tragedy.

'There is wonderfully little difference between the woman you have for five shillings and the one you pay five pounds, excepting in the silk, linen and manners,' wrote Walter in *My Secret Life*. But men were willing to pay vastly different sums of money for sex with high- or low-class tarts, in that twilight social world known as the *demi-monde*. In his survey of London in the 1850s, *London Labour and the London Poor*, Henry Mayhew divided prostitutes into six categories, though he omitted the highest rank of courtesan. There were kept mistresses and prima donnas; women living together in well-kept lodging houses; women living in low lodging houses; sailors' and soldiers' women; park women; thieves' women.

The high-class courtesans of the early part of the century, living in that small, profligate and extremely expensive world which centred on Mayfair and the Steyne in Brighton, were far removed from the prostitutes who touted for custom on the Strand. The latter were known as the Fashionable Impures or the Cyprians. Individually they had such names as The Venus Mendicant, The Mocking Bird, The White Doe, or Brazen Bellona. They had their own boxes at the opera, where they held public court. Men delighted to drive with them in Hyde Park, and considered it an honour to be known to receive their favours. Kept mistresses often had their carriages, phaetons and landaus emblazoned with the coats of arms of their protectors.

The greatest of the courtesans of that period was Harriette Wilson (1789–1846), the veritable Queen of Tarts, otherwise referred to as Harry, or The Little Fellow, not because there was anything diminutive about her, but from sheer affection. The daughter of a Swiss watchmaker and a stocking-mender, Harriette was not the golden-hearted whore of sentimental literature. She was as hard as nails and matey, frank and familiar with her clients, rather than romantic. 'Harry' was not staggeringly beautiful, but she had an alluring figure, fine colouring, and abounding vitality. Sir Walter Scott said she was 'a smart, saucy girl, with good eyes and dark hair, and the manners of a wild schoolboy.' Her *Memoirs* record, without reference to causes or motives, how she took up when she was very young with the Earl of Craven, was established in a succession of elegant apartments, and never looked back. She was a woman of wit, capable of intelligent conversation as well as giving sexual pleasure, and she provided a bracing change from domestic dullness and formality. She was an excellent mimic, an expert in the cut-and-thrust of fashionable badinage, and had the spirit of the age in her gusto and mischief. Her house was always crowded with noble company, mostly male. She had a liaison with the Hon. Frederick Lamb, lived in Paris for a time with Sir Charles Stuart, and became the kept mistress of the Duke of Argyle in 1825, but also intrigued with the Marquis of Worcester, among others. The parsimony of the Duke of Beaufort, who tried to compound a promised annuity to Harriette of £500 by a single payment of £1,200, led to her harbouring a lasting sense of ill treatment.

When she was getting older and society was more puritanical, she announced her intention of publishing her memoirs and naming all her lovers. She needed money, and wrote, 'The Hon. Fred Lamb has called on Stockdale [the publisher] to threaten us with prosecution; had he opened his purse to give me a few hundreds, there would have been no book.' The Duke of Wellington told her to 'publish and be damned'. She duly published the book in four volumes in 1825, was not damned more than she had been already, and made a great deal of money. The publisher's door was 'thronged ten deep on the mornings announced for the publication of a new volume', and over thirty editions were issued in one year. Scott said, 'The gay world has been kept in hot water lately by this impudent publication.' Among those who figured prominently were the Duke of Wellington, the Duke of Leinster, Lord Hertford, Marquess Wellesley, Earl of Fife, Prince Esterhazy, Lord Granville Leveson-Gower, Lord Ebrington, Beau Brummell, Viscount Ponsonby, Lord Frederick Bentinck, Lord Byron and Lord Brougham. Further instalments of the memoirs were threatened, but unnamed former lovers collected money for her, whereupon she buried her past and married a Monsieur Rochefort.

To be a kept woman was the ambition of many intelligent prostitutes, for thus they could escape the hazards of the streets. At the highest levels there was little question as to who was the father of her illegitimate children; and the latter had almost as good opportunities in life as the legitimate children of their father, though of course no titles and less property. For example, the famous actress, Dorothy Jordan, was for twenty years the mistress of the Duke of Clarence, who became King William IV in 1830, and she had ten children by him. He was not a very good provider for her, so she frequently returned to the stage to earn money to pay off the family's debts, and he eventually cast her off in order to do his dynastic duty and marry a suitable princess. None of his legitimate children survived, but he was devoted to his illegitimate children, known as the Fitzclarence brood, and they were all openly received at Court, married into the aristocracy and established in good positions. Some men married their kept mistresses, as when Sir William Hamilton, ambassador at the Court of Naples, married Emma, who had previously also been the mistress of his nephew. Emma was great friends with the King and Queen of Naples, but was not acceptable in respectable English society when she openly became the mistress of the hero Lord Nelson.

Kept mistresses and prima donnas of the Victorian period seem to have been happier than many respectably married women. The successful had to perform well, look well, talk intelligently, and a good singing voice was prized. Later in the century the St John's Wood area of London became famous for the many kept mistresses living there in bijou residences known as 'love nests'. One happy kept mistress told Mayhew in the 1850s, 'I am not tired of what I am doing. I rather like it. I have all I want, and my friend loves me to excess.' It was she who said that she could have married the following day if she had wanted to. The *demi-mondaine* Laura Bell, on the other hand, was looking for eventual marriage and respectability. She made her London debut in 1850, having established her reputation as a courtesan in Dublin, where she had a barouche of her own (a two-seat, four-wheeled carriage with a folding top) drawn by two white horses. After two years of being a favourite of the London 'swells' with money to burn, as well as being the mistress of an Indian prince, she married Augustus Thistlethwayte, grandson of a bishop, and became an evangelical preacher. But she continued to be wildly extravagant, and her husband had eventually to announce that he would not in future be responsible for her debts.

Louisa Turner came to prostitution via the stage. The daughter of a glove-shop owner in Carlton Street, she studied music and went into Italian opera, known as 'the hot-bed of seduction'. The girls in the cast took her to a brothel near Oxford Street, and she decided this was easier work than the theatre. Lord Yarmouth took a fancy to her, and from then on she saw opera from a box instead of singing in it. Amy Johnson, daughter of an army officer, spent the entire fortune of her protector in two years. He went to debtor's prison, but she went from success to success.

One of the most famous *poules de luxe* to entice the upper crust was Catherine ('Skittles') Walters, who proved how misinformed was the moralists' view that all prostitutes lost their looks rapidly and succumbed to gin and syphilis. Skittles lived to the age of eighty-one, dying in 1920. Among her friends were the Prince of Wales, who signed himself in letters to her, *'ton petit Bébé'*; Prime Minister Gladstone who tried unsuccessfully to reform her; and Baroness Angela Burdett-Coutts who took her to the pantomime. In later years she was a familiar sight in Hyde Park, being pushed along in her bath chair by her friend Lord Kitchener, hero of the Boer War, who also had hoped to reform her.

Skittles earned her nickname by her displays of skill in a smart skittles alley in Paris. She made her debut in London in 1861, appearing at the fashionable hours in Hyde Park, riding in Rotten Row in a tightly-laced jacket and riding trousers that showed off her figure. She was instantly a success with the men about town. In 1862 she was such a draw that crowds assembled to look at her, seriously upsetting the traffic arrangements for the great exhibition in South Kensington, a short distance away. She was the centre of a cult, and books were written about her, though journalist and politician Henry Labouchere said, 'She must be the only whore in history to retain her heart intact.' Skittles was deeply loved by the young Marquis of Hartington, known as Harty Tarty. He was heir to the Duke of Devonshire, one of the richest men in England. He wanted to marry her, but was persuaded by his family that this was not possible, so he paid her an allowance of £2,000 a year for the rest of her life.

The prostitutes at the top of the tree were unassailable. Eliza Lynn Linton wrote angrily in 1868, of respectable upper- and middle-class young women, 'The Girl of the Period envies the queens of the *demi-monde* far more than she abhors them. She sees them gorgeously attired and sumptuously appointed, and she knows them to be flattered, fêted and courted.' And Mayhew said of kept mistresses, 'It is a great mistake to suppose [they] are without friends and society: on the contrary, their acquaintance, if not select, is numerous, and it is their custom . . . at the fashionable hour to pay visits and leave cards on one another.' He also thought, contrary to the popular view, that a cast-off mistress had little difficulty in finding another protector.

Prostitutes of lower rank than kept mistresses were called 'prima donnas' by Mayhew. They frequented such places as the smart Burlington Arcade in Piccadilly, or fashionable parks, theatres and concert halls, usually bribing the police or uniformed attendants to allow them in. Dr William Acton described prostitutes who came in 1857 to two dancing rooms known as the Argyll and the Holborn as 'pretty, and quietly, though expensively dressed', using cosmetics, and behaving decorously: 'little solicitation was observable.' He thought they were the daughters of tradesmen and artisans and had been apprenticed in smart shops, but tired of the drudgery. If a woman misbehaved at the dancing rooms she was turned out by the door-keeper and forbidden ever to return, which was a heavy punishment. The woman expected to earn two or three sovereigns (40 to 60 shillings) for sex, and during the evening to get food and champagne 'without stint'. Acton thought such a woman probably had a male friend who visited her regularly, and contributed to her upkeep, but not enough to provide for her entirely. The friend would know that she solicited custom elsewhere, and did not object as long as she was always available for his visits. The novelist Samuel Butler recorded, 'I have a little needlewoman, a good little thing. I have given her a sewing-machine,' and later said he visited a Madame Dumas in Islington every Wednesday at 2.30 pm, took his pleasure, paid her £1, and then returned home.

In the early and middle years of Victoria's reign, being a prostitute in the West End of London was a lucrative and secure business. The women were notoriously extravagant. There was not much danger of being chivvied by the police, since prostitution of itself was not a crime (though soliciting and causing a public nuisance were), and average earnings were between £20 and £30 a week. Some women had their own apartments to which they took clients, but accommodation houses of various degrees of costliness were to be found in all parts of London. One author said that in the 1850s he rented for 5 shillings a room in a gentleman's house. It had 'red curtains, looking-glasses, wax lights, clean linen, a huge chair, a large bed, and a cheval-glass, large enough for the biggest couple to be reflected in.' In the 1860s and 70s any coffee house with the word 'beds' on the windows was also available for sexual use. It was not until the Criminal Law Amendment Act of 1885 that the management or keeping of a brothel became an offence.

Considered a lower class of prostitute in the Haymarket were the domestic servants and daughters of labourers, described by Mayhew as 'dressed in a light cotton or merino gown, and ill-suited crinoline . . . some with pork-pie hat, and waving feather,' who hung around disreputable coffee-shops. They asked half a guinea or a guinea for sex. They came from all over London to share in the spoils of the fast life. The lowest class of prostitute were those who would go with shop boys, errand lads, petty thieves, or labourers, for a few pence.

The prostitutes who lived in houses near the Haymarket with a number of others, because they were excluded from respectable lodging houses, were called by Mayhew 'convives'. They were said to be unusually generous to each other, lending clothes and money. Some were independent of the mistress of the house, but were charged extortionate rents. Board lodgers were those who gave a portion of their earnings to the mistress in return for board and lodging. Dress lodgers were those who got their clothes as well as their board. They were followed around by a 'watch woman' who made sure they did not run off with the clothes. One woman told Mayhew that she ran away from home in Somerset when she was fifteen, and joined a farming gang that went from place to place. She lived with one of the men as his wife for some years, but then he ran off and she became a prostitute in the Seven Dials area of London, living in a lodging house. She said she was not well enough dressed to earn her living in the Strand.

Considered even lower than the convives were women living in low lodging houses in the East End of London. There a class of women known as 'hunters' took lodgings and after a while would run away without paying their rent. One, who had tired of being a domestic servant, was known as 'Swindling Sal' and said she never paid any rent, hadn't done so in years, and never meant to. She was twenty-seven, tall and stout, and 'appeared as if she would be a formidable opponent in a street quarrel or an Irish row.' Her earnings varied from three to ten pounds a week.

Sailors' and soldiers' women congregated where the men were stationed or came ashore. Mayhew thought that few English girls could properly be termed sailors' women, most of the prostitutes being Irish or German. They met clients in public houses on the docks, and in areas such as Shadwell, Spitalfields and Whitechapel, using neighbouring houses as brothels. Some sailors even managed to conceal prostitutes on board ship, when they were at sea.

Dr Acton described army town prostitutes in 1857, saying at that time they 'pursued their calling' unmolested by the authorities, as long as they abstained from 'acts of flagrant indecency'. In Aldershot, Hampshire, however, where there was a large army barracks, no street prostitution was allowed. In most army towns the professional prostitute lived in lodgings, paying about 3s 6d a week, to a landlord who usually kept a beer-house or place of public entertainment where she had to spend her evenings until the soldiers returned to barracks at 9.30 pm. Then she was free to go where she pleased. She had to persuade the soldiers to drink a lot, and accept any drinks they offered her. A soldier was paid little more than a shilling a day, so he could not pay a woman much for sex, and she needed about eight to ten lovers each evening to earn a subsistence. Syphilis was prevalent among soldiers, and promiscuity spread the disease rapidly. This led to demands for a system to regulate prostitution, as we shall see later. The women who were amateur prostitutes, rather than professionals, were generally called 'Dollymops'. They were servant-maids, nursemaids, shop girls and milliners who did not go to casinos or bars, but were hunted by soldiers and made assignations in the park, in the street or in shops. Every nice girl, it seemed, loved a soldier in uniform, and her favours usually cost him little.

The most degraded of soldiers' women were the 'wrens of the Curragh', living in crude huts made of furze on the border of an Irish military base. The *Pall Mall Gazette* published a sensational report on them in 1867, describing them as 'outcast wretches living in communities of fifty or sixty, making just enough money to keep body and soul together'. Some women had followed soldiers to the camp from distant towns – some from love and some from desperation. They had such a horror of the workhouse that they preferred to be 'wrens', although if they strayed from the limits allotted to them they would be fined or sent to prison.

Prior to mid-century the Covent Garden area of London was the most notorious area in the capital for thieves and their women, and according to Mayhew the Barbican in the 1860s was still 'a bad, ruffianly, thievish place.' Women living in streets around Drury Lane, and paying about 2 shillings a week rent, 'would go home with a man for sixpence, and think themselves well paid.' Mayhew described seeing three such women standing talking together, 'innocent of crinoline', dirty, and wearing 'old bonnets and shawls'. They were still prostitutes although their hair was going grey.

Prostitution flourished in England in the nineteenth century, and many highly respectable men were the clients. The Royal Commission which reported on Oxford University in 1852 – where a large proportion of the students intended to become priests in the Church of England – considered 'sensual vice' one of the 'most obvious evils' there, and said opportunities for it were too abundant in the surrounding villages, where university discipline could not be exerted. The French writer Taine, visiting London in the 1860s, noticed that shops and houses in the Strand and Haymarket advertised 'beds to let' by day, and that young men of the respectable classes might be seen entering and leaving them in considerable numbers.

Most men accepted prostitution as an inevitable feature of society, needed for the satisfaction of male sexual desire before and outside marriage. Middle-class men began to marry later in life, especially in the last decades of the century, when parents demanded high incomes from prospective sons-in-law, with which to keep their daughters 'in the standard to which they were accustomed'. There was pressure on young men to remain celibate as bachelors, but many found this impossible. Women of the *demi-monde* were often more attractive and exotic to men than the eligible women they would marry. Upper-class Englishmen often acquired a liking for sex with lower-class women derived from their childhood bonding with their nannies, who bathed them and tucked them up in bed, loved them and kissed them, and with whom they may often have slept when young.

There was a double standard of sexual behaviour, because what was accepted for men was not considered acceptable for women. There was ambiguity in thinking about women, too: though they were lauded as men's conscience and as repositories of virtue, they were also held to be easily corruptible. Eve, not Adam, had been tempted by the serpent, and this showed that women were innately sinful. However, sexual promiscuity was held to be more abominable in a woman than in a man, 'because she violates, as it were, the very law of her nature in a sense in which he does not.' This presumably meant that she took the risk of getting pregnant by a man other than her wedded husband. Towards prostitutes men might feel disgust after the act, but little guilt, since they were thought to have freely chosen the life and to have forfeited the respect to which they were generally entitled as members of 'the weaker sex'. They had renounced purity, the essence of respectable womanhood.

By the 1860s the ideal of purity in sexual behaviour had become sacrosanct, in public at least, to the English middle classes. Love of a noble kind was separate from and superior to sexual desire. Many people thought that sexual intercourse should take place, even within marriage, only for the propagation of the species. This made some men guilty about enjoying sex at all, whether within marriage or with a mistress or prostitute. Taine wrote of the 1860s: 'An Englishman in a state of adultery is miserable: even at the supreme moment his conscience torments him.' How Taine knew this is anybody's guess. He may have been right about the middle class, but not about the upper class who were sexually permissive throughout the nineteenth century. What did change after the Regency period was that upper-class men became more discreet about their vices.

Most nineteenth-century literature portrayed an unbridgeable chasm between respectable and wanton women, and said it was impossible for a 'fallen woman' to rejoin respectable society. Thackeray and Dickens wrote of fallen women with sympathy, but always ostracized them in the end. In *Vanity Fair* Becky Sharp purchases respectability, but her murder of Jos Sedley allows the heartless domestic angel Amelia to shrink from her at the end. In the sensational novels of the 1860s fallen women have a certain degree of good fortune but in the end always pay for their 'crimes'. Publishers knew, of course, that their reading public would not stomach any other conclusion, and forced authors to write appropriately. But some later novels introduced a more resilient heroine. Thomas Hardy's 'Ruined Maid' returns home in triumph – '"some polish is gained with one's ruin", said she', while George Moore's Esther Waters boasts that she was only conscious that she had accomplished her woman's work. Significantly, many woman writers such as Eliza Lynn Linton and Ann Lamb pointed out that mercenary sexuality existed in the respectable marriage market as well as in the *demi-monde*; they suggested that the economic dependency of the prostitute on her male customers was not so different from the general dependency of middle-class women upon their husbands.

Concern about prostitution became the obsession of prime ministers, novelists, clergymen, physicians, philanthropists, and social reformers. The popular view was sentimental. The prostitute was portrayed as 'ruined', her life destroyed by sexual experience, a passive victim of male lust, destined for an early grave. This was not necessarily the case, as was shown earlier, but the Victorians turned the rescue of 'fallen' women into a large-scale activity. Missionaries from churches regularly patrolled the streets around the Haymarket, passing out leaflets and asking prostitutes to forsake their sinful lives, but the shelters they offered were highly punitive and the alternative work available badly paid, so the rescue rate was not high. The attempts of Prime Minister Gladstone to rehabilitate fallen women – as long as they were pretty and walked in the better parts of London – were not very successful either. The prostitutes called him 'Old Glad-Eye' and they suspected his motives. He certainly got a thrill out of his relationships with these girls.

The organized harassment of prostitutes began in Europe at the time of the syphilis epidemics of the late sixteenth century. Degrading and terrorizing punishments were introduced for the women, but no attempts were made to punish their male clients. England was the last of the countries of Europe to adopt a system of state-licensed prostitution (in 1864) and the first to abolish it (in 1886). The great abolitionist struggle was led by Josephine Butler and other distinguished women such as Florence Nightingale, Harriet Martineau and Mary Carpenter.

The Contagious Diseases Acts of 1864, 1866 and 1869 were the work of the military, who were concerned at the high rate of venereal disease among soldiers and sailors, and doctors such as William Acton who saw garrison-town regulations as the first step towards wider medical regulation. The acts provided for periodic genital examination of any woman suspected of being a prostitute and living in a town with a large military population. Women who were found diseased were forced into special 'lock' hospitals until they were cured. Treatment consisted of applications of mercury ointment, which suppressed the symptoms of syphilis but could cause kidney disease, and often caused painful burning. The treatment was compulsory only for women; to support this double standard, a military doctor said periodic examinations of the soldiers 'would tend to destroy the men's self-respect', and other doctors untruthfully said that venereal disease could be spread only from women to men (ie. not the other way round). Women who refused inspection could be imprisoned and even put to hard labour. People could be arrested for allowing a prostitute suspected of having a venereal disease to live with them.

One of the most abusive aspects of these acts was the lack of a clear definition of 'common prostitute'. A magistrate and surgeon at the Portsmouth Lock Hospital said it was 'any woman . . . going to places which are resorts of prostitutes alone, and at times when immoral persons are usually out. It is more a question of mannerism than anything else.' An accused woman bore the burden of proving her virtue. The police in garrison towns were notoriously brutal, and they could not be prosecuted for false arrest of a woman they considered a prostitute. They were careful to approach only lower-class girls, many of them illiterate and unaware of their legal rights. Innocent women as well as practising prostitutes were harassed, and some made formal complaints against the police but were rarely believed by the magistrates. The Contagious Diseases Acts made it increasingly difficult for women to move in and out of prostitution, as they had done previously, since so much unwelcome attention was drawn to them if they were arrested, and those who had other jobs frequently lost them as a result. This had the effect of making prostitution a permanent career.

At first, the CD Acts went unnoticed by the middle classes, but by 1869 an opposition group of liberals, moral reformers, feminists, working men, and prostitutes themselves, was forming. The struggle to repeal these acts was difficult because Victorian sexual decorum allowed only medical men to discuss prostitution and venereal disease; the subjects were off limits to others, even Members of Parliament, and especially respectable women. So the upper-class women who battled on behalf of prostitutes had to be both brave and shrewd, in order to champion them within a conventionally Victorian moral framework which the forces of organized religion could support. Josephine Butler, daughter of an influential landed gentry family of liberal reformers, and married to a like-minded clergyman and educationist, shrank from the task at first, as did her husband also, but they felt called by God to fulfil it.

Josephine and her supporters said that state regulated vice had been ineffective when introduced in other European countries, and it was a source of moral disorder in that it destroyed 'the aversion which vice should inspire' and 'strengthened its power'. Why, they asked, should men's animalism be provided for? They claimed that it was a source of physical disorders, by exciting incontinence and promising immunity, and that it degraded soldiers by assuming they were more immoral than other men. They objected to making prostitution an acceptable necessity, and safe from disease. They objected to the disparity of imposed treatment, calling it morally unfair. Both men and women should be reclaimed from vice, they said. They did not believe that women voluntarily became prostitutes or enjoyed that work.

Josephine Butler organized against the CD Acts on two fronts. She began speaking publicly to working-class audiences, at a time when ladies did not do this, and she organized women of her own class into a Ladies' Association. In her first year she spoke at nearly one hundred meetings, established, edited and wrote for *The Shield*, which defended women's rights, swayed the outcome of a parliamentary by-election, and submitted a protest to Parliament about the CD Acts, signed by 251 prominent women, among them Florence Nightingale. In 1872, Parliament bowed to 'the revolt of the women' and their political allies, and established a Royal Commission on the subject, inviting Josephine to testify. Nothing came of their report, which recommended an end to the forced medical examination of prostitutes but restated the sexual double standard: 'There is no comparison between prostitutes and the men who consort with them. With the one sex the offence is committed as a matter of gain, with the other it is an irregular indulgence of a natural impulse.'

Josephine went on a tour of European state brothels and hospitals for prostitutes in 1874. Revolted by what she saw, on her return she wrote and spoke constantly about the conditions in them, and about the trade in young girls. Her friend, the journalist W.T. Stead, reported in the *Pall Mall Gazette* on child prostitution and the white slave traffic in London. To show how easy it was to buy and sell an English child, he persuaded a reclaimed prostitute named Rebecca Jarret to procure a child named Eliza Armstrong from her mother for £5. Eliza was shipped to the Salvation Army in Paris (instead of to the usual state brothel). The article created a sensation, but Eliza's father (a drunkard) complained to the police that his permission had not been asked for the child to be sent out of the country. For that offence, Stead was imprisoned for three months and poor Rebecca for a year. Bernard Shaw called the whole thing a put-up job. In a later investigation Stead pretended to purchase a virgin of sixteen. He paid £3 to the procuress, and was then expected to give the girl £4 (out of which the girl would pay the procuress a further £2). Stead found his would-be victim eager to go through with the arrangement, though she said she did not want her mother to know about it. When he offered her £1 not to be seduced, she said she would prefer to be paid for the seduction, since she and her mother were so poor. The number of women abducted to foreign countries as sex-slaves was probably very limited, and it was also rare for children to be forced into prostitution against their wills, but Stead's stories drew attention to the poverty and sexual exploitation of many young girls.

Josephine's efforts finally bore fruit. The victory of the Liberal party in a general election in 1880 led on to the suspension and then the abolition of the CD Acts, and the raising of the age of consent for women from twelve to sixteen. Before 1885 it was not an offence to have sexual intercourse with a young girl, with her consent, though her age had a bearing on whether she was capable of consenting to sex. In that year, a law was passed which made it a crime to have sex with a girl under the age of sixteen, and a more serious offence to have sex with a girl under thirteen. Yet the irony was that in 1885 the age at which a girl could marry continued to be twelve (subject to parents' consent); it was raised to sixteen only in 1929, by the Marriage Act of that year.

Prostitution did not come to an end when the CD Acts were repealed in 1886, but a grossly sexist piece of legislation was abolished. Cases of VD among the home forces were exactly the same in number, after twenty-two years of the CD Acts, as they had been before – 260 per thousand. Later on, local authorities set up clinics to which both men and women could go for treatment for VD, but it was the middle of the twentieth century before antibiotics were discovered to cure it. Despite her heroic efforts Josephine Butler was until recently largely forgotten:

no woman has ever worked harder for her sex than she did, but perhaps because she defended the rights of the destitute and prostitutes, she received no honours.

The flagrantly unjust treatment of suspected prostitutes under the CD Acts drew attention to the sexual double standard that applied to women of all stratas, and stimulated the growth of the women's movement. The debate on the causes of prostitution highlighted the exploitation of women at work, including the poor wages they received. But few rescuers were prepared to say, as did feminist Annie Besant, that 'remunerative employment would empty half the streets; pay women the same wages that men receive, for the same work, and women would cease to sell their bodies when they could fairly sell their labour.' It is doubtful whether this solution would have abolished prostitution altogether, but the numbers of women 'on the game' might have been considerably smaller if they could have earned enough from respectable work to keep themselves comfortably.

Conclusion

TO BECOME THEMSELVES

(The vote) has allowed women to be themselves, to choose their own future, or their own present; to choose things for themselves and not be tied by tradition. They're free agents to act as they want . . .

Elizabeth Dean, ex-millworker, aged 102, interviewed 1987

[In the Women's Movement of the 1970s] we wanted to change everything, absolutely everything, every cultural value with which we'd been brought up . . . That moment of complete optimism was quite short-lived, but that's what we wanted.

Sally Alexander, historian and organizer of the first Women's Liberation Movement conference in Oxford in 1970

England was a vastly different country in 1914, compared with 1800. One astonishing change was that, despite so many people dying young, the population had risen from nine to thirty-six million. There were more super-rich people, and many more ranked as middle class, a group which ranged from wealthy business people at the top, down to shopkeepers, farmers, schoolteachers and clerks at the bottom. Within the 'manual labour class', which made up about three quarters of the population, there were large differences in conditions of work and play, and in conduct and morality: some lived in modest comfort, others in dire squalor. About one in seven workmen were skilled, and could earn twice as much as unskilled labourers, but because so much work was seasonal few men could totally support their wives and children, most of whom had to earn money to help maintain the family. Children started work at the age of eight to ten (sometimes younger) at the beginning, and twelve to fourteen at the end of the century.

As modern industry and the population grew, most people moved into towns. In 1801 about a quarter of them lived in towns; by 1851 half did so; and by the end of the century it was three quarters. Victorian women outnumbered men in moving from the countryside to the towns, as they had done for several centuries and for the same reason: the ease with which relatively young and single women could find employment as servants. Although domestic service was an 'old-fashioned' form of employment, a Victorian woman who sought such a position was, or could be, doing so in a very 'modern' frame of mind. The job paid relatively high wages, part of which could be saved, and in an affluent household a young woman could learn valuable social and domestic skills which might lead to a better marriage than she might otherwise expect. Some girls, who were sent off into service by parents who needed their wages, remained emotionally dependent on their families, but others relished their freedom. Women who migrated to towns probably felt the same sense of adventure as men who did so, but compared with movement around the country, migration out of England by Victorian women was very small.

The change from country to town life brought both gains and losses. On the one side there was release from the scrutiny of squire and parson, wider job opportunities for women, more freedom to choose religion and politics, and the camaraderie of the streets. On the other side, there was the claustrophobia of overcrowded, sprawling towns, with their dirt, disease and squalor, more crime and vice, and the interference of nosey neighbours. The two major groups of the working class – the respectables and the roughs – sorted themselves out into distinct areas and streets within towns, which many wives and mothers never left, but neither group could escape an environment polluted by industry, open coal fires in houses, and excrement from humans and animals.

Those who remained in the countryside did not have a less harsh life than town dwellers. In 1801 a third of the working population had some connection with farming; by 1901 it was no more than one in eight. This was due to increased mechanization, the import of cheap wheat from abroad, and the turnover to animal husbandry, all of which made fewer workers necessary. Factories increasingly took away jobs like spinning, knitting, hand lace-making and basket weaving, by which country women had previously supplemented their husbands' miniscule farm wages. In the northern counties farm labourers' wages were kept up by competition from mines and factories, but in the south they were desperately low. Wives scrimped and saved, often working in the fields in all weathers, begging scraps and used tea leaves from the 'big houses', and coming home to damp, draughty cottages with scarcely enough of a fire to cook their food, let alone warm themselves.

Like all the countries of Western Europe, England had in the nineteenth century what is called the 'European Marriage Pattern', established by the seventeenth century, in which the average woman married in her middle to late twenties a man near her own age. Ten to twenty per cent of women never married. The pattern was not confined to the peasantry, but gradually became part of upper- and middle-class life as well. The average age of first marriage for aristocratic women slowly increased, until between 1850 and 1874 it was twenty-six. Finances and dowries obviously affected whether women married or not, but some privileged women simply chose not to. By contrast, in most Third World countries (and this is true even today) the average woman was married by her middle or late teens to a man older than herself, often by as much as ten years. Few women were allowed to remain permanently unmarried, whatever their feelings and preferences. Western Europe was the only cultural area which gave women time to develop a mature sense of identity before subjecting them to constant childbearing. From the standpoint of age, husbands seemed more like partners than father substitutes. Middle-class women who remained unmarried had to find ways of keeping themselves, and gradually developed new lifestyles which were to influence all women.

Because of late marriage West European women never had as many children as they were biologically capable of bearing, and many practised birth control of a crude sort. Despite its importance, little is known about the causes of the momentous shift from traditional to modern fertility patterns which began in Europe and the United States in the nineteenth century. Its onset does not seem to coincide with any specific stage of social or economic development. In France, for example, people began to have fewer children before there was much industrialization or much movement into towns. Peasants were worried about their land being divided up between many children when they died. In England, industrialization and urbanization had been under way for decades before there was any substantial decline in family size. The 1911 Family Census suggests that family size had been declining since the 1850s, and the birth rate itself (per thousand of the whole population) declined from 1877. In 1911, of all working-class groups, married women textile workers had the fewest children, but wives working in other jobs in textile districts, or in other parts of the country, did not have small families, so there seems no obvious link between going out to work and having fewer children. Upper middle-class families may have preferred to have fewer children because of the cost of educating and rearing them, but this can hardly be the reason why ducal families (among the wealthiest and most secure in England) should have had small families, which they did.

Control of the number of children they had was vastly more important to most Victorian women than getting the vote, and this was the basis for an 'unofficial' drive for personal autonomy. Contraception was frowned upon by all the Churches and by doctors, and it was not a major plank in organized demands for women's rights because most feminists either disapproved or were afraid to raise the question. It was an unpopular cause, and espousing it would have undermined the respectability of other campaigns. Doctors at the time were convinced, however, that women of all social classes were secretly using abortion (a woman-dominated form of control) to terminate unwanted pregnancies. A similar situation existed in nineteenth-century America and France. Women clearly played an active role in deciding how many children to have.

One of the most important developments of the early nineteenth century was the gradual transference of the 'social lead', insofar as it influenced national attitudes, to the middle classes. Class distinctions remained, as did snobbery. Outwardly, the elegant life of London society went on with little change, as did much sexual laxity. But outward permissiveness disappeared and accepted standards changed. Men no longer flaunted their mistresses in public, language grew more restrained, religion acquired a new importance. The new manufacturing class grew in numbers, came to provide a greater share of the nation's capital, and with increasing self-confidence laid stress on the values they considered important. After the passing of the Reform Bill in 1832 they had a recognized stake in the political affairs of the country, and they wanted their wives and daughters to play an important part in maintaining high standards of respectability and decency.

The original impetus to transform 'Merry England' into Victorian England was a religious one, but the middle classes utilized it to cement their own plans for a hardworking, highly moral and respectable workforce – both employers and employees. Charles II is reputed to have said that Calvinism was no religion for a gentleman. Most eighteenth-century gentlemen reacted in the same way to Methodism, which appealed to the poor and uninfluential. But groups of serious Anglicans, who believed that laxity, drunkenness and idleness represented a threat to the nation, backed the Evangelical movement in its call for a more vital personal religion of the spirit. Hannah More by her writings persuaded the fashionable world to set a better example to the lower orders, and the unvirtuous began to hide their vices behind a veil of discretion.

By 1850 England had undergone a moral revolution, and the middle class had imposed conformity to its own puritan values on the rest of society, at least to the extent of everyone paying lip service to them. The significance of religion changed over the century, and church attendance was falling from at least 1851 onwards, especially in the large cities. Yet Evangelicalism and Methodism were still a formidable combination of religion, ethics and ideology which governed ideals of behaviour. Many people who did not go to church themselves sent their children to Sunday school, to learn the values of hard work, duty to family, the evils of drink and the perils of sinfulness.

An important and interesting question is how and why, despite their constricted upbringing, so many Victorian women developed strong and distinctive personalities. Surprisingly, religion played a role here, in telling women contradictory things: first, to submit themselves to their husbands because women were inferior to men, but secondly, that we are all equal in the sight of God, and equally worthy of salvation. So the patriarchal ideal came under increasing attack. Also, the intense pressure of parents to mould girls to *their* purposes made some girls rebellious and determined to follow their own inclinations. Telling girls to be the transmitters of culture gave some of them the chance to emerge as innovators and competitors with men. Famous examples were Mary Somerville, Florence Nightingale, Sophia Jex-Blake and Dame Ethel Smyth, the composer and suffragette. She was one of six lively daughters of a colonel who disliked music but capitulated to his daughters' wish to study it. In the working class, too, there were strong-minded women who became local preachers, trade union leaders, suffragists and suffragettes, such as Selina Cooper, Alice Foley and Hannah Mitchell.

We don't know the private motivations of every passionate believer

in women's rights. Upper-class Victoria Lidiard was a suffragette who
went to prison in 1912, for smashing windows in Oxford Street and
throwing a stone through a window at the War Office, as part of the
suffrage campaign. A few years before she died (in October 1992 at the
age of 102), she was interviewed for a BBC television programme. She
said her drive came from her mother, who organized all her daughters
into joining the suffragettes in 1910. Victoria could not recall her mother
ever having a good day's health; she had a child every thirteen months
but, though physically frail, possessed an iron will and was a determined
supporter of women's rights. Drunks and young boys hurled abuse and
rotten fruit at Victoria when she spoke at suffrage meetings, and a local
clergyman spat in her face, but she continued the fight because she considered it 'simply the right thing to do'. Elizabeth Dean, a Lancashire
millworker, became a rebel when she saw the injustices ordinary women
suffered at work, in marriage, in childbirth, and in the courts of law.
She believed that only by getting the vote could women gain some power
over their lives, and she joined the suffragettes in 1912. Emmeline
Pankhurst said she first became militant when she saw in a workhouse
infirmary a thirteen year old pregnant girl with VD. Emmeline Pethwick
Lawrence, another suffragette leader, said the novels she read as a
young girl affected her lifelong interests. Reading novels helped some
women to identify their changing roles, and to recognize the conflict
between their own needs and those of their families.

Early and mid-Victorian novels illuminate emotional conflicts. Some
spread the gospel of self-realization among women who would never
have thought of themselves as rebels or radicals. It has been estimated
that over forty thousand novels were published between 1800 and 1900.
A minority were written by women. Few used fiction to advocate deeply
unconventional behaviour, but, for example, Margaret Oliphant wrote
feelingly of the lack of communication between spouses and the
boredom, fretting and chafing of women. She showed the difficulties
and realities of marriage and warned of the pitfalls, though she disliked
divorce. In her witty novel *Miss Marjoribanks* (1865), Lucilla is a Victorian anti-heroine, unsentimental, large, strong, insubordinate to men
and with a hearty appetite, who bosses everyone around and eventually
marries a man she can regard as a partner. Mrs Oliphant began a trend
of portraying male characters who disappoint or let down their womenfolk; she wrote of alcoholics, wastrels and physically ailing men, a sad
galaxy who reflected her own family experiences. In fact, so many
novels by women were published, in which men were physically

disabled, that male novelists began to complain.

The sensational novels of the 1860s recorded family patterns of hatred and contempt. The death of a husband was often a welcome relief to the wife, and if death did not occur the wife sought remedy in flight, adultery, divorce or murder. No one knows whether women's actual behaviour was affected by their novel reading; many simply enjoyed reading about escapades they would never be able to pursue themselves. Henry Mayhew thought women were debased by reading trashy novels; others worried about women becoming unhappy or undutiful if they read novels that were not meant to improve the mind. Women themselves wanted to be entertained. As Mrs Austin, a friend of John Stuart Mill, remarked:

> Charlotte Yonge's novel *The Heir of Redcliffe* I have not read. It sounded too good for me. I am not worthy of superhuman flights of virtue – in a novel. I want to see how people act and suffer who are as good-for-nothing as I am myself. Then I have the sinful pretension to be amused, whereas all our novelists want to reform us . . .

Though few women novelists were publicly involved with the 'Woman Question', their novels expressed doubts and conflicts about the limited lives women were allowed to lead, and subtly suggested there should be wider opportunities available. In *Middlemarch*, *The Mill on the Floss*, and *Daniel Deronda*, the innate abilities of Dorothea, Maggie and Gwendolyn go unrealized because of the way their lives are circumscribed. Author of these novels, Mary Anne Evans, adopted a conventional device of her time by using a male pseudonym, George Eliot, to gain serious attention to her work, and she used this name throughout her life. But in her private life George Eliot defied convention by living openly with a married man, despite which she became a famous and successful author and was eventually accepted into respectable society and visited by royalty, long before her late marriage to the Revd Mr Cross. Women's actual lives were more complex than many novels suggest. Although the ideal of womanhood may seem to have been static between, say, 1837 and 1873, the heroines of novels changed to reflect new ideas on women's property rights, the need for better education and jobs, and changed marital relations. The New Woman began to emerge. By the 1890s she was independent, pursued a career, sometimes bore a child out of wedlock (but hid it away) and questioned the necessity of marriage.

Victorian England was not ahead of the United States and all other European countries in giving married women property rights. Barbara Leigh Smith's summary of the laws in 1854 pointed out that many other countries had laws more advantageous to women, and the fabric of those societies was not being torn apart. In America most States had repealed property laws originally based on the Common Law of England. Vermont had taken the lead, and many other States had gone further by giving married women control of their earnings if their husbands neglected or deserted them. In 1870, Annie Besant explained that in Germany the law varied in different States; but under one system, known as *Gutermeinschaft* (community of goods) there was no separate property for husband and wife, all being managed in the common stock over which the husband had no more right than the wife. In Austria, the wife retained her rights over her own property.

Nor was England ahead of other countries in giving women access to higher education. The world's first modern woman doctor, Elizabeth Blackwell, trained in the United States, and Britain's first woman doctor, Elizabeth Garrett Anderson, got her medical degree in Paris some years later, because no British university would admit her. Other English women read medicine at the University of Zurich, before London University admitted women. American women were going to college long before British women, but they found it just as difficult to break into male-dominated professions, and in fact they took longer to get the vote.

By 1914, an English woman could operate in a far wider sphere than she could a century earlier. She was a person in her own right, but still not equal to a man. There had been no change in the belief that a woman's place was in the home, and that a woman's work was less valuable than a man's, so there was still plenty of room for improvement. The battle lines for later waves of feminism were drawn up by Victorian women, though most of them thought home and children provided the most important work for married women, and that paid work outside the home should be for spinsters who had to support themselves. They knew that many working-class wives were forced to work or starve, but they disapproved of the double burden this imposed on them. They did not approve of special protective laws for women, since this made them appear weaker than men and worth less pay. Working-class women and their trade union leaders had different ideas: the former were glad to get any protection the law could provide to powerless employees doing exhausting work and getting little sense of personal achievement from it.

More equitable attitudes towards sexual behaviour was a late-Victorian feminist demand. They wanted both men and women to be chaste before marriage and monogamous afterwards. Birth control was not a major plank for feminists until the 1930s. The vote was seen as the most vital issue, since political power could (it was hoped) be used to achieve a wide range of changes. The outbreak of the First World War put an end to suffragette activities, but women's contribution to the war effort shook many traditional ideas, including the view that they were not responsible enough to be given the vote. Given the opportunity, women did men's work as well as the men had done it, ran their homes alone, kept the munitions factories going, drove ambulances in France and organized voluntary work for the forces. When, during the War, it was decided to give the vote to all adult men, it was felt time to reward women, too. Prime Minister Herbert Asquith admitted, 'some of my friends may think that . . . my eyes, which for many years on this matter have been clouded with fallacies and sealed by illusions, at last have been opened to the truth.' In 1918, 6 million out of a total of 13 million adult women got the vote (they had to be over thirty and householders, or wives of men householders, or have been to university).

Within two years of the end of the First World War women seemed to gain enormous ground. In 1919 Parliament passed the Sex Disqualification (Removal) Act, which declared that no one should be disqualified from holding public office or civil or judicial posts by their sex. The number of women entering the professions remained small, but the rate of entry was higher during the decade following the passing of the Act than for any other decade in this century so far. One profession left untouched by the Act was the civil service. In many jobs women could work only as long as they remained unmarried; the 'marriage bar' meant they had to resign from the job when they married. This bar was rigidly applied in the 1920s to the legal profession, the civil service, local government, teaching, nursing, work in banks and the BBC. During the Second World War employers found it necessary to keep married women on, yet the marriage bar for women teachers was not finally lifted until 1944. The marriage bar did not apply to manual jobs. Even in the Depression the BBC employed married women as lavatory attendants, cleaners and wardrobe women, because it was 'normal custom for women of this class to have outside employment'. From 1911 to 1951

the fastest growing of all women's employment groups was the category
of clerks, which includes secretaries and stenographers but excludes
sales personnel. By 1951 women comprised 60 per cent of this white-
collar, service-oriented, but low-paid group. Women also continued to
be employed in ever greater numbers in the lowest status and most
poorly paid of the manual jobs.

Women stood for Parliament from 1918 (though they had to wait
until 1958 to sit in the House of Lords), and became lawyers, jurors and
magistrates. It took another ten years for all women over twenty-one
to be given the vote, in 1928. Feminists such as Ray Strachey (*The Cause*,
1928) said the vote had yielded women a new status in public life, law,
employment, sexual expression and social life. It is often thought that
the small band of women MPs had little impact on the House of Commons, yet sixteen Acts protecting women's interests were passed in the
early 1920s, ranging from improved maternity services; pensions for
widows; divorce on equal grounds to men; better maintenance terms for
illegitimate children and separated wives; and equal guardianship rights
to children; to an Act protecting women who could prove they were still
suffering from the effects of childbirth from being accused of the crime
of murder if they killed their newborn baby. Millicent Fawcett said she
noted a remarkable improvement in MPs' attitudes to women when
millions of them had the right to vote. By 1987 there were forty-one
women MPs, the highest number ever, but they were still only 6 per cent
of the total. The first woman cabinet minister was Margaret Bondfield
(Labour) in 1929; the first woman Prime Minister was Margaret Thatcher (Conservative) in 1979. Mrs Thatcher's path to the top was eased
by her marriage to a millionaire, which allowed her to pay others to do
her housework and childcare. This is not an option for most women.

The feminists of the 1920s were more concerned with women's needs
as wives and mothers – birth control and family allowances, for example – than with their need to broaden their horizons and look beyond
the house. The 1930s was not a good time for feminists; the movement
was fragmented and younger women were not clear which cause they
should support. Rising poverty, the slump and the international situation eclipsed other issues. There was widespread agreement that in tough
economic times men should have the jobs rather than women, and
women's employment returned to pre-war levels. The theory was that
all men had wives and families to keep (which was not true) and that
no woman was the sole breadwinner for a family (which also was not

true). Many women went into domestic service because no other work was available.

The Second World War gave women the opportunity to join the armed forces, firewatch, drive ambulances, and take over men's jobs as they had done in the First World War. Two successful campaigns waged by the Women's Freedom League (a splinter group from the suffragettes) gave women the right to keep their nationality when they married a foreigner, and the right to the same compensation as men for war injuries. Not surprisingly, equal pay became an issue once more. As a result of government intervention during the First World War, women's wages reached two-thirds of men's. During the next two decades they slid back to one-half, and there they remained until the 1960s. Teachers, civil servants and local government officers were granted equal pay in 1955, to take full effect in 1961.

Married women continued to work when the War ended, despite propaganda attempts to persuade them to go home. A boom in the economy provided plenty of jobs, and women wanted to work, yet they were also told they ought to be at home with their children. The belief that children of working mothers are neglected is raised over and over again, despite evidence to the contrary. A problem which continues to this day, however, was that working mothers were usually overburdened by housework and child care, as well as their work outside the home. Women in industry grew more assertive as their numbers rose; for example, in 1968 there was a strike by women machinists at Ford Motor Company for recognition as skilled workers. Barbara Castle, then Minister for Employment and Productivity in the Labour Government, promised to push through an Equal Pay Act, and this was passed in 1970. But employers were given until 1975 to implement the Act, and together with male trade unionists they found plenty of ways to evade its provisions. There was no concept within the Act of equal pay for work of equal value.

The Sex Discrimination Act of 1975 made illegal discrimination on grounds of sex in employment, advertizing, and provision of goods, facilities and services. Few people understood it, and the Equal Opportunities Commission set up to oversee implementation of the Act had no teeth to enforce it. In 1974, contraceptive advice and supplies were made available through the National Health Service. The 1975 Protection of Employment Act made it illegal to dismiss a woman because she was pregnant, and gave her the right to maternity leave and some pay, and to return to work within twenty-nine weeks of giving birth. An Act of 1980 reduced these maternity rights. The 1984 Equal Value Amendment Act said women in low-paid jobs could claim equal value with men doing similar but different work. Women's pay was still only three-quarters of men's. In 1985, Britain was the only member of the European Economic Community to veto the introduction of parental leave, (not maternity leave given to the mother at the time of a birth, but leave for either parent to take care of a sick child). Today Britain offers poorer social provisions for women than any of its European partners.

Despite the Victorian legislation on married women's property, this was an issue of continuing ambiguities and difficulties. Sixteen different Acts of Parliament were passed between 1907 and 1963 concerning matrimonial causes, inheritance, property and maintenance. For example, under a 1938 Inheritance Act a widow could, for the first time, appeal against a will that neglected to provide for her and her children. The Married Women's Savings Act of 1963 laid down (for the first time) that a wife had a legal right to half the savings she may have made from the housekeeping money she received. Between 1964 and 1975 there were eight further major pieces of legislation on finance, divorce reform, title to the matrimonial home etc. The 1969 Divorce Reform Act redefined the grounds for divorce in terms of the breakdown of the marriage rather than the fault of either partner. A 1971 Act gave women equal rights with men on custody of children. In 1974 British women married to foreigners were given the same rights as men for their spouses to live in Britain. A 1976 Act gave some rights to battered wives, and from 1978 the magistrates' courts have had greater powers to deal with matrimonial and family disputes.

The modern women's movement emerged in the late 1960s in the United States, born partly of a struggle for civil rights in which women came to see themselves as underdogs. Women workers questioned why they were so badly paid compared with men. Educated women refused to accept that housework and childcare were the only jobs they were fit for. Betty Friedan's book, *The Feminine Mystique*, was the spark that lit the brushfire in America, followed in England by Germaine Greer's *The Female Eunuch*. The new feminists were young intellectuals, and they wanted liberation, not emancipation. Many older feminists just did not understand them. The first British conference of the Women's Liberation Movement, in Oxford in 1970, demanded equal pay immediately, equal education and job opportunities, 24-hour nurseries for children of working mothers, free contraception and abortion on demand. Many of these demands were later met, but changes in the law did not quickly overcome ancient customs and prejudices.

The Women's Movement was never a single entity, but an amalgam of special interest groups. Its achievements were many, but political and ideological differences eventually fragmented it. There were women who thought that only the overthrow of capitalism would permit true equality. There were those who liked men and wanted to improve relations between the sexes, believing that it was too easy to blame men for everything and that men, too, could be victims of the system. And there were those who thought men were irredeemably the enemy: they regarded heterosexual women as collaborators. The loss of momentum and fragmentation of the Women's Movement resembles the lull after the vote was won. The arguments continue about what women should now be fighting for, and how best to achieve it. Each succeeding generation has to struggle for its own ideals. Established pressure groups such as the Fawcett Society, which (with various name changes) stretches right back to the early struggles for the vote in the nineteenth century, continue to fight against specific and clear injustices.

The battle for women's rights is far from over. As in the nineteenth century, most women want to marry and have children, but they now expect to work outside the home for most of their married lives, taking time out when the children are small and then opting for part-time work which they can fit in with growing children and the housework. Poverty is increasingly a woman's problem. One in eight families is looked after by a woman alone (compared with one in 200 by men alone) and most women have lower earning power than men. Formal education has become identified in this century as an avenue of social mobility, a road which to some extent offsets the advantages of birth or wealth. It is not clear, however, that modern English women achieve much social mobility through educational achievement. Women now fill almost half the places for undergraduates in universities, but it is unusual for them to reach the top of any of the professions they enter. A few, such as Mary Quant and Anita Roddick, are self-made business millionaires, but most women are in badly paid 'ghettos' of occupations allocated to them by tradition, or stuck in the lower ranks of professions and corporations. Women themselves often bow out of the race because of the demands of family life. Few men even consider such a choice, let alone make it.

Asked to sum up the costs and benefits to English women of the two-hundred-year movement for women's rights, women's emancipation, women's liberation, older women would know what improvements they have actually seen in their lifetimes. Victoria Lidiard said, when she was ninety-eight, that 'many, many laws have been passed affecting women and children which would not have been passed unless women had the vote.' The daughter of a father who thought education for girls was unimportant, but a mother who thought otherwise, Victoria became an optician; she thought access to education had been the single biggest improvement in women's lives in her lifetime. At the end of her life she was still battling for the ordination of women in the Church of England, and it is sad that she died just before the Synod voted in favour of this in 1992. Elizabeth Dean, who worked in a Lancashire textile mill for most of her life, was asked when she was 102 if she thought the vote had brought equality to women. She had not the slightest doubt it had:

Now a woman can get married or not as she likes, she doesn't mind. Nobody throws things at her [is rude], or sneers. It has allowed women to be themselves, to choose their own future, or their own present: to choose things for themselves and not to be tied up by tradition. They're free agents to act as they want and as they feel they really need to act, without people sneering or people talking. It's a marvellous feeling to feel free to do just what you want to do after being down so long.

Victoria and Elizabeth saw women gradually break free from the restrictive world they were born into in the 1880s. Looking around in the 1980s they saw a different breed of woman, and were delighted. Younger women may argue that this is an unduly optimistic view, that equality has come only for a fortunate few, that the world is still controlled by men to their own advantage, and that the majority of women are always in second place. Few would deny that there are still plenty of battles to be fought, but all women can be grateful to whatever forces produced in the nineteenth century those strong-minded, rebellious, independent women who refused to accept themselves as inferior to men, and broke the mould once and for all.

SELECT BIBLIOGRAPHY

Unless otherwise indicated, all titles were published in Britain

INTRODUCTION

Colquhoun, Patrick, *A Treatise on Indigence*, 1806
Parkes, Bessie Rayner, *Essays on Woman's Work*, 1865
Sewell, Elizabeth, *Principles of Education, Drawn from Nature and Revelation, and Applied to Female Education in the Upper Classes*, 1865
Walker, Alexander, *Woman Physiologically Considered*, 1840

CHAPTER 1

Asquith, Margot, *Off the Record*, 1944
Balsan, Consuelo Vanderbilt, *The Glitter and the Gold*, NY, 1952
Barker, Priscilla, *The Secret Book*, 1888
Booker, B.L., *Yesterday's Child*, 1937
Bottome, Phyllis, *Search for a Soul*, 1947
Burnett, John, *Destiny Obscure*, 1984
Burstall, Sara, *Retrospect & Prospect: Sixty Years of Women's Education*, 1933
Chorley, Kathleen, *Manchester Made Them*, 1950
Corke, Helen, *In Our Infancy: Autobiography 1882–1912*, 1975
Cruikshank, Marjorie, *Children and Industry*, 1981
Cullwick, Hannah, *Diaries* (ed. Liz Stanley), 1984
Davies, Margaret L. (ed.), *Life As We Have Known It*, 1931
Davies, C. Stella, *North Country Bred*, 1963
Harrison, Jane Ellen, *Reminiscences of a Student Life*, 1925
Holdsworth, Angela, *Out of the Doll's House*, 1988
Hughes, Mary, *A London Child of the Seventies*, 1977

Johansson, Sheila, 'Sex and Death in Victorian England', in *A Widening Sphere* (ed. Martha Vicinus), 1980

Lewis, Judith Schneid, *In the Family Way*, Rutgers UP, 1986

Lochhead, Marion, *Young Victorians*, 1964

Menzies, Mrs (published anon.), *A Woman of No Importance*, 1917

Mitchison, Naomi, *All Change Here*, 1975

Mitchell, Hannah, *The Hard Way Up*, 1968

Nevill, Lady Dorothy, *Reminiscences*, 1906

Paston, George, *Little Memoirs of the Nineteenth Century*, 1902

Perkin, Deborah, original interviews for 'Out of the Doll's House' series, BBC Archives held at Fawcett Library.

Thompson, Flora, *Lark Rise to Candleford*, 1939

Villiers, Marjorie, *The Grand Whiggery*, 1939

Walvin, James, *A Child's World*, 1982

Webb, Beatrice, *My Apprenticeship*, 1926

Weeton, Ellen, *Journal of a Governess, 1807–11*, 1936

CHAPTER 2

Beckwith, Lady Muriel, *When I Remember*, 1950

Cobbe, Frances Power, *Life of F.P. Cobbe. By Herself*, 1894

Chorley, Kathleen (see Chapter 1)

Dyhouse, Carol, *Girls Growing Up in late Victorian and Edwardian England*, 1981

Faithfull, Lilian, *In the House of My Pilgrimage*, 1924

Foakes, Grace, *My Part of the River*, 1974

Hughes, Mary (see Chapter 1)

Kamm, Josephine, *Rapiers & Battleaxes*, 1966

Martineau, Harriet, *Autobiography*, 2 vols., 1877

Marshall, Sybil, *Fenland Chronicle*, 1967

Murray, Janet, *Strong-Minded Women*, NY, 1982

Pankhurst, Emmeline, *My Own Story*, 1914

Peck, Winifred, *A Little Learning, or A Victorian Childhood*, 1952

Sewell, Elizabeth, *Autobiography*, 1907

Sewell, Mary, *Life and Letters* (ed. Mrs Bayly), 1889

Smith, Mary, *Autobiography*, 1892

Somerville, Martha, *Personal Recollections from Early Life to Old Age of Mary Somerville*, 1873

Swanwick, Helena, *I Have Been Young*, 1935

Webb, Beatrice (see Chapter 1)

Woolf, Virginia, 'A Sketch of the Past' (1939) in *Moments of Being: Unpublished Autobiographical Writings* (ed. Jeanne Schulkind), 1985

CHAPTER 3

Acland, Eleanor, *Goodbye for the Present*, 1935
Arbuthnot, Harriet, *Journal 1820–1832*, 2 vols., 1950
Asquith, Margot (see Chapter 1)
Benson and Esher (eds.), *The Letters of Queen Victoria, 1837–61*, 3 vols., 1907
Besant, Annie, *Autobiography*, 1893
Blackwell, Elizabeth, *The Human Element of Sex*, 1885
Carlyle, Jane, *Letters to Her Family*, 1924
Chitty, Susan, *The Beast and the Monk*, 1974
Davies, Margaret L. (ed.) *Maternity*, 1915
Davies, Margaret L. (ed.) *Life as We Have Known It*, 1931
Fulford, Roger (ed.), *Dearest Child: Letters between Queen Victoria and the Princess Royal*, 1964
Gillis, John, *For Better, for Worse*, 1985
Holdsworth, Angela (see Chapter 1)
Hunt, Peter, *The Madeleine Smith Affair*, 1950
Jalland, Pat, *Women, Marriage, Politics 1890–1914*, 1986
Lamb, Ann Richelieu, *Can Women Regenerate Society?*, 1844
Lewis, Judith Schneid (see Chapter 1)
Marshall, Mary Paley, *What I Remember*, 1947
McLaren, Angus, *Birth Control in Nineteenth-Century England*, 1978
Mitchison, Naomi (see Chapter 1)
Perkin, Joan, *Women and Marriage in Nineteenth-Century England*, 1989
Penn, Margaret, *Manchester Fourteen Miles*, 1947
Reeves, Magdalen Pember, *Round About A Pound A Week*, 1913

CHAPTER 4

Branca, Patricia, *Silent Sisterhood: Middle-Class Women in the Victorian Home*, 1975
Burnett, John (see Chapter 1)
Glyn, A., *Elinor Glyn: A Biography*, 1968
Holland, Lady, *Journal 1791–1811*, 1908
Martin, Anna, *The Married Working Woman*, 1911
Nevill, Lady Dorothy (see Chapter 1)
Perkin, Joan (see Chapter 3)
Reeves, Magdalen Pember (see Chapter 3)
Stuart, Lady Louisa, *Gleanings from an Old Portfolio*, 1895
Tonna, Charlotte Elizabeth, *Personal Recollections*, 1854

CHAPTER 5

Cunnington, C. Willett, *The Perfect Lady*, 1948
Davies, Margaret L. (*Life*, see Chapter 3)

Dayus, Kathleen, *Her People*, 1982
International Journal of the History of Sport, May 1988
Perkin, Harold, *The Origins of Modern English Society, 1780–1880*, 1969.

CHAPTER 6

Cobbe, Frances Power, 'Wife Torture in England', *Contemporary Review*, April 1876
Fingall, Countess of, *Seventy Years Young*, 1937
Holland, Lady (see Chapter 4)
Mayhew, Henry, *London Labour and the London Poor*, 4 vols., 1861
McGregor, O.R., *Divorce in England*, 1957
Menefee, Samuel, *Wives for Sale*, 1981
Nevill, Lady Dorothy (see Chapter 1)
Webb, Beatrice (see Chapter 1)
Weeton, Ellen (see Chapter 1)

CHAPTER 7

Burnett, John (see Chapter 1)
Fawcett, Millicent Garrett, *What I Remember*, 1924
Liddington, Jill, *The Life . . . of Selina Cooper*, 1984
Martineau, Harriet (see Chapter 2)
Mayhew, Henry (see Chapter 6)
Montague, Elizabeth, *Her Life and Friendships*, (n.d.)
Pankhurst, Emmeline, *My Own Story*, 1914
Pinchbeck, Ivy, *Women Workers and the Industrial Revolution 1750–1850*, 1930
Shaw, Charles, *When I Was a Child*, 1903

CHAPTER 8

Bishop, Isabella Bird, *A Lady's Life in the Rocky Mountains*, 1879
Brimley Johnson, R. (ed.), *The Letters of Mary Russell Mitford*, 1925
Burstall, Sara (see Chapter 1)
Cobbe, Frances Power (see Chapter 2)
Collet, Clara, *Educated Working Women*, 1902
Craik, Dinah Mulock, *A Woman's Thoughts About Women*, 1858
Grey, Maria, *Last Word to Girls on Life in School and After School*, 1869
Haldane, Elizabeth, *From One Century to Another*, 1937
Lamb, Ann Richelieu (see Chapter 3)

CHAPTER 9

Burnett, John (see Chapter 1)
Children's Employment Commission Report, 1843

Children's Employment Commission Report, 1867
Drake, Barbara, *Women in Trade Unions*, 1920
Divorce Commission, 1912–13, *Parliamentary Papers XVIII*
Factory Inquiry Commission, *Parliamentary Papers*, 1833
Hellerstein, Hume and Offen (eds.), *Victorian Women*, 1981
Holdsworth, Angela (see Chapter 1)
Pinchbeck, Ivy (see Chapter 7)
Snowden, Philip, *The Living Wage*, 1912

CHAPTER 10

Black, Clementina, *Married Women's Work*, first edition 1915
Cadbury et al., *Women's Work and Wages*, 1906
Hamilton, Cicely, *Marriage as a Trade*, 1909
Jeffries, Richard, *The Toilers of the Field*, 1892
Rowntree et al., *How the Labourer Lives*, 1913

CHAPTER 11

Bamford, Samuel, *Passages in the Life of a Radical*, 1841
Bell, E. Moberly, *Octavia Hill: a biography*, 1942
Strachey, Ray, *The Cause*, 1928
Webb, Beatrice (see Chapter 1)

CHAPTER 12

Besant, Annie, *The Legalisation of Female Slavery in England*, 1885
Butler, Josephine, *Personal Reminiscences of a Great Crusade*, 1911, reprinted
  1976
Linton, Eliza Lynn, *Modern Woman*, NY, 1886
Marcus, Steven, *The Other Victorians*, 1969
Mayhew, Henry (see Chapter 5)
Pearsall, R., *The Worm in the Bud*, 1969
Walkowitz, Judith, *Prostitution and Victorian Society*, 1980
'Walter', *My Secret Life*, 1972

CONCLUSION

Fawcett, Millicent Garrett (see Chapter 7)
Hall, Ruth, *Marie Stopes: A biography*, 1977
Holdsworth, Angela (see Chapter 1)
Kenney, Annie, *Memories of a Militant*, 1924
Pankhurst, Emmeline (see Chapter 2)
Perkin, Deborah (see Chapter 1)
Strachey, Ray, *The Cause: A short history of the Women's Movement in Great
  Britain*, 1928

Index